TOUGHER
THAN THE REST

★ ★ ★ ★ ★ ★ ★ ★ ★ ★ ★

100 BEST
BRUCE
SPRINGSTEEN

★ ★ ★ ★ ★ ★ ★

JUNE SKINNER SAWYERS   SONGS

FOREWORD BY CHRISTOPHER PHILLIPS

OMNIBUS PRESS
Part of **The Music Sales Group**
New York/London/Paris/Sydney/Copenhagen/Berlin/Tokyo/Madrid

Omnibus Press
A Division of Music Sales Corporation, New York

Exclusive Distributors:
Music Sales Corporation
257 Park Avenue South, New York, NY 10010 USA
Music Sales Limited
14 - 15 Berners Street, London W1T 3LJ England
Music Sales Pty. Limited
120 Rothschild Street, Rosebery, Sydney, NSW 2018, Australia

Order No. OP51557
International Standard Book Number: 0.8256.3470.9

Printed in the United States of America

Visit Omnibus Press on the web at www.omnibuspress.com

Library of Congress Cataloging-in-Publication Data

Sawyers, June Skinner, 1957-
  Tougher than the rest : 100 best Bruce Springsteen songs / June Skinner Sawyers.
      p. cm.
  Includes index.
  ISBN 0-8256-3470-9 (pbk.)
  1. Springsteen, Bruce. Songs. 2. Rock music—United States—History and criticism. I. Title.
  II. Title: 100 best Bruce Springsteen songs.

  ML420.S77S3 2006
  782.42166092—dc22

                                                                                        2006026804

Special thanks to Mona Okada at Grubman, Indursky & Shire, P.C. (Bruce Springsteen's management company)

"Where there is no hope, one must invent hope."
—Camus

*"A song ain't nuthin' in the world but a story
just wrote with music to it."*
—Hank Williams

Table Of Contents

Acknowlegments vii

Foreword by Christopher Phillips ix

Introduction xiii

Greetings From Asbury Park, NJ. 1

The Wild, The Innocent & The E Street Shuffle 11

Born To Run 23

Darkness On The Edge Of Town 35

The River 51

Nebraska 67

Born In The U.S.A. 89

Tunnel Of Love 105

Human Touch 121

Lucky Town 125

The Ghost Of Tom Joad 133

The Rising 159

Devils & Dust 173

LIVE CONCERTS AND COMPILATIONS 185

Bruce Springsteen & The E StreetBand Live/1975–85 187

Bruce Springsteen Greatest Hits 195

Tracks 203

18 Tracks 225

The Essential Bruce Springsteen 231

...And Sixty More 247

Further Reading 261

About the Author 269

Index 271

Acknowledgments

I wish to thank the many Springsteen fans everywhere, but especially those truly dedicated folk who worked so hard to organize and participate in Glory Days: A Bruce Springsteen Symposium, a truly remarkable mélange of scholarship, music, and fun. Organized by Penn State, it was held from September 8–11, 2005, at the Sheraton Eatontown Center in Eatontown, New Jersey, and on the campus of Monmouth University in West Long Branch, New Jersey. In particular, I thank the following for their support and opinions (whether they agreed with me or not): the Glory Days contingent of Nancy Bishop, Karen Chapman, Woody Dresden, Alison MacLennan, and Marya Morris and Glory Days organizers Mark Bernhard, Ken Womack, and Jerry Zolten. My fellow panelists at the conference—Paul D. Fischer, Jeffrey B. Symynkywicx, and especially Stephen A. Horan—were more helpful than they probably realize. Theresa Albini took many of the photographs that appear while artist Kreg Yingst provided the evocative linocut of Springsteen set against a backdrop of smokestacks. You can view his artwork at *www.kregyingst.com.* The exhibits at the Johnstown Flood Museum in Johnstown, Pennsylvania, helped me better understand the magnitude of the disaster. My editor, Andrea Rotondo, was a pleasure to work with as well as remarkably patient.

Many people—some in conversation, others through their work—helped me shape my thoughts. They include Springsteen biographer Dave Marsh, author Bobbie Ann Mason, songwriter Gretchen Peters, writer Dale Maharidge as well as Bryan K. Garman, Robert Santelli, Joe Grushecky, Don McLeese, Jefferson Cowie, Jim Cullen, Colleen Sheehy, Craig Werner, Samuele F. S. Pardini, Ellie Deegan, and Dave Romano. Whenever I've had the pleasure of bumping into photographer extraordinaire Frank Stefankon, he has been both supportive and gracious as has Springsteen scholar Bob Crane. In addition, I thank Stan Goldstein and Jean Mikle for offering their wonderful Asbury Park and Freehold tours. May they long continue. I am also indebted to Daniel Wolff, author of the truly marvelous *4ᵗʰ of July, Asbury Park: A History of the Promised Land,* for making the connection in his book between Springsteen and Stephen Crane.

Finally, thanks to *Backstreets* editor Christopher Phillips for writing the Foreword. We may not always agree (how boring would that be?) but I always value and respect his opinion, nevertheless.

Foreword
By Christopher Phillips

June Skinner Sawyers is just asking for trouble. Compiling a list of the "best" Bruce Springsteen songs is a tricky business, as you know if you've ever compiled a Springsteen mix to try to turn on a friend, or just drawn up a *High Fidelity*-style list of your own. You know the agonizing decisions that have to be made, the various sides of his songwriting that have to be represented, the sentimental favorites that you can't imagine your life without, but really, do they make *the list*? Those internal debates are one thing; June's doing it for all of us to see. Considering the wealth of top-notch songs and the passion—in some cases, rabidity—of many of Springsteen's fans, whittling down the catalog is bound to invite debate.

Take Springsteen's 1995 *Greatest Hits* release, the first compilation of its kind and an "official" take on the Best Bruce Springsteen Songs—with "Rosalita" nowhere to be found. In fact, there wasn't a single cut from the first two albums on *Greatest Hits*: no "Blinded By The Light," no "Spirit In The Night,' no "Growin' Up." Granted, it was a "hits" collection, not a "best of," but the omission seemed to suggest that Bruce didn't start writing good songs until 1975. And later actual hits like "I'm On Fire" and "Tunnel Of Love" fell by the wayside as well. If, as a Springsteen fan, you've been on this train for a while, you might remember the outcry. (A more representative studio retrospective, 2003's two-disc *The Essential Bruce Springsteen*, gave "Rosie" and some of her kin their rightful place in the canon.)

Greatest Hits boiled it all down to 14 songs. June gave herself a more expansive limit of 100. Surely that casts a wide enough net to make this a cinch, right? But simple math tells you that she's still up against it—with more than 250 officially released songs, by her count, we're talking 60 percent of Springsteen's babies left brokenhearted from the start.

Then she goes and leaves off half of *Born To Run*. She's really asking for trouble.

But lists like these are subjective, so I won't take issue with her picks. Though, of course, that's half the fun of this whole list-making business. Just as an audience is integral to a great Springsteen show—he has applied the alternate meaning of "in concert," as a phrase that should describe the relationship between the performer and the crowd—lists like these wouldn't be nearly as meaningful without someone else to nod with approval, raise an eyebrow, or cry foul. You know, those fans and trainspotters with their but-what-abouts and how-could-yous.

So, just for the sake of doing my part, I'll gripe about *Born To Run*. My guess before cracking these pages was that all eight songs would make the cut. Maybe "Meeting Across The River" might have to go... but you can't have "Jungleland" without "Meeting," and surely "Jungleland" would be on the list, no?

No!

Okay, though "Jungleland" would make my top 20, it's hard to argue with June's description of the song as overwrought. And "Backstreets"—a song near to my heart—is the epic chosen in its stead, so we'll let "Jungleland" go. But cripes, no "She's The One" or "Night"? Oh, the perennially underrated "Night"—a headlong rush of a song that, thanks to its mere excellence compared with the perfection of the rest of the album, has always seemed like the ugly stepkid among the songs on *Born To Run*. To a rational mind, I guess that's reason enough to drop it on down the ranks. But that's also the very reason why it's a favorite of mine— it's a song I want to wrap my arms around, tell it I understand, that it's loved. "Night" is a song I can root for. And the couplet "The world is busting at its seams / And you're just a prisoner of your dreams" is right up there with any quintessential Springsteen lyric you can name. Not even in the top *160*? Well, I guess that'll make me love it all the more.

June's got plenty of her own underdogs—"I Wanna Marry You" hits me as a bold choice, a beauty of a song I somehow tend to lump in with *The River's* throwaway puff-pieces like "Crush On You" and "I'm A Rocker." She makes a good case for it here, tracing a nice through-line from "Thunder Road" and accurately noting that if "I Wanna Marry You" "had been released in the Sixties, it probably would have been a huge hit." Fair enough.

Many of her underdog favorites are also my own—she plucks "Seeds" from *Live/1975-'85,* "County Fair" from *Essential,* "Wages of Sin" and "Shut Out the Light" from *Tracks.* Those feel good—it's partly the validation that any good list gives, and partly the idea that a more casual fan reading this book might be moved to explore these overlooked corners of Springsteen's catalog.

It's gratifying, too, to see *Tunnel Of Love* and *Nebraska,* my two favorite albums other than the in-its-own-league *Born to Run,* get so many songs in the upper echelon here. In fact, the just-as-deserving *Nebraska* nearly gets the treatment I imagined for *Born To Run*—nine of its 10 songs make this list. Much as I hate to see "Used Cars" kicked to the curb, there's something poetically apropos about leaving that one song behind. Your number still hasn't come in, kid.

On the other hand, like *Greatest Hits,* June's list leans away from the first two albums. My taste runs in a similar vein, but there are still some clear but-what-abouts here. "Incident on 57th Street" and "Does This Bus Stop at 82nd Street" don't make the top 100—but "Working On The Highway" does? How could you? And while I'm at it, "Balboa Park" over "Be True"? "Factory" over "Fire"? "Rockaway The Days" over... well, just about anything else?

But as I say, this is a subjective list; I'll resist the urge to bitch and moan. And June has more on her mind than just list-making. With the heart of a fan and the head of a scholar she uses these songs as a jumping-off point for rumination, information, and cogitation that just might make you hear some of these songs differently. She connects "Walk Like A Man" with "Mystery Train," and "Thunder Road" with Whitman's "Song Of The Open Road"; she hears Rod Stewart's "Every Picture Tells A Story" in the hair-combing of "Growin' Up" and "Dancing In The Dark." She notes that "Rosalita" is the only song on *The Wild, the Innocent & the E Street Shuffle* with a chorus, that "Thunder Road" "reads like the opening lines of a screenplay." (It's true—"The screen door slams. Mary's dress waves." Those are stage directions!)

As the songs pile up, so do their themes, and June is on it. She follows the recurring symbol of the Promised Land throughout Springsteen's work: from its first appearance on "Thunder Road," to its predominance as an image on *Darkness On The Edge Of Town,* to its ambiguous place in *The River's* "The Price You Pay." She traces the influences that have inspired these songs, from all the movies—*Thunder Road, Badlands, Night Of The Hunter, Alamo Bay, Inherit The Wind,* and of course, *The Grapes Of Wrath*—to artists like Hank Williams and Flannery O'Connor. She offers history lessons: "Sandy" and "My City Of Ruins" become opportunities to chronicle the ups and downs of Asbury Park, and songs like "Nebraska" and "Roulette" lead to the true-life tales that inspired them, connecting Springsteen's songs to the real world.

Waitasec. Real world... "Real World" doesn't make the list? You're telling me that "All Or Nothin' At All" is a better song than "Real World"? Okay, Mister Trouble come walkin' this way—go give him hell.

Introduction

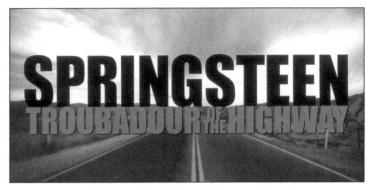

"Troubadour of the Highway." (Author collection)

B ruce Springsteen has written roughly more than 250 songs. And those are just the ones that have been officially released. Who knows how many more are hidden somewhere in the vaults.

In *Tougher Than The Rest,* I have chosen what I think are his best 100. I realize, of course, that my idea of best is not necessarily the same as yours. Springsteen fans are among the most passionate in the world. Identification between *this* singer and *his* audience is fierce and sincere. Not all of your favorite songs will be mentioned in these pages (although a good many will). Undoubtedly, there will be much difference of opinion, but I suspect we will agree more than we will disagree.

Tougher Than The Rest is not intended to be a musical analysis. Rather, it is a synthesis of history, anecdotes, interpretation, and personal opinion. I describe the narrative structure of the song—if there is one—and, when appropriate, place the song in its historical and cultural framework. When appropriate, I also trace the origin or inspiration of a song. Not every song warrants lengthy discussion. Sometimes a song just *sounds* great and the less said the better. Essentially, I draw my commentary from a combination of published interviews, personal reflection, and my own interpretation, but I also share the opinions of other critics and pundits.

I also include sidebars—some just for the fun of it (Ten Funniest Springsteen Songs, for example); others offer additional information that didn't quite fit in the text proper. In addition, the text is augmented by photographs, postcards, and other paraphernalia that, I think, will considerably enhance your enjoyment of the book. As a bonus, I also include brief snippets of an additional 60 songs.

The songs are arranged chronologically from *Greetings From Asbury Park, N.J.* in 1973 to *Devils & Dust* in 2005. Individual songs from compilations, greatest hits, and other collections are discussed if they contain original material. For this reason, *We Shall Overcome: The Seeger Sessions*—Springsteen's interpretations of traditional songs that was released in spring 2006—is not included (although I do discuss aspects of it in a sidebar).

What makes a song great? More to the point, what makes a Bruce Springsteen song great? Sometimes it can be a combination of a great lyric and a terrific piece of music. Sometimes, the story may be so powerful that to ignore it would be a crime. Some songs pack a wallop, others are more delicate. And sometimes it's just pure emotion—the way a song makes you *feel*—that makes you want to listen to it over and over again. Songwriting may be a craft, but it is also a mystery.

"Good songs work on many different levels; that's what makes them good, that's what makes them last," Springsteen once said. That's why his songs can be such a joy. They do work on many levels. Often, they are complex organisms with quite distinctive lives of their own.

Springsteen has written about himself, especially during his early days when he composed what he called "twisted autobiographies." As he got older, though, he began to look outside of his immediate environment—beyond New Jersey and the East—and wrote about other people and their often-difficult circumstances. Like a novelist or short story writer, he creates characters. More and more, he has learned to say more with less (quite a contrast from his early attempts at songwriting). He has become a master of economy. With just a few lines, he is able to create a set of believable characters in a recognizable milieu. He is, in other words, a minimalist of the finest order.

Much has been written about the special relationship that exists between Springsteen and his fans. And, it's true, when it comes to Bruce Springsteen, music is more than just mere entertainment. It's a calling, a form of collective salvation.

When he was a young man, Springsteen believed that rock 'n' roll could save lives. It saved his life. As he matured, he realized that he needed more than just music, and this new-found maturity is reflected in his music. But the excitement of being onstage, of connecting with the audience, is still very much the reason he does what he does. A perennial question—some say *the* human question—is, How do I live my life with meaning? This is the question that has consumed Springsteen his entire adult life. It is the question that gives his songs their remarkable strength and durability.

"Walking offstage is a clearing experience," he says. He has called the act of picking up a guitar and singing as "self-medication." Performing, getting onstage, "was the only recourse to the roaring confusion that was my internal life. To this day, I feel re-centered when I come down those steps. I feel a sense of communication and connectedness and a reason to get up in the morning. I've spoken to the people, and they've spoken to me."

Springsteen is both a consummate performer *and* a consummate storyteller. These then are among the best of his stories, among the best of his songs.

A final word. All 160 of these songs speak to me on some level—some more so than others. I've tried my best to explain their significance, what set them apart, but ultimately it all comes down to one crucial question, do they pass the goosebump test or a variation of it? Such a subjective question requires subjective responses. Here they are.

Greetings From Asbury Park, NJ.
(Columbia, 1973)

An exuberant debut, Springsteen displays his musical influences prominently on his sleeve, ranging from Bob Dylan of course, but also Van Morrison and The Band. (*Rolling Stone* thought Springsteen's *Greetings* sounded like "'Subterranean Homesick Blues' at 78.") *Greetings* received mostly excellent reviews but the record sold poorly—less than 50,000 copies. But this is where it all started.

Musicians:

Bruce Springsteen: acoustic guitar, electric guitar, conga, harmonica, bass, piano

Vincent Lopez: drums, background vocals, handclaps

Clarence Clemons: sax

Garry Tallent: bass

David Sancious: piano, organ

Harold Wheeler: piano

Richard Davis: upright bass

Producers: Mike Appel and Jim Cretecos

Recorded at: 914 Sound Studios (Blauvelt, NY)

Tracks:

"Blinded By The Light" (5:02)

"Growin' Up" (3:05)

"Mary Queen Of Arkansas" (5:20)

"Does This Bus Stop At 82nd Street?" (2:05)

"Lost In The Flood" (5:14)

"The Angel" (3:23)

"For You" (4:39)

"Spirit In The Night" (4:48)

"It's Hard To Be A Saint In The City" (3:13)

Running time: 35:79

Titles in boldface refer to songs discussed in the text. Titles in italics refer to songs discussed in the bonus section.

"Blinded By The Light"
from *Greetings From Asbury Park N.J.*
(Columbia, 1973)

Of all the early Springsteen songs, "Blinded By The Light" is among the most Dylanesque. With its prolix lyrics, impressionistic writing style, and full-throttled rock 'n' roll, it most reflected the characteristics of Bob Dylan. Springsteen was well aware of the Dylan comparisons at the time, and to his credit, took it in stride.

"Bob Dylan? I like the cat," Springsteen once said, displaying his 1970s patois to full effect. He admitted some similarities "somewhere," but he emphasized, "[w]e come from two totally different scenes…" And then he listed the musicians who directly influenced him: Elvis Presley, Otis Redding, Sam Cooke, Wilson Pickett, The Beatles, Fats Domino, and even Benny Goodman. "You can hear them all in there if you want."

"Blinded By The Light" is a wild piece of music, a frothy, loosey-goosey concoction of utter abandon. A flood of images come at you with little or no warning and yet the language itself is simple, the characters ordinary people (eccentric perhaps but still ordinary). It's clear that Springsteen is having a blast here, not only playing with the inherent musicality of the English language, but also poking fun at himself and his ragtag bunch of New Jersey street rats.

The song itself may not make much sense from a conventional point of view—it will never be confused with anything from Tin Pan Alley or the Brill Building songbooks—but the images are among the most vibrant in the Springsteen canon. Fleshpot mascots, a bloodshot forget-me-not, or a rolling stone preacher from the East are not the types of people you meet in most pop songs. And the names Springsteen gives this motley crew of characters—go-cart Mozart, little Early-Pearly—live in a weird alternate universe somewhere along the Jersey Shore. Indeed, most of the songs, notes Springsteen, were "twisted autobiographies."

Several years after it was released, "Blinded By The Light" became a Number One hit on the *Billboard* charts in early 1977. But significantly, it was a hit not for Springsteen but for the English group Manfred Mann, previously known for such Sixties classics as "Pretty Flamingo" and the Dylan-penned "The Mighty Quinn."

The entire album was cut in three weeks. But after it was finished, Clive Davis, president of the Columbia record label at the time, came back to

OTHER PEOPLE'S VOICES

Springsteen knows where he came from. As a rock 'n' roll historian, he has impeccable taste in other people's music. Most of the songs he has covered over the years are heavy on Chuck Berry, soul, and Sixties classics (especially Creedence Clearwater Revival). The following is a sampling of covers that Springsteen, thus far, has *not* committed to vinyl:

"On Top Of Old Smokey"
"Waltz Across Texas"
"Twist And Shout"
"Follow That Dream"
"Mountain Of Love"
"I Want You"
"Who'll Stop The Rain?"
"Run Through The Jungle"
"Rockin' All Over The World"
"Proud Mary"
"Deportee (Plane Wreck At Los Gatos)"
"Precious Memories"
"Dream Baby Dream"
"Wooly Bully"
"Mony Mony"
"Do You Love Me?"
"Highway 61 Revisited"
"Across the Borderline"
"Satan's Jewel Crown"
"Jole Blon"
"Quarter To Three"
"Oklahoma Hills"
"Long Black Veil"
"When The Saints Go Marching In"
"Dirty Water"

Springsteen and complained that nothing on the record sounded even remotely commercial. In other words, there was no single material. Springsteen went home and wrote two songs, "Blinded By The Light" and "Spirit In The Night."

The songs from *Greetings* were written during a particular moment in time. Springsteen himself admitted that he never wrote in that spontaneous, stream-of-conscious style again. "Once the record was released I heard all the 'new Dylan' comparisons, so I steered away from it," he said. Springsteen wrote the songs on *Greetings* from a very "unselfconscious place. Your early songs come out of a moment when you're writing with no sure prospect of ever being heard. Up until then, it's just you and your music." Mostly, he was writing for himself and for the hard-core fans who found in his music a reflection of themselves.

The critical response was almost visceral. The legendary *Rolling Stone* critic Lester Bangs called Springsteen "a bold new talent with more than a mouthful to say…"

Greetings was the beginning of something big, and "Blinded By The Light" its apotheosis.

"Growin' Up"
from *Greetings From Asbury Park, N.J.*
(Columbia, 1973)

"Growin' Up," one of the essential Springsteen songs, contains one of the most telling Springsteen lyrics: *And I swear I found the key to the universe in the engine of an old parked car.*

There it is—the very essence of the Springsteen persona—summed up in a single line: his yearning for something better, his spirituality, the worship of the automobile, and the promise of mobility, freedom, and independence it can bring. The most important thing to remember here is to move forward, to not look back or, to borrow a later Springsteen phrase, to go on further down the road.

Basically, "Growin' Up" is Springsteen's autobiography in three minutes and five seconds. But there is more. Much more. When he admits to combing his hair "till it was just right," it conjures up the image of Rod Stewart's rock classic "Every Picture Tells A Story," released two years earlier, wherein the protagonist of Stewart's randy tale combs his hair "a thousand ways" and ends up looking just the same. And a little more than ten years later in "Dancing In The Dark," Springsteen again looks in the mirror and finds the face looking back at him lacking—in something. "I wanna change my clothes, my hair, my face."

In 1963 Springsteen enrolled as a freshman at Freehold High School in his hometown of Freehold, New Jersey, during a time of racial tensions. A loner at heart—he had no interest in sports or school activities—music was the only thing that kept him going. He joined a rock band, the Castiles, two years later in 1965. Despite being in a band (or perhaps because of it), he still felt like an outcast among the larger student body. So much so that when he graduated he was barred from commencement exercises because his peers did not appreciate his long hair.

"I suffered daily, daily defeat and humiliation in front of my peers in high school," Springsteen admitted in October 1984 during a performance at the Oakland Coliseum. "When fall comes around I'm still glad that I don't have to go to high school."

Life at home wasn't much better. In one of his many loquacious introductions before a live audience, Springsteen described what it was like growing up in a household headed by a remote, taciturn, emotionally challenged father who worked too many hours at tedious jobs that he hated:

> When I was growing up, there were two things that were unpopular in my house. One was me, and the other was my guitar. We had this grate, like the heat was supposed to come through, except it wasn't hooked up to any of the heating ducts; it was just open straight down to the kitchen, and there was a gas stove right underneath it. When I used to start playing, my pop used to turn on the gas jet and try to smoke me out of the room. And I had to go hide on the roof or something.

Springsteen's childhood home, Freehold, NJ. (Theresa Albini)

Throughout the length of the song, Springsteen is contrary ("when they said 'Sit down' I stood up"), rebellious ("I broke all the rules"), and in a state of inner turmoil ("I swear I lost everything I ever loved or feared…"). But he also finds in the most commonplace of things, in the ordinariness of everyday life, something approaching the transcendental.

"Growin' Up" was recorded at CBS Studios in New York on May 3, 1972, one of 12 songs performed at Springsteen's audition for the legendary producer John Hammond. It remains one of his signature songs, as eagerly awaited today in concert as it was more than 30 years ago. But, like the singer itself, it has changed over the years, becoming, in retrospect, a haunting memory of a life as it was once lived. When Springsteen offered a marvelous and considerably slowed-down version during the *Devils & Dust* tour of 2005 played on, of all things, a ukulele, it no longer felt like a song written by someone barely out of high school. It triggered many emotions: a touch of wisdom, a smattering of whimsy perhaps, and more than its share of regret.

PASSING THE AUDITION

In early May 1972, Bruce Springsteen performed at the Gaslight in Greenwich Village. Although there were no more than a dozen people in the crowd, the audience member that mattered the most, the audience of one for whom Springsteen was playing *to*, was the legendary Columbia Records producer John Hammond. In fact, with the exception of Hammond, no one gave the scruffy Dylan look-alike much heed. According to writer Dunstan Prial, the 22-year-old Springsteen, who had something of a folkie reputation at the time, was wearing "scuffed motorcycle boots, ragged blue jeans, and an ill-fitting T-shirt…" and "looked more like James Dean in *Rebel Without a Cause* or Marlon Brando in *The Wild One* than Woody Guthrie or Jack Kerouac." Earlier in the day, Springsteen and his then-manager Mike Appel had stopped by Hammond's office at Fifty-second Street and Sixth Avenue. Hammond had been impressed by the New Jersey native's storytelling abilities, by his passion, and by his natural charisma. The next day Springsteen recorded a handful of songs: "Growin' Up," "It's Hard To Be A Saint In The City," "Mary Queen Of Arkansas," "Does This Bus Stop At 82nd Street?," and "The Angel"—all would appear on his first album—as well as "If I Was The Priest," "Southern Son," "Street Queen," and "Cowboys Of The Sea." It was the beginning of a beautiful, if short-lived, friendship. Hammond died on July 10, 1987. At a memorial service held in Manhattan several months later, Springsteen sang Dylan's "Forever Young" in his honor.

"For You"

from *Greetings From Asbury Park, N.J.*
(Columbia, 1973)

It was a hit for the Greg Kihn Band but the only version that counts was sung by Springsteen on his first album. From the moment the first chord strikes, we sense the song's urgency. And as we soon learn, the story involves a matter of life and death. A woman has attempted suicide "with no apparent motive" and the narrator is there for her. "I came for you," and then repeats as if there was any doubt, "for you."

It is a song set in a real place—the attempted suicide occurs in the Chelsea neighborhood of Manhattan—and a patient is brought to a real hospital ("'Cause they're waiting for you at Bellevue with their oxygen masks"). But, ultimately, it is the very real emotions that ring true. The grittiness of it seems even more authentic because we can believe that these people actually exist. It is their story and, in this particular case, the fate of a very real life is truly at stake.

The relationship is not an easy one but the narrator is committed to saving this lost soul, to seeing this through no matter what. Her pulse is weakening by the moment. He urges her—no, dares her, as she lies prostate in the ambulance—to open herself up to him, to reveal her secrets before it is too late ("while you've got the strength to speak"). He is not ready to let her go. If he could, as he makes clear, he would give up his own life for her ("if only you could ask"). And yet he admires her ability to hang on, even as she is fighting for a life that she herself chose to put into jeopardy.

He then recalls the time when he was the strong one and she the broken shell, when he would reach out to her—but at arm's length—not quite sure perhaps if this vulnerable and troubled young woman was worth the pursuit. Both were looking to get away—who knew where?—but nevertheless were always on the lookout for something better. She is the one who left her own home to find a better life or at least a better reason to live "than the one we were living for."

What is most striking about "For You" is its humanity and the fact that someone can care so much about someone else that he would be willing to put his life on the line for her. It is this very vulnerability that appeals to Springsteen fans, especially women.

Perhaps the best example of how the song affected people, how this particular song encapsulates the special relationship that exists between Springsteen and his fans, is found in Elizabeth Wurtzel's *Prozac Nation,* a disquieting memoir about clinical depression. Like many young people who feel isolated from society, Wurtzel turned to music for solace. So many Springsteen fans feel they have a personal connection with the singer, as if he is singing directly to them and singing directly about their experiences. For Wurtzel, Springsteen, more than anyone, seemed to understand her, seemed to empathize with her, even if it was only in his songs.

Wurtzel identifies with Springsteen and his Jersey roots so much that she wishes she could be a boy in New Jersey. In vain, of course, she tries to convince her mother that they should move there. "I want so badly to have my life circumstances match the oppressiveness I feel internally." She realizes both the absurdity and the irony of it all. Springsteen is trying to get out of New Jersey while she is trying to get in.

Not surprisingly, given its subject matter, Wurtzel is particularly taken by "For You." She identifies with the suicidal victim of the song. "That's me," she writes. "I'm the girl who is lost in space, the girl who is disappearing always, forever fading away and receding farther and farther into the background." With each passing day, she feels more and more invisible. The one thing that separates her from the girl in the song, though, is she has no one to rescue her. No New Jersey savior waiting in the wings. No one to pick up the pieces to put her back together again. No one to save her from herself.

"Spirit In The Night"
from *Greetings From Asbury Park, N.J.*
(Columbia, 1973)

If one had to choose a single cut from *Greetings* that truly captured the heady exuberance, the sheer giddiness of its singular listening experience, that song would be "Spirit In The Night," a tale about a late-night joyride by a bunch of Jersey losers. They bear names like Crazy Janey and Wild Billy and his friend G-man along with Hazy Davy and Killer Joe. Talk about an egalitarian mix. With the exception of Crazy Janey, they are adolescent males who usually travel as a pack.

Billy is the one who asks his mates if they want to go up to Greasy Lake. "It's about a mile down on the dark side of Route 88." The narrator brings along a bottle of wine—Springsteen is very specific here about the kind of wine (a bottle of rosé). He picks up Hazy Davy and Killer Joe and the party begins.

Living up to his name, Wild Billy is a bit of "a crazy cat" with a preference for coonskin caps. Before you know it, everyone is dancing under a moonlit night. Billy and Davy end up near the lake in a mud fight, essentially stoned out of their mind, Killer Joe passes out and the narrator and Crazy Janey make love "in the dirt singin' our birthday songs."

T.C. Boyle wrote a short story called "Greasy Lake" that was inspired by the Springsteen song. And like the song, Boyle's characters are party animals, although with a slightly more dangerous edge to them. "We wore torn-up leather jackets, slouched around with toothpicks in our mouths, sniffed glue and ether and what somebody claimed was cocaine." They drink gin and grape juice and are all of 19. Boyle's story takes place in early June, on the third night of summer vacation. Everyone is terminally bored, aimless, and restless. They cruise up and down the strip, go in and out of every bar, eat bucket chicken and cheap hamburgers, and throw raw eggs at mailboxes and hitchhikers.

Boyle's Greasy Lake is fetid and murky, "the mud banks glittering with broken glass and strewn with beer cans and the charred remains of bonfires." For these small-town drifters, Greasy Lake was the place to be. "We went up to the lake because everyone went there, because we wanted to snuff the rich scent of possibility on the breeze, watch a girl take off her clothes and plunge into the festering murk, drink beer, smoke pot, howl at the stars, savor the incongruous full-throated roar of rock 'n' roll against the primeval susurrus of frogs and crickets." If this short paragraph doesn't sum up early Springsteen, I don't what does.

Did Greasy Lake ever exist? That's one of the perennial questions on the minds of Springsteen fans. According to Vini Lopez, the first drummer in the E Street Band, Greasy Lake is really a composite of places. "88" is said to refer to Exit 88 off the Garden State Parkway. The band members would drive north "onto an undeveloped road," and, writes Springsteen expert Bob Crane, "reached a lovers lane complete with swamps and a lake." The lake, Crane adds, is gone now, absorbed by an industrial park development.

"Spirit In The Night" is Springsteen at his ebullient, infectious best. Listening to it you can't help but manage a goofy grin and shake your head at the sheer brassy impudence of it. He would never quite sound this unaffected again, never quite seem as if he was having this much fun on a record (well, he sure comes close though on *We Shall Overcome: The Seeger Sessions*). The crazy cast of characters that Springsteen sings about in the song function as the alter egos for the cast of characters who were either members of his band or friends and associates or simply hangers-on. In this case, life not only imitated art, it preceded art.

The Wild, The Innocent & The E Street Shuffle

(Columbia, 1973)

By the time of the release of his second album, *The Wild, The Innocent & The E Street Shuffle*, the mainstream rock press thought Springsteen a "considerable new talent." The songs depict teenage street life—more specifically, Asbury Park street life—in all its manifestations and moods: tough, wistful, and longing to escape. To *Creem*'s Ed Ward, it was "either a flawed work of genius or else a work of flawed genius. It's irregular as hell, inconsistent, annoying sometimes, but once you've listened to it a couple of times…you forgive all that and just *get off.*" To *Crawdaddy!*, it was a more "musically mature and eclectic" work. Springsteen himself described the sound on the album as being the work of "a little carnie band." It features two of Springsteen's most durable classics, the wistful "4ᵗʰ Of July, Asbury Park (Sandy)" and the crowd-pleasing rave-up, "Rosalita (Come Out Tonight)."

Musicians:

Bruce Springsteen: guitars, harmonica, mandolin, recorder, lead vocals

Clarence Clemons: saxophone and background vocals

David L. Sancious: piano, organ, electric piano, clavinet, soprano sax, background vocals

Vini "Mad Dog" Lopez: drums, background vocals, coronet

Danny Federici: accordion, background vocals, piano, organ

Garry W. Tallent: bass, tuba, background vocals

Richard Blackwell: congos and percussion

Albany "Al" Tellone: baritone sax

Producers: Mike Appel and Jim Cretecos

Recorded at: 914 Sound Studios (Blauvelt, NY)

Tracks:

"The E Street Shuffle" (4:31)

"4th Of July, Asbury Park (Sandy)" (5:36)

"Kitty's Back" (7:09)

"Wild Billy's Circus Story" (4:47)

"Incident On 57th Street" (7:45)

"Rosalita (Come Out Tonight)" (7:04)

"New York City Serenade" (9:55)

Running time: 45:27

Vintage Asbury Park postcard. (Author collection)

"4th Of July, Asbury Park (Sandy)"

from *The Wild, The Innocent & The E Street Shuffle*
(Columbia, 1973)

What Yoknapatawpha County was to William Faulkner, what Dublin was to James Joyce, Asbury Park is to Bruce Springsteen. The song that encapsulates so beautifully the enigma of Asbury begins with the strum of an acoustic guitar. It captures a moment as ephemeral as a sunny day along the shore and immediately sets the laidback, elegiac mood of the song. "4th Of July, Asbury Park (Sandy)" is Springsteen's musical love letter to his adopted home town of Asbury Park, that backwater, working-class resort town that, despite already being down on its luck, miraculously gave *him* hope. Ironically, an earlier famous son of Asbury Park, the novelist Stephen Crane, saw not hope here but despair and hypocrisy. Springsteen a century later saw something else—a sense of purpose and meaning. Amid the ruins of the seaside town that was collapsing before his very eyes, Springsteen found himself.

Asbury Park boardwalk. (June Sawyers)

"Sandy" epitomizes the Asbury Park that Springsteen knew in the late 1960s and early 1970s, its seediness, certainly, but also its faded charm. It is no coincidence that in the song he refers to Asbury as his "Little Eden," his version of an earthly paradise, even though it is located in a rough-and-tumble Jersey Shore town populated by "switchblade lovers" and "wizards" who play on Pinball Way "way past dark"; boys from the casino who dance with their shirts open, and lovers who sleep on the beach. To Springsteen, the ruins of Asbury Park functioned as a "metaphor for the end of a summer romance." It is also a deeply romanticized portrait of a place that had witnessed better days.

As anyone who has been to Asbury Park knows, Springsteen uses in this song—and elsewhere, especially in "My City Of Ruins" written some 30 years later—actual settings, cultural landmarks that he knew so well: the eponymous boardwalk, of course, but also the casino at the southern end of the boardwalk and most evocatively perhaps, Madam Marie (Marie Castello), the now legendary fortuneteller who, at least in song, was arrested by the cops (a nice piece of poetic license here) "for tellin' fortunes better than they do." Years later, Springsteen talked to Ed Bradley on *60 Minutes* about Madam Marie. "Sure, she told me I was going to be rich and famous. But she probably told that to all the guitar players." And even today, the fortune-telling booth still stands along the boardwalk—family members run it nowadays—her name screaming out in red neon and the misspelled words (somehow adding to her charm) and beckoning all to enter:

Madam Marie, Asbury Park, NJ. (June Sawyers)

WORLD FAMOUS
MADAM MARIE
FOR IMEDIATE APPOINTMENT
HER LEGEND CONTINUES
WITH A NEW BEGINNING

Sandy was a composite of the girls Springsteen knew along the Jersey Shore. "The stuff I write is what I live with," Springsteen said at the time. "The stories are all around me. I just put 'em down."

"4ᵗʰ Of July" is a love song about two Jersey tramps, drifters on the boardwalk and drifters in life, who manage to survive in a gritty yet still fairy-tale like setting of amusement parks, penny arcades, and sandy beaches. Jimmy Guterman, author of Springsteen bio *Runaway American Dream,* has called "4ᵗʰ Of July" "a warm tale of failure"—in this case, failure to get the girl, failure to keep a job, failure even to enjoy a simple carnival ride (he gets his shirt caught on a tilt-a-whirl) without something going wrong (in an almost-spoken voice, he sheepishly admits, that he didn't think he would ever get off it).

One hears in the song an almost palpable yearning for something more satisfying than an amusement park ride or the superficial relationships symbolized by fleeting summer romances. It doesn't help that the narrator can't keep his mouth shut. He blurts out to Sandy that his affair with a waitress who worked "that joint" under the boardwalk is over ("she won't set herself on fire for me anymore"). He hears too that she was seen by the local kids dressed like a starlet in one of the cheap little seaside bars that are scattered along the Shore. He himself sees her with her lover boy in a parked car. The emptiness of the "carnival life" now overwhelms him and he asks Sandy to leave all of it behind and join him for a more meaningful life. "I mean it, Sandy girl…Yes, I promise, Sandy girl," he sings at the end of the song but somehow we doubt his resolve.

The song is also an absolute joy to listen to as the complex arrangements—Springsteen's acoustic guitar, Danny Federici's irresistible accordion, David Sancious' delicious keyboards, and the ethereal vocals—weave in and out like the ebbing and flowing of the ocean waves. You can almost taste the salt water taffy. According to Guterman, Springsteen wanted to include a children's chorus in the song but, unable to do so, he overdubs violin player Suki Lahav's voice to approximate the sound of children along the shore.

The story of Asbury Park is the story of America in microcosm, or at least the part of America that has fallen on tough times and struggles to reinvent itself. One can see why Springsteen fell in love with its faded charm so easily. Did he see in its roughness a part of himself? Did the fact that the town once held out so much promise resonate with him?

Daniel Wolff is a journalist and a poet. With the publication of the wonderful *Fourth Of July, Asbury Park: A History Of The Promised Land* in 2005, he also could be considered the unofficial biographer of Asbury Park itself. He believes that the city can—and does—represent the nation's history (and makes a convincing case of it). What's more, in the town's up and down history he senses too the "shape and feel of rock 'n' roll." Rock 'n' roll, he writes, "keeps jumping to what moves us, hurrying to the next climax, deliberately repeating itself as it tries to get and keep our attention."

In 1870, New York brush manufacturer James A. Bradley bought 500 acres along the Jersey Shore for approximately $90,000 and a year later founded a town that he called Asbury Park named in honor of Francis Asbury, considered the father of American Methodism and the first Methodist bishop in the United States.

Thus, Asbury Park began life as a religious community much like its neighbor to the south, Ocean Grove. Bradley strove to create a moral community, a dream city populated by moral citizens. It is he who is responsible for the broad boulevards and the promenade next to the sea (called appropriately enough Ocean Avenue). The large Victorian homes with mansard roofs and wraparound porches that still exist also owe a lot to Bradley's vision of a seaside promised land. Street names such as Kingsley, Heck, and Webb commemorated Methodist bishops and ministers. Bradley was also responsible for building the beachfront and boardwalk.

It's hard to believe now, but before World War II, swanky hotel after swanky hotel lined the boardwalk—in fact, more than 200 hotels and boarding houses, many of them set back from the beach. Its summer population often swelled to as much as 50,000 people (it only had 3,000 year-round residents). In the early 1880s, young women in their flowing, long dresses and men in their top hats promenaded along the boardwalk. One of the most popular schemes that Bradley concocted was the annual Baby Parade, where infants dressed as adults and competed for prizes. The layout of Asbury was inspired by European cities with their leafy parks, tranquil lakes, and broad avenues leading down to the sea. Alas, Asbury was the victim of its own success, becoming in the end an oxymoron: a religious resort town. Something had to give.

During the postwar years, Asbury's middle class began moving out to the suburbs or further down the coast, a shift that was made more accessible by the opening of the Garden State Parkway in 1955. What's more, shopping malls lured businesses out of town. Adding insult to injury, people who used to flock to the Shore chose instead far-flung, hot-weather resorts in Sun Belt states like Florida and Arizona. By the 1960s and 1970s, the well to do had been replaced by hippies, rockers, bikers, and other assorted counterculture figures.

Asbury Park's other famous son, Stephen Crane, has surprisingly much in common with Springsteen. Although Crane was raised in a respectable

Methodist family (his mother was president of the Women's Christian Temperance Union of Ocean Grove and Asbury Park), he was considered one of the local riffraff. Crane was in a hurry to grow up. He had little patience for the proper behavior that his religious parents so aggressively promoted. A part-time reporter as a teenager, he spent a great deal of his time along the shore, taking his girlfriend on the merry-go-round that had recently opened and listening to the calliope music that wafted in the tangy, sea-salt air. Basically, he was the kind of person that Bradley abhorred and railed against, the prototype of Springsteen's tramps. "[A]n outcast, a renegade," says Wolff. "Tramps like us," indeed. In fact, Crane despised middle-class values and middle-class mores while sympathizing with the plight of the chronically poor, effectively blaming a system that was the result of neglect and spawned by greed and corruption.

As Wolff points out, a literary precursor of sorts to "4th Of July" is Crane's short story, "The Pace Of Youth." Written in 1893 and originally published in the January 18-19, 1895, issue of the New York *Press*, Crane's story is ostensibly about a summer romance along the Jersey Shore between the daughter of the town's leading businessman and an employee who works at Stimson's Mammoth Merry-Go-Round. Remarkably, in it one hears echoes of Springsteen ("Runnin', laughin' 'neath the boardwalk with the boss's daughter")—in its themes, in its description of the town, in its very characters. Asbury Park hasn't really changed that much after all.

During the heyday of the big band era, musicians such as Tommy Dorsey, Benny Goodman, and Paul Whiteman played the Convention Hall, which still stands at the northern end of the boardwalk. But several decades later, in an ominous and prophetic turn of events, a racial riot broke out outside the hall during Fourth of July weekend 1956 when, believe it or not, Frankie Lymon and the Teenagers headlined. How could the sweetly innocent, seemingly innocuous sounds of Frankie Lymon instigate a riot? In Asbury Park, things aren't always as they seem.

The group had just started their second number when a fistfight broke out. After the fighting continued, the concert was canceled and the kids were told to go home. That's when things turned really ugly. Angry youths, both white and black, began fighting in public on the boardwalk and, worse, roving packs of teenagers began smashing windows in the heart of the business district. It went down in history as the Convention Hall Riot, and it gave the new music—rock 'n' roll—a black eye. For a time, the music was banned.

By a decade or so later, in 1967, 35 percent of the city's black population lived below the poverty line; most settled on the West Side, across the railroad tracks. And on July 4, 1970, the inevitable happened.

It all started innocently enough: a car driven by a white man stopped at a red light on the West Side of town. Some black kids were running around and chasing each other and throwing bottles. One of the bottles hit his car, and the man sped off, his car tires screeching in the darkness. Soon, the kids thought they had a good thing going and began hitting cars driven by both black and white drivers. The police were called. Two officers, African Americans, arrived on the scene. A crowd gathered and tension mounted. One of the officers raised his gun in the air, warning everyone to move back. Soon, at a few minutes past midnight, two teen West Side dances let out. Then things really spiraled out of control. One of the officers was struck on the head, the other on the shoulder. They retreated and the crowd—a large group of black teenagers—went wild, breaking into liquor stores and drugstores. Looting erupted, and the mayor declared a state of emergency. The rioting continued for several days, as crowds smashed shop windows in the business district and the police fired their guns in response. According to Wolff, 46 people were injured by gunfire.

The riots were the beginning of the end for Asbury Park. Despite being surrounded by wealthy communities (posh Spring Lake is only a 10-minute drive away), Asbury Park had been left behind and, almost overnight (or so it seemed even though turmoil was festering for many years), it turned into a virtual ghost town.

At the time of the riots, Springsteen was living, writes Wolff, "in a surfboard factory on the edge of town" and playing in a heavy-metal band called Steel Mill, packing them in at places like the Sunshine In, a short distance from the boardwalk. For even though Asbury Park was a ghost of its former self, the music, and specifically, rock 'n' roll, still attracted a crowd.

But Steel Mill apparently wasn't enough for Springsteen. He had other ideas, more ambitious musical aspirations. Inspired by Van Morrison's funky His Band and The Street Choir, Springsteen had visions of forming a new band—one that combined his love of soul music with rock. It would be an integrated band, a bold and risky move in racially tense Asbury Park. The new band didn't last long though—finances got in the way. So, by the winter of 1971, Springsteen was living above an abandoned beauty salon on Cookman Avenue in the heart of Asbury. It was here where he wrote the songs that appeared on *Greetings*.

Years later, conditions are slowly improving in Asbury Park. According to *Travel + Leisure* magazine, real estate prices have risen 300 percent during the three-year period from 2001 to 2004. New Yorkers, in particular, many of them gay and lesbian, are buying up property. There are other signs of revival, too: a $1.25 billion development project is in the works. When all is completed, it will consist of 3,000 apartments and condominiums, a seaside hotel, and 450,000 square feet of shopping and entertainment space—spread out along the oceanfront.

If things go according to plan (and in Asbury Park, that is never a guarantee), Springsteen will barely recognize the place.

What is life on the Shore really about? Perhaps Cathy Newman in *National Geographic* magazine said it best:

> Nothing connects the towns of the Jersey Shore other than the shore itself. Asbury Park is as different from Atlantic City as a penguin is from a pelican…. There is no common ground—except the frail connective tissue of nostalgia. The shore is about memory. It is about family ritual. It's about childhood softened by the haze of distance…
>
> The shore is the Lost City of Atlantis in us all—a submerged longing for innocence and simplicity, for how we once were. And so we go again and again (if only in our minds) to places like Ocean City, Asbury Park, and Cape May. Places where we don't have to grow up. Places where we can grow back down.

Oh, Sandy…

UNDER THE BOARDWALK

New Jersey has 127 miles of coastline from Sandy Hook to Cape May Point and a boardwalk culture like no other. Atlantic City's Boardwalk (note the capital B) is, at five miles in length, the longest; Sea Bright, at 200 feet, the shortest. In 2004, Asbury Park's mile-long boardwalk was rebuilt.

"Rosalita (Come Out Tonight)"
from *The Wild, The Innocent & The E Street Shuffle*
(Columbia, 1973)

An irresistible showstopper in concert—the song that ended virtually every show from 1974 to 1984—"Rosalita (Come Out Tonight)" has a jumpy, push-and-start melody and a full-bodied wall of sound with traces of Motown, Stax/Volt, and Chuck Berry in its mix. It is a celebratory as well as hilarious homage to freedom and one of Springsteen's legendary epic-like short-story songs. It also has Springsteen's patented collection of idiosyncratic characters with goofy nicknames: Little Dynamite and Little Gun, Jack the Rabbit and Weak Knees Willie, Sloppy Sue and Big Bones Billy. What's more, it is the only song on *The Wild, The Innocent & The E Street Shuffle* that has a chorus. And to boot, it is just downright infectious; indeed, one of the friendliest songs in the history of rock 'n' roll. It is a song that is almost impossible not to *like*.

"Rosalita" functions as Springsteen's musical autobiography—up until that time. "I wrote it as kiss-off to everybody who counted you out, put you down, or decided you weren't good enough," Springsteen admitted in his book, *Songs*. (An early composition, "Seaside Bar Song," resembles "Rosalita" in structure, theme, and lyrics although, like "Thundercrack," it is much wilder. Before "Rosalita," "Thundercrack"—a glorious mess of a song—served as the crowd showstopper.) A middle of summer song, "Rosalita" is the ultimate us-against-the-world teen romance circa the Jersey Shore, 1973.

The song's protagonist has small dreams. Hanging out, playing pool, skipping school, and acting "real cool" are high on his list. "Stay out all night," he recommends, "it's gonna feel all right." What's not to like? "So Rosie come out tonight," he sings.

But there's a problem. Rosie's mother doesn't think highly of our hero because he sings in a rock 'n' roll band. Similarly, Rosie's father shares much the same opinion. In fact, the father has locked Rosie in her room. It is up to the Springsteen alter ego to "liberate" her, "confiscate" her. After all, he just wants to be her man. "Someday we'll look back on this and it will all seem funny," he offers (even then, Springsteen could look at his situation with bemused detachment). And yet Rosie's mother is angry and, worse, the father knows that the down-and-out singer has no money (as if to emphasis the point, Springsteen repeats this line three times).

But things aren't as dire as they seem. There is hope after all for, as the singer screams (almost unable to believe it himself), the record company just gave him a big advance. Now, with money jingling in his pocket, he offers if not salvation at least some hope of a promising future, even if it's only a longing to escape to a little café in San Diego "where they play guitars all night and all day."

But it's the live performances of "Rosalita" where the song comes into its own. Anyone who has seen Springsteen perform it in concert, especially during those manic, crazy days of the 1970s, knows what a whirling dervish of a song it can be. Just when you think Springsteen and company have spent every last drop of precious energy, they come back for more.

Born To Run
(Columbia, 1975)

Springsteen's most famous album, considered by many to be his masterpiece, *Born To Run* offers neo-religious songs with big themes (the Girl, the Car, the Quest) and music to match. The songs here stake a claim—that rock 'n' roll literally can save lives. Springsteen here sings as if his life—if not his career—depended on it. *Born To Run* combines Dylan's lyricism and Roy Orbison's operatic voice all wrapped up in Phil Spector's larger-than-life production values. Springsteen called the songwriting on *Born To Run* as the most theatrical of his career.

In November 2005, Columbia Records released the *Born To Run: 30th Anniversary Edition* box set which includes a two-hour concert DVD "Hammersmith Odeon, *London, '75*" and a documentary *Wings For Wheels: The Making Of* Born To Run." If *Greetings From Asbury Park, N.J.*, started Springsteen's career, *Born To Run* cemented it.

Musicians:

Bruce Springsteen: guitar, vocals, harmonica

Garry Tallent: bass guitar

Max M. Weinberg: drums

Roy Bittan: Fender Rhodes, glockenspiel, piano, harpsichord, organ, background vocals

Clarence Clemons: saxophones

Randy Brecker: trumpet, flugel horn

Dave Sanborn: baritone saxophone

Wayne Andre: trombone

Ernest "Boom" Carter: drums

Danny Federici: organ

Richard Davis: bass

Suki Lahav: violin

Mike Appel: background vocals

Steve Van Zandt: background vocals

Producers: Bruce Springsteen, Jon Landau, and Mike Appel

Recorded at: Record Plant Studio (New York)

Tracks:

"Thunder Road" (4:50)

"Tenth Avenue Freeze-Out" (3:11)

"Night" (3:01)

"Backstreets" (6:29)

"Born To Run" (4:30)

"She's The One" (4:30)

"Meeting Across The River" (3:16)

"Jungleland" (9:33)

Running time: 38:00

"Thunder Road"
from *Born To Run*
(Columbia, 1975)

The first thing you notice about "Thunder Road" is its cinematic quality. The history of the cinema is written all over it from its title (Springsteen took the name from a 1958 movie of the same name, starring Robert Mitchum) to its sharp, incisive images ("The screen door slams / Mary's dress waves"). It reads like the opening lines of a screenplay.

Significantly (or perhaps not), Springsteen has made it clear that he never actually saw *Thunder Road*. He just fell in love with the idea of the movie and the images associated with it. "It was about these moonshine runners down south. I only saw the poster in the lobby of the theater, and I took the title and I wrote the song. But I didn't think there was ever a place that was like what I wrote in the song. I didn't know if there was or not."

But there is something else going on here as the plaintive notes of a harmonica open the song. What is the destination of Thunder Road? The promised land, wherever that may be. Is it a physical place? Or is it a figment of the imagination? Springsteen doesn't say. All we know is that it is somewhere, elsewhere. And it is these dreams of elsewhere that motivate his characters and allow them to believe that there may be a better place. Out there. Somewhere.

At the time he wrote the songs on *Born To Run*, Springsteen was living in a house in West Long Branch, New Jersey, not far from Asbury Park. He recalls in *Songs* that he had a record player by the side of his bed. "At night I'd lie back and listen to records by Roy Orbison, The Ronettes, The Beach Boys, and other great '60s artists." In "Thunder Road," the radio is playing an Orbison song. He sings, as he often does, for the lonely. Think about it. Springsteen evokes the figure of Roy Orbison, the anti-Elvis. What pop singer is more vulnerable than Roy Orbison? The narrator identifies with Orbison, identifies perhaps with his very ordinariness ("Hey that's me"). He goes to Mary's place, daring her to take a chance on life, on him ("show a little faith, there's magic in the night"). Years later, on *The Rising*, "Mary's Place" becomes a center of refuge, a haven from despair.

He knows that it's a lot to ask. He knows that she can choose instead to stay home, to place it safe, and hope that a stronger figure—"a savior to rise from these streets"—than our hero will come to rescue her. He makes clear that he's no hero ("that's understood"). All he can offer her is a chance—"one last chance, in fact,"—for a better life. Indeed, the only kind of redemption he can give—and when he sings this line it is a barely audible, garbled—lies beneath the dirty hood of the car that waits outside her front door. Two lanes will "take us anywhere," he sings, perhaps even to the mythical Promised Land.

"Thunder Road" is the first time on record that Springsteen uses "promised land," a phrase that is so fraught with hope and the veiled possibility of liberation that it sometimes feels that Springsteen invented the words so much is it associated with him. But, of course, the idea of a promised land or, more accurately, The Promised Land, is centuries old:

> *I am bound for the promised land,*
> *I'm bound for the promised land;*
> *O who will come and go with me,*
> *I am bound for the promised land.*

So rang out the old hymn about that elusive "promised land" that beckoned one and all across the Jordan River, a "fair and happy land" of "sweet fields" and "rivers of delight" where "milk and honey flow." These were the reassuring words that helped the pioneers and early settlers endure life in their hard land. During the Great Revival of the Nineteenth century that swept across the American South, people flocked to the campgrounds to hear evangelists preach their baleful tales of salvation and eternal damnation—they were all sinners, they were constantly reminded—but it was the hope that snuck in between the brimstone that meant the most, that cut the deepest. In song after song, Springsteen echoes the difficulty of life as lived by thousands upon thousands of his fellow contemporary Americans, but he might just as easily be singing about the many others who came before.

And yet Springsteen's promised land has more of a secular quality about it, an egalitarian appeal that owes its inspiration to the Nineteenth century American poet and journalist, Walt Whitman. In "Song Of The Open Road," Whitman invites the reader to join him on a journey that leads to who knows where. Springsteen in "Thunder Road" and in other songs recalls Whitman's vision of a wide-open, democratic America; an America big enough—and big-hearted enough—to include everyone. Like Whitman, too, "Thunder Road" is characterized by a muscular simplicity. But as always with Springsteen, there is no free ride. Risks are involved—success most definitely is not guaranteed—but the singer does offer the sweet possibility of escape. As in earlier songs, the lyrics of "Thunder Road" conjure up images of dusty beach roads that haunt the Jersey Shore and, in one particularly searing image, burned-out husks of old Chevrolets.

It is these extinct metal dinosaurs that seem to echo the lost dreams of his often quietly desperate characters.

Springsteen was just 24 when he wrote the song and yet it contains one of his most heartfelt and most profound lines ("So you're scared and you're thinking that maybe we ain't that young anymore"). It is a remarkable lyric, all the more remarkable since it was written by someone with, presumably, the future and all that it represents spread out before him. Years later, during an interview with Neil Strauss of the *New York Times,* Springsteen wonders himself where he got the wisdom to write such a line. "I have no idea where I was conceivably coming from at that time," he says.

"Thunder Road" is many things to many people: a liberating celebration of freedom to some, "a haunting hymn to the past" to others (as writer Nick Hornby once described the acoustic version). And even now, so many years after it was first released, the song continues to resonate. During the funeral for one of the victims of the World Trade Center attacks, mourners sang a few plaintive lines.

Show a little faith, indeed.

TALKING ABOUT THE PROMISED LAND

The first time the phrase "promised land" appears in a Springsteen song is in "Thunder Road." Of course, he built an entire song around it in "The Promised Land," but it also shows up in "Racing In The Street," "The Price You Pay," "Johnny Bye-bye," "Goin' Cali," and "The Ghost Of Tom Joad."

"Tenth Avenue Freeze-Out"
from *Born To Run*
(Columbia, 1975)

One town leads into another along the Jersey Shore, from upscale Deal—hometown of Springsteen's wife and E Street Band member Patti Scialfa—and Allenhurst to Asbury Park and pious Ocean Grove. And then there's tiny Avon-by-the-Sea, Bradley Beach, Belmar, South Belmar, and finally, elegant Spring Lake.

The name of Springsteen's E Street Band has its origins in the attractive beach town of Belmar. The corner of E Street and 10th Avenue is a favorite—and much-photographed—landmark of Springsteen fans. David Sancious, the original keyboard player for the E Street Band, used to live at 1105 E Street.

So it's not surprising that the second cut on *Born To Run,* the raucous "Tenth Avenue Freeze-Out, " has come to personify, perhaps more than any song in the Springsteen catalogue, the special relationship that exists between Springsteen and the audience. It is, after all, a buoyant, street-wise party song that celebrates life at its fullest. During the shows in the Seventies, this was the song Springsteen would sing when he wanted the full attention of the crowd, whether on his home turf in New Jersey or in tougher, show-me-the-goods-first climes such as London or Hamburg: Sliding down to his knees and almost begging, pleading, cajoling the audience to meet him on an equal plane, or as equal a plane as a rock singer and his fan base can approximate. Years later, during the 1999 to 2000 E Street Band reunion tour, Springsteen transformed the song into a spiritual call and response (rock-critic Dave Marsh called it "a 20-minute, gospel-soul rave-up"), turning what was a musical icon of the *Born To Run*-era into a soulful version that mixed and matched various artists and sounds, bits and pieces, from the glorious rock and soul past: Al Green's "Take Me to the River," Curtis Mayfield and the Impressions' "It's All Right"—with a touch of Jimmy Swaggart and maybe a little Jerry Lee Lewis for effect. During these performances, Springsteen would rhapsodize about "the power, the glory, and the *majesty* of rock 'n' roll." Like a latter-day preacher, he would exhort the crowd until they were in a frenzy:

Tenth Avenue, Belmar, NJ. (June Sawyers)

I want to go to that river of resurrection, where everybody gets a second chance…but you gotta work at it! You just don't stumble onto those things, you don't find those places by accident. You've got to seek them out and search after them. And that's why we're here night after night after night after night. Because you can't get to those things by yourself. You've got to have *help*.

"Tenth Avenue Freeze-Out" is a festive, triumphant celebration of camaraderie in all its levels: from band member to band member (one member, in particular, Clarence "Big Man" Clemons, is mentioned in the song) and, more important, from singer to individual fan. If an older Springsteen no longer believed that rock 'n' roll could save the world, it could at least bring a goodly number of people together—at one place, at one time. No, Bruce the Preacher cannot offer eternal life, but he can offer to anyone willing to listen—that is, his imagined community of like-minded souls—the true spirit of rock 'n' roll.

"Right here! Right now!" he shouted at the top of his lungs.

In an interview that appeared in the English music magazine *Q*, Springsteen discussed the artist-audience connection: "I always want my shows to be a little bit like a circus, a touch of political rally, a little touch of a lot of different things. Really, in the end I want people to go away feeling more connected to each other and connected in their own lives and to the whole world around them, and to accomplish that you got to be connected…"

"Backstreets"
from *Born To Run*
(Columbia, 1975)

"Backstreets" is essential Springsteen. (There's a reason why the Springsteen fanzine of the same name is named after it.) All of his quintessential themes are: friendship, faith, loyalty, love, betrayal, and faithlessness. There are lines that he would recycle elsewhere ("dancing in the dark," "it don't matter to me now") but it all started here first. It has a sense of urgency to it as well as an everything-is-on-the-line quality.

Roy Bittan's poignant piano solo opens the song. On a "soft infested summer" Terry and the narrator became friends (initially, we are not quite sure if Terry is male or female). They sleep in old abandoned beach houses, get wasted under the summer sun, and fall in love so deeply that it is almost doomed from the start.

Coca-Cola sign. (Theresa Albini)

Their world appears menacing ("We sat with the last of the Duke Street Kings") but also glamorous and wildly romantic in a seedy kind of way: Endless summer nights spent slow dancing in the dark at dimly lit juke joints. Awash in the glory of youth, they feel they will live forever, that their torrid love affair will never end. But then it all comes crashing down. Lies and a betrayal that hurts so badly that the narrator hates the man Terry had an affair with and hates Terry for leaving him. And then Springsteen lets out a ghastly wail of sheer anguish. His little fantasy world has come crashing down. At night, lying in the dark, he recalls the movies they used to go see "trying to learn how to walk like the heroes" up there on the big screen before realizing that they are "just like all the rest."

At six and a half minutes long, "Backstreets" is of epic-length proportions with larger-than-life themes. Compare the song to another cut of similar length and ambition on *Born To Run,* "Jungleland." Whereas, to this listener at least, "Jungleland" sounds ponderous and heavy-handed, pompous almost, weighted down by its overwrought tale of urban street rats on the prowl, "Backstreets" pulls back just enough that we want to know more about these people. Whereas "Jungleland" is all archetype, "Backstreets" is idiosyncratic, with distinctive characters. But in its larger-than-life themes, too, it falls under the epic category. Springsteen's tale of defeated characters, bitter with the taste of disappointment on their tongues, is the consummate tour de force performance, with one of the best vocals of his career. Some may call it histrionic, but given the subject matter, it's warranted. Springsteen gives it all he's got. Nothing less would do.

"Born To Run"
from *Born To Run*
(Columbia, 1975)

> *"We were discussing* Born To Run *by Bruce Springsteen. I said that
> it was the most Roman Catholic record album ever made.*
>
> *"'Look what you've got,' I said. 'You've got Mary dancing like a
> vision across the porch while the radio plays. You've got people trying
> in vain to breath the fire they was born in, riding through mansions of
> glory, and hot-rod angels, virgins and whores.'*
>
> *'And 'She's The One,' said Arthur. 'It's Mariolatry city.'"*
>
> —characters in Michael Chabon's novel *The Mysteries Of
> Pittsburgh* (1988)

From the opening power chords to the defiant closing line, "Born To Run" is a singular achievement and a great rock anthem. It has been called Springsteen's masterpiece, a rock opera in miniature with everything that such a statement implies. Indeed, it has it all: the Stax Records sound, the vulnerability of a Roy Orbison song, the poetry of Van Morrison. It is for these and other reasons that "Born To Run" is considered by many critics to be the greatest song Springsteen has ever written—period.

The first track to be recorded on the album, "Born To Run" reached Number 35 on the Pop 100 and was named one of the 100 greatest pop songs, compiled jointly by *Rolling Stone* and MTV. It is also among the 50 selections added in early 2004 by the Library of Congress to the National Recording Registry.

Springsteen spared no cost in making the album (according to *Rolling Stone*, more than a dozen overdubs are on "Born To Run" alone). Ironically, the creative process was a miserable period for Springsteen. He found it difficult to translate the sound that was in his head—the grandeur of opera, the melodrama of the best of the teenage love ballads that he grew up on, the dynamism of his already legendary live shows—onto vinyl. At one point, he was so frustrated that he even considered canceling the entire album and replacing it with a live set. What a tragedy that would have been.

Born To Run was a turning point for Springsteen. By the spring of 1974, he had already recorded two albums that went nowhere. He knew his record company, Columbia, was growing impatient. He felt the pressure. He knew that in order to do what he wanted to do in the music business, he had to create not only a masterpiece but also a *commercial* masterpiece.

Born To Run was recorded during a transitional time in Springsteen's career, a time between what he was and what he would become. "Here was the moment when the loose gypsy rocker who favored frantic R&B rave-ups and epic arrangements started moving toward the type of crafted anthems that could conquer a hockey arena," wrote Greg Kot of the *Chicago Tribune*. The song itself took six months to complete. At various times, it went through several versions, including one rendition that included strings and a backing choir.

The album was also the first time Springsteen used the studio as a tool "and not an attempt to replicate the sound of when we played," he told *Mojo* magazine's Mark Hagen. If writing the songs was a difficult process, recording and getting the right sound was next to impossible, or so it seemed. "I was striving for something very specific that I didn't know how to get," he admitted.

Whatever Springsteen wanted, he knew it had to be extraordinary. "We were not in it to do something average," manager Jon Landau told Jon Pareles of the *New York Times*. "We were not in it to get any particular song on the radio. We were in it to do something great."

Born To Run proved to be transitional from an artistic perspective, too. As Springsteen notes in *Songs*, his characters became "less eccentric….they could have been anybody and everybody." The songs, he said, confronted issues of "faith and a searching for answers." Springsteen thought of it—still thinks of it—as being a very personal album.

But the pressure on him at the time was almost unbearable. This was his last chance, and he couldn't afford to blow it.

Springsteen began recording *Born To Run* in between club dates in 1974 at 914 Sound Studios in Blauvelt, New York, in an old studio where the piano was perennially out of tune. At Landau's suggestion (Landau had already written his famous "I've seen rock 'n' roll's future and its name is Bruce Springsteen" quote), he moved to a higher caliber studio—the Record Plant in Manhattan—to finish the record. But the "Born To Run" single was completed before the rest of the album, which led to a strange and frustrating situation for everyone involved. Deejays were playing the record on the radio even though the song was not officially for sale.

What is *Born To Run* about? Many things. Finding a soul mate and finding yourself. Freedom and security. Love and heroism—all of this and more surrounded by soaring arrangements and the most exquisite kind of street poetry.

It is an album of endless summer nights. The Circuit ("full of switchblade lovers") that Springsteen sings about refers to the stretch of road in Asbury Park along Kingsley Street and Ocean Avenue. It was the place to be in the

1960s and early 1970s and a right of passage for any self-respecting Asbury Park teen. "When you got your driver's license, you made the circuit," Helen-Chantal Pike, the city's historian, writes. Teens drove down the boulevard with their radios cranked up to full volume, preening for each other and vying for attention. And then there is the figure of Wendy.

Typical for Springsteen (but untypical in the rock pantheon) is his egalitarian treatment toward women. He wants not only to be Wendy's friend but also the guardian of her dreams and visions. Together, he tells her, they can escape from the trap of their dreary dead-end lives. He admits he doesn't know where he's going ("I'm just a scared and lonely rider") but he is willing to give all he has to find out if the love he feels for her is real. In an aside that is not on the lyric sheet, Springsteen actually asks "Can you show me?" He is ready to make the commitment. Then he looks around him. Beyond the amusement park, cars race down the boulevard, as "girls comb their hair in rearview mirrors / And the boys try to look so hard." In this desperate, rundown town, he is ready to leave it all behind ("baby we'll never go back") for his "last chance power drive" on the open road.

The song is all about movement. In the Springsteen worldview, mobility equals hope. Despite its ominous trappings ("death trap" and "suicide rap" in the first few lines alone), "Born To Run" is brimming with optimism, albeit of the cautious variety. The optimism takes its form in the promise of taking action—of getting out of the place that makes the characters feel trapped.

And yet there is a deep undercurrent of melancholia, too. In the live version performed at the Los Angeles Sports Arena on April 27, 1988, Springsteen—accompanied by only his acoustic guitar and harmonica—brings out the essential sadness and, yes, inherent gloominess of the song. Never has it sounded so heartbreakingly poignant, never so touching, never so utterly soulful. Did Wendy and our hero get to that place where they really wanted to go? Based on this rendition, we're not so sure.

In Michael Chabon's novel *The Mysteries Of Pittsburgh,* one of the characters calls *Born To Run* the most Catholic album ever. Springsteen himself has called it a "religiously based" record, "in a funny kind of way. Not like orthodox religion," he emphasized, "but it's about basic things, you know? That searchin', and faith, and the idea of hope."

When it was released in August 1975, it was everything people expected it to be—and more. Springsteen, of course, appeared on the cover of both *Time* and *Newsweek* simultaneously—a feat usually reserved for politicians and heads of state. In *Creem* magazine, Lester Bangs called Springsteen's music "majestic and passionate with no apologies." Meanwhile, Greil Marcus in *Rolling Stone* said the album was magnificent, the music exhilarating and "Born To Run" in particular "the finest compression of the rock 'n' roll thrill since the opening riffs of 'Layla'..."

Born To Run turned Springsteen from New Jersey's favorite son to rock 'n' roll phenomenon. At the age of 26, he was compared to the best of the best—Presley, Lennon, Jagger, Dylan. The album and the song remain a milestone in rock history and one of the many highlights in Springsteen's long career.

CATHOLIC BOY

Springsteen on his Catholic upbringing:

"Catholic school, Catholic school, Catholic school. You're indoctrinated. It's a none-too-subtle form of brainwashing, and of course, it works very well. I'm not a churchgoer, but I realized as time passed, that my music is filled with Catholic imagery. It's not a negative thing. There was a powerful world of potent imagery that became alive and vital and vibrant, and was both very frightening and held out the promise of ecstasies and paradise. There was this incredible internal landscape that they created in you.

"As I got older, I got a lot less defensive about it. I thought, I've inherited this particular landscape and I can build it something of my own."

—to Jon Pareles of the *New York Times,* April 24, 2005

Darkness On The Edge Of Town
(Columbia, 1978)

With *Darkness On The Edge Of Town*, Springsteen "figured out" what he wanted to write about: "the people that mattered to me, and who I wanted to be. I saw friends and family struggling to lead decent, productive lives and I felt an everyday kind of heroism in this." He added, "Still do." The result is a dark, brooding meditation, at turns celebratory and somber, angry and pensive.

Musicians:

Clarence Clemons: saxophone

Danny Federici: organ

Roy Bittan: piano

Bruce Springsteen: vocals, lead guitar, harmonica

Garry Tallent: bass guitar

Steve Van Zandt: guitar

Max Weinberg: drums

Producers: Jon Landau and Bruce Springsteen

Recorded at: Record Plant (New York)

Tracks:

"Badlands" (4:01)

"Adam Raised A Cain" (4:32)

"Something In The Night" (5:11)

"Candy's Room" (2:51)

"Racing In The Street" (6:53)

"The Promised Land" (4:33)

"Factory" (2:17)

"Streets Of Fire" (4:09)

"Prove It All Night" (3:56)

"Darkness On The Edge Of Town" (4:28)

Running time: 40:91

"Badlands"
from *Darkness On The Edge Of Town*
(Columbia, 1978)

In 1977 Springsteen was living on a farm in Holmdel, New Jersey, where he wrote most of the songs on *Darkness On The Edge Of Town.* Far removed from the distractions of New York or even, for that matter, from the goings on of the Jersey Shore, Springsteen began seriously to think about his past, about where he came from, and what he wanted to write about. He also began to think about class consciousness—in *Songs* he admits he always identified with English rock that addressed those concerns, especially the music of The Animals. It wasn't an issue that made it into the lyrics of most rock songs even though so many rockers came from working-class backgrounds. Springsteen felt a need to discuss it directly. Or, as he puts it, "I felt a sense of accountability to the people I'd grown up alongside of."

"Badlands" cover. (Author collection)

It was around this time too that Springsteen discovered country and folk music. The simplicity and dark truths of Hank Williams in particular epitomized the kind of music he now wanted to make; music that would "resonate down the road." He would turn to Williams and then Woody Guthrie again and again for inspiration in subsequent albums such as *Nebraska, The Ghost Of Tom Joad, Devils & Dust,* and *We Shall Overcome: The Seeger Sessions.*

"Badlands," the first cut on *Darkness On The Edge Of Town,* is about the everyday heroism that was becoming more and more important to Springsteen. What concerned him most were the stories that could be told of people struggling to lead decent, meaningful lives.

From the opening chords of "Badlands," the listener knows that Springsteen has given his all to the song. The narrator may be lost and confused, yet he is determined to turn his life around. He revels in life ("it ain't no sin to be glad you're alive," he reminds us at one point). No longer patient for "just the in-betweens," he demands to take control "right now." He has spent too long—his entire lifetime, in fact—waiting for something good to happen ("for a moment that just won't come"). Nobody is going to give him a free ride. He understands that. Instead he must rely on his own devices and the love of a woman to get him through. But not only love. He expects faith, hope, and a prayer to raise him above the fray. More than anything, the defiant chorus makes us believe that anything is possible. It's not surprising that "Badlands" remained a stalwart of Springsteen's live shows with the E Street Band.

INFLUENCES AND INSPIRATIONS

"He mixes the past like a hip-hop deejay," once said music critic and historian Craig Werner about Springsteen's avowed eclecticism. Indeed, Springsteen, the great synthesist, has spoken frequently about his influences and inspirations, which includes not only music but also cinema and literature. Here they are (some of them anyway) in roughly chronological order:

- Walt Whitman
- Robert Johnson
- Carter Family
- Hank Williams
- Woody Guthrie

Springsteen contributed "We Shall Overcome" on *'Til We Outnumber 'Em: Live From Cleveland.* The concert was the grand finale of a 10-day celebration in 1996 co-organized by the Rock and Roll Hall of Fame Museum and the Woody Guthrie Foundation and Archives. Produced by

Ani DiFranco and released on her Righteous Babe Records, it also featured Billy Bragg, Ramblin' Jack Elliott, Arlo Guthrie, Indigo Girls, Dave Pirner, Tim Robbins, and DiFranco. On *Folkways: A Vision Shared: A Tribute To Woody Guthrie And Leadbelly* in 1988, he contributed renditions of two Dust Bowl ballads, "Vigilante Man" and "I Ain't Got No Home." He has performed several Guthrie songs in concert, including "Deportee (Plane Wreck At Los Gatos)" and, most famously, "This Land Is Your Land."

- Author John Steinbeck (especially *The Grapes Of Wrath* but also *East Of Eden*)
- Filmmaker John Ford (especially *The Grapes Of Wrath* and *The Searchers*)
- Chuck Berry ("Open All Night," "Johnny Bye-Bye")
- Doo-wop
- Elvis Presley
- *Night Of The Hunter* ("Cautious Man")
- Roy Orbison ("Thunder Road," "Leah")
- Bob Dylan (especially early Dylan)
- The Beatles (on "Take 'Em As They Come," bassist Garry Tallent pays homage to Paul McCartney's bass guitar on The Beatles' "Rain")
- The Animals
- Van Morrison (especially his album *St. Dominic's Preview*)
- R&B
- Stax
- Soul
- Smokey Robinson
- Wilson Pickett
- Sam Cooke ("Mary's Place" in *The Rising* is a rewrite of Sam Cooke's "Meet Me At Mary's Place")
- Major Lance
- Girl groups ("Give The Girl A Kiss" is said to be loosely inspired by The Shangri-Las' classic hit, "Give Him A Great Big Kiss")
- Power pop ("I Wanna Be With You" pays homage to The Raspberries, in both title and spirit)
- Short story writers (James M. Cain, Jim Thompson, and especially Flannery O'Connor)

- Novelists (Pete Dexter, especially *Paris Trout*)
- John Huston's film adaptation of Flannery O'Connor's novel *Wise Blood.*
- Jonathan Kozol's *Amazing Grace: The Lives Of Children And The Conscience Of A Nation* ("Black Cowboys" was inspired by Kozol's book and is set in the South Bronx neighborhood of Mott Haven, one of New York's poorest, where the protagonist hails from).

On the night of November 5, 1980—the day after Ronald Reagan was elected president—Springsteen stood onstage at Arizona State University in Tempe, Arizona. He tuned his guitar "nervously," according to critic Mikal Gilmore, and then told the audience: "I don't know what you guys think about what happened last night, but I think it was pretty frightening." Then he sang his heart out, "with an unprecedented fury," adds Gilmore, performing an incendiary version of "Badlands" that few in the audience would ever forget.

"Badlands" is a timeless Springsteen classic, as significant today as when it was first written.

"Adam Raised A Cain"
from *Darkness On The Edge Of Town*
(Columbia, 1978)

"Then the Lord said to him…'Whoever kills Cain will suffer a sevenfold vengeance.' And the Lord put a mark on Cain, so that no one who came upon him would kill him. Then Cain went away from the presence of the Lord, and settled in the land of Nod, East Of Eden."

—Genesis 4:15–16

"The greatest terror a child can have is that he is not loved, and rejection is the hell he fears. And with rejection comes anger, and with anger some kind of crime in revenge for the rejection, and with the crime guilt—and there is the story of mankind."

—John Steinbeck

"Man has a choice and it's a choice that makes him a man."
—James Dean as Cal Trask in the movie version of *East Of Eden*

Inspired by the film version of John Steinbeck's 1955 novel *East Of Eden,* "Adam Raised A Cain" is Springsteen's take on the Cain and Abel murder. The troubled son, Cal Trask, played by James Dean, struggles with his father, Adam Trask, played by Raymond Massey. Like God in the Bible, Adam refuses Cal's gift—in this case, a gift of money—with a brisk, "If you want to give me a present, give me a good life. That's something I can value."

Steinbeck used the Bible, reportedly among his favorite books, as not only a model for the plot of *East Of Eden* but also as a vehicle for his own creativity. In *East Of Eden,* he offers an adaptation of the fourth chapter of Genesis. Abel is the favored son, Cain the outcast. Abel is the keeper of sheep, Cain a tiller of the soil. Cain offers God fruit from the ground, Abel the first offspring from his flock. God gladly accepts Abel's gift but rejects Cain's gift. As in life, there is no explanation.

Given his own difficult relationship with his father, one can see why the biblical story of parental rejection resonated so deeply with Springsteen. Springsteen sings the lines of "Adam Raised A Cain" with such splenetic fury—he spits out the words—that we just know he is writing it from personal experience. The narrator in the song understands why his father is so bitter and although he doesn't want to repeat the sins of the past, he realizes too that he and his father share an indelible bond; he recognizes what Springsteen scholar Jim Cullen aptly describes as "a temperamental kinship." After all, the son seeks to escape the fate of the father, an Adam figure condemned to spend his mortal life in misery and sorrow. Who would want to follow in those footsteps? Who would consciously want to repeat a past sheathed in such pain and agony, to live in such a forsaken land? The son compares his predicament to the biblical story of Cain and Abel, two brothers trapped in a deadly game of rivalry; he too is lost but, unlike the Genesis tale, his land is far from an Edenic paradise.

Springsteen begins with a striking religious image, although a decidedly Protestant, almost Pentecostal, one. In the summer when he was baptized, the narrator recalls how his father held him to his side and placed him in the water. The baby cries out loud, echoing the father's own anguish and reminding us that the love that exists between them is a love forever locked "in chains." It's crucial, I think, that in the next line we see the father at the door, hovering on the threshold, not quite sure whether to enter or leave the family home while the now grown-up son stands in the rain, always the outsider. Adam did indeed raise a Cain. What's more, old faces from the son's boyhood come back to haunt him; hardly the prodigal son, they ask him why he has returned.

"In the Bible Cain slew Abel," Springsteen sings, and East Of Eden "he was cast." But then history keeps repeating itself. The son pays for the sins of his forefathers until it becomes a never-ending cycle of misery. "Daddy worked his whole life for nothing but the pain," he cries. His father blames others for his misfortune; his dark heart of a dream has become a living nightmare.

"Adam Raised A Cain" is a song of elemental passions, yet rich in nuance and the secrets that we often hide from one another. Both father and son are cut from the same cloth. Both are the victims of a repetitive past, caught in a drama, ultimately, of their own making. But it is also a song about the choices that we make. Just because something has always been done a certain way doesn't necessarily mean that that way is the right way.

Steinbeck considered the story of Cain and Abel to be the "father" of all stories. In the Bible, Cain is ostracized by his family, cursed as a fugitive, and destined to live outside the confines of civilization for the rest of his days. He fears he will be a dead man but the Lord puts a mark on him as a precautionary measure, thus assuring that no one will hurt him. If the Old Testament centers on actions and their consequences, then Springsteen's "Adam Raised A Cain" also recalls the lessons of the past. Like Steinbeck, Springsteen is saying the past does not have to be repeated ad nauseam. We can rewrite the story, our story. There *is* such a thing as choice. This is why "Adam Raised A Cain," which some dismiss as simply an angry diatribe, is really one of Springsteen's most optimistic songs.

"Racing In The Street"
from *Darkness On The Edge Of Town*
(Columbia, 1978)

On August 9, 1978, at the Agora in Cleveland, Springsteen described the Circuit, as it was when he was living in Asbury Park:

> Back in Asbury Park there's these two roads, there's Kingsley Avenue [actually Kingsley Street] and Ocean Avenue and they form sort of an oval. And on Friday night they burn about half the gas in the United States in between stoplights down there. But outside of town, there's this little fire road, and that's where they go Racing In The Street.

"Racing In The Street" is a gorgeous ballad, one of Springsteen's best, an almost seven-minute paean to the marginalized, the shunned, and the forgotten. Roy Bittan's slow, elegant, graceful piano introduction sets the scene. The narrator has a dead-end job and a crumbling relationship, but what he does have—his pride and joy—is a '69 Chevy "with a 396/fuelie heads and a Hurst on the floor." (To those who know nothing about cars, Springsteen might as well be speaking a foreign language—but he does get his point across. Author Nick Hornby, a quintessential Englishman, hates cars but he loves the song.) He and his partner Sonny built it from scratch, and they race for money throughout the American Northeast. He divides the world into two kinds of people: those who have given up living ("and start dying little by little, piece by piece") and those who come home from work yet still do what they consider important, who, that is, haven't given up on life. Clearly, he thinks of himself as falling into the second category.

Diner Grill. (Theresa Albini)

All is not well. The narrator's girlfriend is miserable. She cries herself to sleep at night with the lights dimmed. Other times she just sits on the porch of her father's house, her life bitterly wasting away. She has no purpose, no future. The dreams that she once had, the dreams that once sustained her—whatever they were—have vanished; she even regrets being born.

And yet Springsteen concludes on a hopeful note with a reference to a promised land. In a stunning image, he and his lover ride down to the sea to wash their sins off their hands; a baptismal starting over by the ocean side. The song ends with a lovely coda of piano, organ, and drums, one of the most moving conclusions in rock.

"My whole life, I was always around a lot of people whose lives consisted of just this compromising—they knew no other way," Springsteen told Paul Nelson of *Rolling Stone* when the record was released. "That's where rock 'n' roll is important, because it said there could be another way, you know."

In this song, Springsteen, the great synthesizer and rock 'n' roll historian, recalls the rock 'n' roll past. The title of "Racing In The Street" closely resembles Martha and the Vandella's "Dancing in the Street," but its mournfulness and poignancy recall the Beach Boys' great "Don't Worry, Baby."

"The Promised Land"
from *Darkness On The Edge Of Town*
(Columbia, 1978)

> *"Tell the folks back home this is the promised land callin'*
> *And the poor boy's on the line"*
>
> —Chuck Berry

Chuck Berry wrote "Promised Land" in the Federal Medical Center in Springfield, Missouri, where he was serving out a three-year prison sentence for violation of the Mann Act, a federal statue that forbid transporting minors across state lines for the purpose of prostitution. He was released on his birthday: October 18, 1963.

Berry's "Promised Land" is about a young man who leaves his home in Norfolk, Virginia, bound for the Promised Land of California. Springsteen, a long-time Chuck Berry fan, borrowed the title for his own song. As any Springsteen fan knows, Springsteen has performed numerous Berry songs in concert over the years, including "Around And Around," "Back In The U.S.A.," 'Little Queenie," "No Money Down," "Sweet Little Sixteen," and "You Never Can Tell" but curiously not, as far as I know, "Promised Land."

Why does the notion of a Promised Land, and Old Testament imagery in particular, resonate so deeply with Springsteen, especially in *Darkness On The Edge Of Town?*

In the Bible, the Promised Land refers to the land that was promised the Jewish people after God told Abraham to leave his homeland to go to a new home in the land of Canaan, where, it was said, milk and honey flowed. It is called the Promised Land because of God's promise as cited in Genesis to give the land to the descendants of Abraham. The Romans exiled the Jews from the land in 135 C.E. From Genesis and later First Testament books, such as Exodus, Jewish and Christian hymns and spirituals were developed. Some of the best known today are those spirituals adopted first by African slaves, then by African-Americans, which came to be identified with the mid-20th century Civil Rights Movement. What then is the Promised Land but something that is out of reach, something that beckons but remains forever maddeningly elusive? As we well know from Springsteen songs, promises are meant to be broken. When the promise is broken, then what?

"The Promised Land" begins and ends with the warm, earthy sounds of the harmonica. The narrator of the song acknowledges the problems in his life ("there's a dark cloud rising from the desert floor") but longs for something better. In fact, he is ready to face his problems head-on—he refuses to run away from them. He works all night in his father's garage and in the evening passes the time driving toward something—toward what neither we nor he seem quite sure ("chasing some mirage"). Like the character in "Badlands," though, the narrator here is also ready to take control. He has done his best "to live the right way"; to conform, in other words, to societal expectations. But that doesn't relieve the anger he feels inside. He has made a commitment to change what he can change and to ignore what needs to be ignored; or, as he puts it, to blow away everything that "ain't got the faith to stand its ground." Ultimately, he refuses to abide by any of the broken dreams or terrible lies that threaten his very existence. Sometimes, though, the urge to start over—to not take no for an answer—can flirt with violence. Springsteen will explore the repercussions of dreams deferred more thoroughly in *Nebraska* but even here, on *Darkness*, the possibility of violence is very real. As independent scholar Larry David Smith notes, the key word in the song is faith: "faith will provide the fuel that ensures that the struggle will yield victory. Faith provides the path to the promised land."

On the *Devils & Dust* acoustic tour, Springsteen sang an even more desolate version of "The Promised Land," using the board of his guitar to create an ominous syncopation and paint an aural portrait of a world beyond redemption. Now, more than ever, the words that he wrote so many years ago echo an ordinary kind of heroism. "I do my best to live the right way, I get up every morning, go to work each day," he sings, and it is a sentiment that recalls the day to day nobility of his parents and, really, Springsteen himself. In interview after interview, Springsteen often refers to what he does as a "job"—something that is required of him, something that he has to do, something that he cannot help but do.

Until he campaigned for Senator John Kerry during the 2004 presidential campaign, Springsteen had never actively supported a candidate before. After playing "The Promised Land" at a campaign rally in Madison, Wisconsin, though, Springsteen made clear his opinions about the country he lived in and about the hope he had for it:

> As a songwriter, I've written about America for 30 years. I've tried to write about who we are, what we stand for, what we fight for.

He then listed the topics that matter the most to him, including economic justice, health care, homelessness, a living wage, the environment, and a "sane and responsible foreign policy."

In the Springsteen mindset, then, it appears that the Promised Land represents none other than America itself or rather an American ideal—the promise of an America that is truly inclusive *and* fair *and* just. It is this America, the America of our better angels, that Springsteen has, indeed, been singing about for more than 30 years and, one imagines, he will continue to write and sing about until his dying day.

BRUCE AND THE BIBLE

For a lapsed ex-Catholic, Springsteen sure uses a lot of biblical imagery in his songs, much of it of the fire-and-brimstone, Old Testament variety. Biblical imagery ("Adam Raised A Cain," "The Promised Land") crops up quite frequently. In "Soul Driver," he pulls an image straight out of Exodus ("forty nights of the gospel's rain" in which a black sky pours down snakes and frogs). He has sung about Jacob ("Jacob's Ladder") and Jesus ("Jesus Was An Only Son") while Moses has appeared several times (including "The Price You Pay," "Leap Of Faith"). He has made reference to Daniel in the Lion's Den ("Lion's Den") and has used biblical names as a matter of course ("Leah"). The devil himself shows up too in the guise of Jesus ("It's Hard To Be A Saint In The City"). Some songs, such as "Into The Fire," The Rising," and "My City Of Ruins" function as prayer itself. Springsteen's characters often pray openly (Bill Horton in "Cautious Man," Janey in "Spare Parts," Puerto Rican Jane in "Incident On 57th Street," to name but a few). Sometimes, though, prayer isn't enough as when the narrator in "The New Timer" acknowledges that even the love of Jesus himself would not be sufficient to rid him of murderous thoughts. Finally, such themes as atonement, redemption, salvation, and penance are riddled throughout his songs.

"Factory"

from *Darkness On The Edge Of Town*
(Columbia, 1978)

Just as Walt Whitman in "Song Of Myself" granted the ordinary laborer a dignity commonly absent from everyday experience, Springsteen too accords the working-class worker in "Factory" a similar, dogged respect. Springsteen's father, who was at various times a bus driver, a prison guard, and a rug mill worker, inspired the song. The whistle of the rug mill factory in Springsteen's native Freehold blew every morning at 8 a.m. sharp, calling the workers to the plant, and it is this deadening monotony that the song best captures with its dirge-like rhythm and repetitive use of the word "working."

"Factory" opens with the sound of a chain clanking as the day begins and ends with a chilling reminder of what can happen when a person's soul gets broken down, day in and day out, more than hinting of its potentially dire consequences ("And you better believe, boy / Somebody's gonna get hurt tonight").

With its somber and deliberate tone, "Factory" has an almost sacred quality to it. In its very anonymity—no character names are given—and its impersonal narrative, it is reminiscent of the ballad tradition, where the story becomes representational. "Factory" then is nothing less than a graceful yet powerful homage to faceless workers through the centuries.

"Prove It All Night"

from *Darkness On The Edge Of Town*
(Columbia, 1978)

At its simplest level, "Prove It All Night" is about a young couple proving their love to each other on a nocturnal trip from Monroe to a place called Angeline. It boasts a catchy melody and an inspirational lyric. And it is another quintessentially Springsteen song.

In "Prove It All Night," as in most of the songs on the album, much of the action takes place in cars or on the road or at night. The couple may be driving from a specific place to a specific destination but, mostly, they are going from nowhere to nowhere. Springsteen wanted the songs on *Darkness* to have a "drive-in quality" about them. "It's like everybody's always in transit. There's no settling down, no fixed action. You pick up the action, and then at some point—*pssst!*—

the camera pans away, and whatever happened, that's what happened. The songs I write, they don't have particular beginnings and they don't have endings. The camera focuses in and then out."

IT'S THE WORKING LIFE

Springsteen's characters work various jobs, mostly of the blue-collar variety. Considering that Springsteen himself has only held two jobs in his life—gardener and rock star—that's saying quite a lot. Here's an occupational breakdown of some of his characters:

Waitress — "4th Of July, Asbury Park (Sandy)"
Garage worker — "The Promised Land"
Factory worker — "Factory," "Shut Out The Light"
Dockworker — "Out In The Street"
Construction worker — "The River"
Firefighter — "Roulette," "Into The Fire," "The Rising"
Pumping gas at a Texaco station — "I Wanna Be With You"
Autoworker — "Johnny 99"
Refinery worker — "Born In The U.S.A."
Car wash worker — "Car Wash"
Office worker — "The Wish"
Truck driver — "Lucky Man"

Darkness was written during a time when Springsteen was watching a lot of John Ford westerns and American and French film noir, movies such as Arthur Ripley's *Gun Crazy* and Jacques Tourneur's *Out Of The Past*. The lyrics of "Prove It All Night," in particular, read like scenes from a screenplay. It has an urgency, an immediacy about it that recalls the best of American independent cinema. But it also feels desperate. The characters are trapped in small towns on the edge of nowhere, living small-town lives that they don't know how to escape from. Despite the open highway imagery in "Prove It All Night"—the promise of leaving everything behind—there is also an insular quality to it, a suffocating feeling that the world is closing in on them.

There is a strong moral edge to "Prove It All Night." The narrator is a sinner who is trying to "get" his hands clean, to rinse all the sins from himself, to become a better person. On their nocturnal journey through the American night, the narrator promises to buy his girlfriend a gold ring and a pretty blue dress and all he asks from her is a kiss. It is no ordinary kiss though—it has ominous connotations—but rather a kiss "to seal our fate." He will prove his love to her if she proves her love to him.

Both share a hunger within. Both want more than what they have. Both believe they deserve more than what they have. It would be nice if all our dreams could come true but in the real world, which is the world of Springsteen's songs, there is no happy ending, no fairy-tale promise that everything will turn out right. On the contrary, to get what you want, you have to grab for it ...and "pay the price," a phrase he would use again.

People warn the girlfriend to stay away from the narrator. (Is he the same character from "Rosalita" whose parents also warned Rosie to be leery of him?) He tells her to pull her hair back in a long white bow and to meet him in the fields "out behind the dynamo." The doomsayers have made their choices but now it is up to his lover to make up her own mind, to pursue her own destiny.

"Darkness On The Edge Of Town"
from *Darkness On The Edge Of Town*
(Columbia, 1978)

Everything on *Darkness On The Edge Of Town* leads up to this snarling, bitter powerhouse of a ballad, a simmering fusion of angst and despair. It is about the dark side of the American dream. If in *Born To Run*, the characters were trying to escape, in this song, they are stuck and do not know what to do about it or where to turn.

By the time Springsteen recorded the songs on *Darkness*, everything in his life had changed. After the success of *Born To Run*, the stakes were higher. People demanded more from him. The record company, in particular, now had expectations. "All of a sudden you're being watched a lot more closely; all of a sudden your actions have implications," Springsteen told journalist Mark Hagen. "I began to think about who I was and where I came from."

The plainspoken, stripped-down sound of "Darkness" best epitomizes the mood that Springsteen wanted to capture. To some, the songs on the album recalled the simplicity of country music and the old traditional ballads. "The music is like Phil Spector melted down and mixed with backroads gravel to model a new kind of folk music, an urban folk music that quotes rock 'n' roll the way Jimmie Rodgers and Hank Williams quoted black and Appalachian spirituals," wrote Joyce Millman on *Salon.com*. To Millman, the darkness that Springsteen is referring to is "the thing that lies just out of reach, that pulls you out of bed in the morning, that seems to get further away the faster you drive toward it but, still, *you gotta have it*. The darkness feeds your ambition. The darkness is your dream." The darkness is also the Promised Land that Springsteen returns to again and again.

In "Darkness," Springsteen acknowledges the secrets that we all harbor inside of us, safely hidden away until someone forces it out into the open. Some people, he writes, are lucky enough to be born into "a good life." And then, he seems to imply, there is the rest of us. These are the people who will get their share of the good life in whatever way possible. The narrator has lost everything—his life savings, his wife—so nothing much matters to him now.

And yet, there is still hope. Despite being down on his luck, our narrator refuses to give up entirely, refuses to give up on the dream of a better life— somewhere. As Springsteen once said, "there's always hope." Even though the dream may never come true, dream on.

The River
(Columbia, 1980)

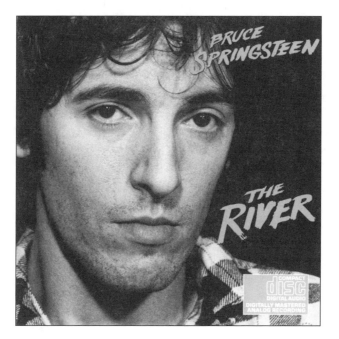

A double album, *The River* gave Springsteen a hit single ("Hungry Heart"), but it is also his most eclectic work: garage band rockers, frothy pop songs, goofy ravers, *and* thoughtful, pensive story-songs and ballads. The musical genres are all over the place too—epic rock, Sixties-style pop, R&B, rockabilly, folk, country, even blue-eyed soul. A prelude to *Nebraska,* it is Springsteen's most mature album up until that time, the album where he began writing about real people and real relationships.

Musicians:

Bruce Springsteen: vocals, electric 6- and 12-string guitars, harmonica, piano

Roy Bittan: piano, organ, background vocals

Clarence Clemons: saxophone, percussion, background vocals

Danny Federici: organ

Garry Tallent: bass

Steve Van Zandt: acoustic and electric guitars, lead guitar, harmony vocals, background vocals

Max Weinberg: drums

Mark Volman and Howard Kaylan (Flo & Eddie): background vocals

Producers: Bruce Springsteen, Jon Landau, Steve Van Zandt

Recorded at: Power Station (New York)

Tracks:

"The Ties That Bind" (3:33)

"Sherry Darling" (4:02)

"Jackson Cage" (3:04)

"Two Hearts" (2:42)

"Independence Day" (4:46)

"Hungry Heart" (3:19)

"Out In The Street" (4:17)

"Crush On You" (3:10)

"You Can Look (But You Better Not Touch)" (2:36)

"I Wanna Marry You" (3:26)

"The River" (4:59)

"Point Blank" (6:05)

"Cadillac Ranch" (3:02)

"I'm A Rocker" (3:34)

"Fade Away" (4:40)

"Stolen Car" (3:53)

"Ramrod" (4:04)

"The Price You Pay" (5:27)

"Drive All Night" (8:26)

"Wreck On The Highway" (3:53)

Running time: 79:65

"Independence Day"

from *The River*

(Columbia, 1980)

"Independence Day" is a song about growing up, facing responsibilities, and leaving the past behind as a son says goodbye to his father and to his hometown. If, as author Bobbie Ann Mason maintains, the struggle of the artist is to grow and change, then Springsteen epitomizes that inner tension between despair and joy, between staying put and moving on.

The first sound we hear is an organ, almost naïve in its simplicity and directness. A son is telling his father to go to bed now. It is late. It is clear they have endured a lifetime of confrontations. Nothing they can say or do can change anything now. We learn that he will be leaving in the morning not only to escape the darkness that has blanketed the house but also the darkness—the suffocation—that has descended on the town itself. The son is determined and defiant. Nothing anybody says and does—whether his neighbors, the townsfolk, or his own family—can do anything to him. "They ain't gonna do to me / What I watched them do to you," he cries. He is above the fray.

The son admits that he can't always explain just what it is that separates them, that makes them always at each other's throat. But then he thinks that, in the end, they are just too much alike.

By the midsection, the childlike simplicity of Danny Federici's organ has given way to the more grown-up, urban-based sounds of Clarence Clemons' saxophone. Formerly busy places in the narrator's hometown are empty and the highway is deserted. The son knows that when he leaves he will have plenty of company. Many people are leaving town, leaving their friends and families behind. The beat now turns almost funereal. It is the same slow death knoll that Springsteen used in "Factory," inevitable, unavoidable, and absolute.

"It's about how generations pass," comments music critic and poet Daniel Wolff, "about the other side of progress, about the way each vision of a better world destroys the one that came before. And it's about how we are bound to each other. The son knows all the things his father wanted. And looking out over this empty promised land, he swears, 'I never meant to take those things away.'"

During one of his long monologues on the concert circuit, Springsteen often discussed the strained relationship that he had with his father and the stifled existence that his father endured in Springsteen's hometown of Freehold, New Jersey. A quite remarkable quote from a 1981 performance in Stockholm appears in Larry David Smith's *Bob Dylan, Bruce Springsteen And American Song:*

I grew up in this little town. As I got older, I started looking around me, and it didn't seem there was any way I was going to get out of there. I looked back at my father, and the only time he got out of that town was to go to World War II. When he came out of the Army, he got married, settled down, and went to work in a plastics factory. And his father had done the same thing. It seemed that the one thing we had in common was that we didn't have enough information; we didn't have enough knowledge about the forces that were controlling our lives. I watched my old man end up as a victim, and he didn't even know it.

But Springsteen was different from his father. He was determined not to repeat the same mistakes, not to fall victim to the same pattern of circumstances. What turned his life around, as we all know, was rock 'n' roll—and the promise that it held out. He would lie in bed at night, listening to Top 40 radio. "It seemed that in those songs by The Drifters and in those songs by Smokey Robinson, there was a promise. There was a promise of a right to a decent life…The only thing that kept me from giving up when I was young was in the rock 'n' roll music I heard—that there was a meaning in life, a meaning in living."

Springsteen could never talk to his father; his father could never talk to him or anyone else, for that matter. But gradually things changed and the once-frayed relationship between father and son improved, if not a healing then a mending of the ways. When, during *The River* tour, Springsteen learned that his father had fallen ill, he visited him in a California hospital "I started thinkin' on the way out about all the things that I always wanted to say to him that I never said," he said, "and I always figured, well, someday we'll sit down and we'll talk about all this stuff—talk about why it was the way it was when I was young, talk about why he felt the way he did."

Douglas "Dutch" Springsteen died many years later, at the age of 73 in May 1998, in Belmont, California. In a statement released announcing his death, Springsteen said: "My father and I had a very loving relationship. I feel lucky to have been so close to my dad as I became a man and a father myself."

But certain things between people often remain unsaid. What Springsteen couldn't quite say to his father instead found its way into "Independence Day"—a song he undoubtedly wrote for himself but also for anyone who ever wanted to say something but didn't know quite how to say it.

"I Wanna Marry You"

from *The River*

(Columbia, 1980)

One of Springsteen's most gorgeous ballads, the sweet-tempered "I Wanna Marry You" owes its debt to the doo-wop songs and soul ballads that Springsteen loved so much growing up. If it had been released in the Sixties, it probably would have been a huge hit.

Danny Federici's swirling organ immediately sets the romantic mood. The narrator sees a young woman walking down the street with a baby carriage. He notices a "lonely ribbon" in her hair and wishes that he was the reason that she put it there.

But the woman of his dreams remains an elusive figure. She never smiles, she never speaks. All we really know about her is that she is a working girl and that she is raising two children on her own.

Although he may sound naïve, our narrator is also a realist. He doesn't want to cramp her style but he thinks now might be the time for her to think about having a home and facing up to adult responsibilities. (How many rock songs have that as their subject matter?) He realizes that may sound foolish, and he knows that true love is the stuff of fairy tales. He is no prince in shining armor; his ambitions are much more modest. Like the character in "Thunder Road," he is not a hero (could the young woman here be "Thunder's" Mary?) and he can't promise that he'll make all her dreams come true, but maybe, just maybe, he can "help them along." (Sometimes, though, you wonder if this guy is a bit too obsessed with his object of affection.)

Then he talks about the unfulfilled life that his father had, and how it made him hard; his father, right before he died, called true love a lie. But the narrator has no interest in being like his father (shades of "Independence Day"). An unabashed romantic, he carries his love "without shame" and would be proud if she would "wear" his name.

The song closes with its full-blown romanticism intact, as the organ now accompanied by Clarence Clemons' saxophone reaches an emotional crescendo.

How true to life is "I Wanna Marry You"? Springsteen seems to have channeled the thoughts of his father into the song. During the *Devils & Dust* tour, he mentioned his father's cynical attitude toward romance (his mother, on the other hand, adored love songs):

Bruce, all love songs are a government conspiracy. That is propaganda. Don't be fooled, don't fool yourself, all those men are paid servants.' The idea was to get you married and you would have to pay taxes. That was his theory.

Springsteen was introducing "The River" but it could easily apply to "I Wanna Marry You."

"The River"
from *The River*
(Columbia, 1980)

I went down to the river to watch the fish swim by
But I got to the river so lonesome I wanted to die..., Oh Lord!
And then I jumped in the river, but the doggone river was dry.
She's long gone, and now I'm lonesome blue.
—Hank Williams, "Long Gone Lonesome Blues"

The harmonica sounds distant, slightly ominous, foreshadowing the grimness that is to follow. And then there are the vocals—sung in a muffled, constricted voice that does its best to hide the pain and disappointment. Dave Marsh has described Springsteen's singing on "The River" as "that odd combination of soul hoarseness, rockabilly twang, and Jersey nasality..."—that and an ample dose of Hank Williams.

The narrator of the tale comes from a place where things don't change much and where you pretty much do what is expected of you. He rushes into marriage when his high school sweetheart, Mary, becomes pregnant (she was "just seventeen"). There is no time for a conventional wedding, "no walk down the aisle," just a rush to the courthouse to say the perfunctory vows and get on with life.

The narrator finds a job working construction for a local company but that soon proves a disappointment too. In Springsteen's America, working hard and putting in long hours does not guarantee success. Everything that once seemed so important to him—work, marriage, family—have vanished. He acts like he doesn't remember; Mary acts like she doesn't care, he sings. But, of course, they both do—very much—and that's the problem, that's why the pain of their life never ends. The memories of better times haunt him "like a curse." And then follows one of the most famous lines in a Springsteen song: "Is a dream a lie if it don't come true or is it something worse."

And then there is the image of the river itself. The river serves as a metaphor for hope. It was the place the young couple would go to when they were courting. Later, after the impromptu marriage ceremony, it was the place they went to feel some kind of solace. Later still, after all expectations have vanished, it is still the place that they go to even though the narrator knows, in Williams-esque fashion, that "the river is dry."

Ah, Hank Williams. The ghost of Hank Williams hovers all over *The River* and its subsequent release, *Nebraska*. According to Marsh, Springsteen modeled "The River" on Hank Williams' country classic "Long Gone Lonesome Blues." It's not hard to understand what Springsteen saw—or rather, heard—in Hank Williams. In "Long Gone Lonesome Blues," Williams sings in a voice soaked with tears, before bellowing out an anguished yodel. But Springsteen himself indicates in *Songs* that the actual Williams song that inspired "The River" was not "Long Gone Lonesome Blues" but instead the more upbeat (upbeat for Williams, that is) "My Bucket's Got A Hole In It," which Springsteen listened to one night in a New York hotel room. "I drove back to New Jersey that night," he recalled, "and sat up in my room writing 'The River.' I used a narrative folk voice—just a guy in a bar telling his story to the stranger on the next stool."

Although the ghost of Hank Williams is everywhere on the record, Springsteen based the content of "The River" on true-to-life situations such as the crash of the construction industry in late 1970s New Jersey and his own family members' experiences. Indeed, when he first performed "The River" live at the "No Nukes" concert in 1979, he dedicated it to his sister Virginia and her husband Mickey.

What is it exactly about country music that appeals so much to Springsteen? Springsteen has commented on country music's beauty and purity, as well as its mystery. Like Dylan, who had equally wide-ranging influences, Springsteen had no desire to mimic his musical mentors. Instead he borrowed what he wanted and branded it with his own stamp in order to fit his own musical needs.

Like country music legends Hank Williams, Jimmie Rodgers, Bill Monroe, and Johnny Cash, the core of Springsteen's music, his musical center, rests firmly within the storytelling ballad. Songs such as "The River" follow in the tradition of the English and Scottish ballads—the Child ballads—where telling a story is a crucial ingredient. Springsteen's attitude is remarkably similar to that of country singer Marty Stuart.

"As a country performer," says Stuart, "my mentors taught me to be a correspondent, to tell people's stories." Springsteen is also a correspondent, a storyteller who shares stories through the voices of his characters. Or, as singer-songwriter Gretchen Peters so succinctly put it, "songs can be things of substance," just as important as novels.

And like Williams, Springsteen here—as well as in so many other songs—creates realistic depictions of his own social environment. Another trait Springsteen has in common with Williams is his sincerity. Both singers approached their material with utmost honesty and, it must be said, humility. Country historian Bill C. Malone has commented on how Williams "lived" the songs he sang. Much the same can be said of Springsteen.

"The River" may be among Springsteen's darkest ballads, but it is also one of his most humane.

"Point Blank"
from *The River*
(Columbia, 1980)

"Point Blank" is a song of shadows, of lives going nowhere, of broken relationships, and broken promises. The characters are stuck in a circle of their own making, repeating themselves over and over again and wishing in vain that things would turn out better.

Musically, it's a beautiful, grown-up ballad. Roy Bittan's understated piano strikes all the right chords of heartbreak and deception, a portentous rumble of what is to come. Springsteen's vocal too is one of his best—at times vulnerable, at times disbelieving, at times brimming with anger.

It offers a wonderfully paranoid Springsteen lyric as well. The narrator asks if the woman, an ex-lover, he is addressing the song to still says her prayers every night before she goes to bed, praying that everything will be alright. He then tells her story. She grew up fast but things did not turn out as she had planned. Rather than living the life that she wanted, she ends up waiting for the welfare check to arrive every month.

In a chilling dream sequence, he dreams that they are together again, dancing in their old haunts. They stand at the bar but the music of the band makes it difficult to have a conversation. She shouts something in his ear, pulls his jacket off, and then grabs his hand and drags him onto the dance floor. Waking up from his reverie, he remembers that he saw her the previous night, her face in shadows, standing in a doorway trying to stay dry from the rain. He calls out her name, but she doesn't answer. And then comes the violent denouement: Bang, bang.

On paper it reads like a sordid little tale of white lies and falsehoods, something out of a Raymond Chandler novel. The music also helps to sustain the mood of suspense and uncertainty.

The song, like the rest of the album, is a paradox. It expresses the way Springsteen was feeling at the time. "[T]he only thing you can do with paradox is live with it," he told his biographer Dave Marsh. "On the album, I just said, 'I don't understand all these things. I don't see where all these things fit. I don't see how these things can work together.' ...It was just a situation of living with all those contradictions. And that's what happens. There's never any resolution."

"Fade Away"
from *The River*
(Columbia, 1980)

Pain has never sounded so gorgeous. Springsteen's forlorn ballad of lost love and one man's desperate attempt to regain what he once had is a great song, one of the best, on *The River*.

"Fade Away" has a Sixties feel to it—all aching vocals and the soulful organ playing of Danny Federici; a lush homage to something you can't have. Even though things have not been good between the characters—she lost has her love for him, he has lost his trust in her—he is not ready to give up just yet. It offers one of Springsteen's more concise lyrics too—poetic and touching—and is sung with great emotion. You can actually hear the desperation—the deep *yearning*—in Springsteen's voice, as he clings to the slightest hope of reconciliation.

In another era, "Fade Away" would have been a Top 10 smash. But when it was released as a follow up to Springsteen's hit, "Hungry Heart," the best it could muster was a feeble Number 20 on the charts. Its lowly showing though doesn't diminish its power or longevity. It still sounds terrific.

"Stolen Car"
from *The River*
(Columbia, 1980)

"Stolen Car," Bruce Springsteen told *Mojo* magazine "is about a guy who felt disconnected and felt that he was fading away, disappearing; felt invisible. Growing up, I felt invisible. And that feeling is an enormous source of pain for people. To make your life felt, it doesn't have to be in some big way, maybe it's just your family and with the job, the basic things you live for." In other words, "Stolen Car," like many of Springsteen's songs, is about the struggle to create meaning for oneself, whatever form that meaning happens to take. The song itself is presented without judgment. It just tells a story, honestly and simply, offering one of Springsteen's most precise lyrics.

The protagonist is an open wound, a lost and confused soul who drives around town in a stolen car hoping that one day he will get caught. "But I never do." He has drifted apart from his wife but can't exactly explain why. At first, he chalks it up to restlessness but then realizes it was something deeper, something more fundamental than just that. Throughout the song, Springsteen the lyricist searches and finds the heart of the song, finds its emotional truth.

As Springsteen writes in *Songs*, "'Stolen Car' was the predecessor for a good deal of the music I'd be writing in the future. It was inner-directed, psychological; this was the character whose progress I'd soon be following on *Tunnel Of Love*. He was the archetype for the male role in my later songs about men and women."

Springsteen has recorded two entirely different versions (both lyrically and musically) of "Stolen Car," first on *The River* and then on *Tracks*. The original release is a shorter and darker cut, the musical accompaniment, especially Danny Federici's organ, slightly detached. The character appears more desperate, his voice trails off at the end of lines as if he truly believes that he has already disappeared. He has already given up. Max Weinberg's drums too sound an ominous note.

On *Tracks* though, Springsteen's voice sounds stronger, more confident, his phrasing clearer. It has a fuller arrangement and the lyrics themselves are more fleshed out. In this second version, the protagonist still has hope of some kind of reconciliation. He adds a scene where there is a party going on. He lies in the shade by the river that runs "down into the sea." From this vantage point, he can see party lights. As a dreamlike organ swirls in the background, he wonders if his wife is inside and if she is looking for him. He dreams that he called her and swore to return "and stay forevermore." He dreams of their wedding day but then in a flash the vision turns dark. Just when he is about to kiss the bride and leans over to touch her lips, he feels it all slipping away.

The details too are different—minor but significant. Whereas in the original the character "met a little girl" and settled down in a little house on the edge of town, in the *Tracks* version, he "found me a girl" and settles down. Interestingly, Springsteen adds "pretty" to the description of the house and the town.

Like fugitives from film noir, the narrator drives by night and travels in fear. In the original version, he fears that the darkness will swallow him whole, making him invisible. In the second version, though, he already has disappeared. No matter what he does or where he goes, nobody ever sees him when he drives by.

Two terrific covers of the song appear on Springsteen tribute albums: Elliott Murphy on *One Step Up, Two Steps Back* chooses the *Tracks* version while Patty Griffin on *Light Of Day* selects the original version. Driven by the rhythms of her guitar, Griffin sings it as if it is a traditional ballad, centuries old, not even changing the gender of the narrator. In the liner notes to *Light Of Day*, Griffin explains why she chose to record "Stolen Car." "It's like he's saying, 'The drama has ended and I don't know what to do.' The guy's not staring at the abyss. He's in the abyss."

"The Price You Pay"
from *The River*
(Columbia, 1980)

"This is the land of which I swore to Abraham, to Isaac, and to Jacob, saying, 'I will give it your descendants.' I have let you see it with your own eyes, but you shall not cross over there."

—Deuteronomy 34:4

The Book of Numbers and the Book of Deuteronomy—two of the first five books that comprise the Old Testament—covers a span of some 40 years in Israel's history, from 1440 B.C. when the Israelites left their encampment at Mount Sinai and wandered aimlessly in the desert for 40 years until 1400 B.C. when they crossed the Jordan River near Jericho and entered Canaan, the very same land that God had promised as their homeland; in other words, the Promised Land.

The humble hero of the Promised Land is Moses, who, some 400 years after Jacob's family emigrated to Egypt to escape a famine, freed the Israelites from Egyptian slavery and helped turn their plight into the founding of a nation. Moses was born in Egypt to an Israelite slave but raised by an Egyptian princess in the Pharaoh's court. At age 40, he fled the country after killing an Egyptian whom he saw beating an Israelite. He settled east of Egypt, married, and became a shepherd. One day while Moses was grazing his flock on the mountainside, God spoke to him in the guise of a burning bush and commanded him to return to Egypt to demand the release of the Israelites. Reluctantly, Moses did as he was told.

So in a nutshell goes the story according to the Bible.

"The Price You Pay" is laced with biblical imagery. Was Springsteen inspired by the Bible when he wrote it? Who knows? But it certainly does serve as the perfect blueprint for this defiant tale of broken promises and lost dreams. Like Moses, the unnamed hero of the song has to learn to live with consequences. Everything has a price. It is significant, I think, that Springsteen refers back to imagery from the Bible, for in the Old Testament no one who disobeys the Lord walks away unscathed. Similarly, no one in the song can walk away without a fight. Lyrically, the song is ambiguous—there is no real story here, just a vague impulse of an ongoing struggle for social justice and living with the decisions that we make.

"Drive All Night"
from *The River*
(Columbia, 1980)

The characters in the remarkable "Drive All Night," a seven-minute song of such deep longing that the pain is almost palpable, are prisoners of their own minds. Boasting one of Springsteen's most soulful and impassioned vocals, it is an epic paean to lost—and re-discovered—love. "I swear I'd drive all night again," he begins in the chorus, to buy his sweetheart something as simple and ostensibly mundane as a pair of shoes, anything to redeem himself in her eyes and sleep in her arms one more time. It's such a wildly romantic song—and a powerful one—that it's no surprise that it was one of the selections chosen for the CBS television series *Cold Case*.

In January 2006 an episode of the series aired that built a murder mystery involving high school friends, set in the Eighties around nine Springsteen songs. The show's creator and writer of the episode, Meredith Stiehm, used Springsteen's lyrics to advance the story line. "No Surrender" is overheard on graduation day; a murder scene is set to "Atlantic City." Most effectively, "Drive All Night" is used to convey the desperation of one of the show's characters.

Lyrically and musically, the song straddles both *Born To Run* and *Darkness On The Edge Of Town*—the long saxophone solo in the middle recalls the milieu of the small-town hoods in "Meeting Across The River" and evokes the dark romanticism of a Raymond Chandler novel. But "Drive All Night" is more optimistic. The narrator reunites with his estranged love. As they prepare for bed, they are tempted by "fallen angels" to go out on the street one more time— one senses that it is this street life that got them into trouble in the first place— but these distractions can't hurt them anymore. Springsteen uses repetition ("through the wind, through the rain, the snow, the wind, the rain") to express absolute commitment.

It is a masterful performance.

COLD CASE

On January 8, 2006, the television series *Cold Case* used nine Springsteen compositions to advance the story line, building a murder mystery around the lyrics of his songs: "No Surrender," "Bobby Jean," "Brilliant Disguise," "Glory Days," "I'm On Fire," "Drive All Night," "Stolen Car," "Atlantic City," and "Two Steps Back." One of the characters even mentioned "Born To Run" in the dialogue. It was, he said, about a "disappointed working guy." Written by series creator Meredith Stiehm, the episode followed four highschool friends from 1980 to 1988, when one of them is found dead, to the present day where detectives crack the unsolved crime. "The idea originally was to use no dialogue at all," says Stiehm. "[Springsteen's] songs are that rich, so full of characters and vignettes."

In previous seasons, the series used two other Springsteen songs, "Walk Like A Man" and "Secret Garden."

"Wreck On The Highway"

from *The River*

(Columbia, 1980)

"Their whiskey and blood mixed together. . . I heard the groans of the dying, but I didn't hear nobody pray."

—Roy Acuff, "The Wreck On The Highway"

"When the Lord made me, he made a ramblin' man."

—Hank Williams, "Ramblin' Man"

"I really think of him as a country singer," Emmylou Harris once said about Bruce Springsteen. The South Jersey cowboy might well agree. "Country asked all the right questions," he acknowledges. "It was concerned with how you go on living after you reach adulthood. I was asking those questions myself. Everything after *Born To Run* was shot full with a lot of country music—those questions."

Country music and road songs go hand in hand. Country music celebrates the road and everything that it represents. Whether the lost highway of Hank Williams or the hillbilly highway of Steve Earle, the road promises mobility and freedom. The destination may be uncertain but it is the journey that matters. Off in the distance, though, lurks disaster. The road can be a treacherous place—highway accidents form a huge part of the country tradition (and, before the automobile age, train disasters). Among the best-known highway accident songs is Roy Acuff's "The Wreck On The Highway." Originally titled "Didn't Hear Nobody Pray," it essentially preaches against drunk driving.

Although Springsteen lifted the title from Acuff's somber country classic, his "Wreck On The Highway" is a simple yet powerful and ultimately very moving ballad about mortality. As Springsteen describes it, "On a rainy highway the character witnesses a fatal accident. He drives home and lying awake that night next to his lover, he realizes that you have limited number of opportunities to love someone, to do your work, to be part of something, to parent your children, to do something good."

Whereas the Acuff song seems to be chastising the crash victims for not having the fortitude, and good sense, to pray before their untimely death, Springsteen offers a more nuanced and considerably less sentimental portrait of tragedy. At first, "Wreck On The Highway" appears to be nothing more than a straightforward account on the aftermath of an accident. A good Samaritan comes upon a wreck, gets out of his own car to see if he can help. But the driver is already dead. He stands as the rain pelts down, almost unable to move. He sees a reflection of himself. That might have been him or a loved one. There but for the grace of God go I. The image of the mangled body on the wet highway continues to haunt him all the way home, and when he goes to bed at night, he tells himself he will not take anything for granted anymore. He holds his sweetheart in his arms, and the music softly fades away.

"Wreck On The Highway" is a perfect song, a masterpiece in miniature, and a haunting meditation on mortality and what it means to be alive.

All-night diner. (Theresa Albini)

Nebraska
(Columbia, 1982)

In *Nebraska*, Springsteen navigates moral gray areas using the state and its flat, open, featureless landscape as an emotional shorthand for the bleak portraits of murderers, loners, and other assorted misfits from the other side of Ronald Reagan's America. The moral here is that anybody can do anything; evil and good reside in the same person.

More than any other Springsteen album of new material, *Nebraska* reveals the folk roots of rock 'n' roll. The songs that make up *Nebraska* were recorded as a demo tape in Springsteen's "home studio," that is, his living room. To say it was a technical challenge to transfer the demo to a master tape is an understatement. When it was released, *Nebraska* received overwhelmingly critical praise. *Rolling Stone* named it among its best albums of the year and, even a few decades later, the accolades continue. Author Jimmy Guterman calls *Nebraska* "a once-in-a-lifetime album, as close as Springsteen will ever get to blues feeling, if not blues form." In 2000, a *Nebraska* tribute album was released and, in 2006, the New York Guitar Festival celebrated its twenty-fifth anniversary with "The Nebraska Project."

Audience reaction was mixed—people either loved it or hated it (probably still do)—but it did manage to reach Number Four on the *Billboard* album charts. *Nebraska* is the aural equivalent of an Edward Hopper painting, *Nighthawks* on vinyl.

Musicians:

Bruce Springsteen: lead vocals, guitar

Recorded at: Springsteen's in New Jersey by Mike Batlin on a Teac Tascam Series 144 4-track cassette recorder

Tracks:

"**Nebraska**" (4:30)
"**Atlantic City**" (3:57)
"**Mansion On The Hill**" (4:05)
"**Johnny 99**" (3:40)
"**Highway Patrolman**" (5:36)
"**State Trooper**" (3:12)
"Used Cars" (3:06)
"**Open All Night**" (2:54)
"**My Father's House**" (5:04)
"**Reason To Believe**" (4:10)

Running time: 38:54

"Nebraska"
from *Nebraska*
(Columbia, 1982)

"But dad i'm not real sorry for what i did cause for the first time me and Caril have [sic] more fun."

—Charles Starkweather, while in his prison cell awaiting transfer back to Nebraska, in a letter to his parents

"I can't deny we had fun though."

—Kit, the character based on Charles Starkweather and played by Martin Sheen in Terrence Malick's 1974 film *Badlands*

"I can't say that I'm sorry for the things that we done / At least for a little while, sir, me and her we had us some fun."

—Bruce Springsteen, "Nebraska"

A deep sense of loneliness—of being unable to connect—lies at the heart of *Nebraska* that recalls the work of Hank Williams and countless other country voices through the years. During this post-*Born To Run*-era, Springsteen was feeling pretty lost himself. "You've got your Saturday night, but you're gonna have to wake up the next morning, pal," he once said, "and you'll have to pay the consequences of the choices you make. Rock had been mainly about avoiding those choices. Country musicians like Hank Williams and Merle Haggard asked the hard questions I was beginning to ask myself. After *Born To Run*, it was, O.K., now what? Country was concerned with how you go on living after you reach adulthood. I said, well why can't rock ask those same questions. Because the audience is going to ask those questions real soon."

Years later, in 1999, he again discussed the reasons why he felt so disconnected, both from his family and from his community. "I think in my own life I had reached where it felt like I was teetering on this void. I felt a deep sense of isolation, and that led me to those characters and to those stories—people I remembered growing up, my father's side of the family, a certain way they spoke, a certain way they approached life, and that resonated through that music."

It is not surprising then that Springsteen turned so forcefully to country music during the late Seventies and early Eighties—its yearning, directness, and intensity must have appealed to him on a visceral level. The traditional themes of abandoned lovers and sinners going to their deathbed without the possibility of redemption that so riddles the songs of Hank Williams and Roy Acuff are themes that resonated with Springsteen even though he may not might have expressed his thoughts in the same way. Williams, in particular, shared much of the same lyrical vocabulary: words like temptation, the promised land, Judgment Day, and heaven pepper his songs. Ironically, while Williams wrote so beautifully about the rambling life, Springsteen was looking for something else, a semblance of community and an end to rambling.

"Nebraska," the first cut on the album of the same name, is Springsteen's version of the Charles Starkweather-Caril Fugate murder spree of the late 1950s. Their deadly rampage inspired a number of movies, including Terrence Malick's *Badlands* in 1974 starring Martin Sheen and Sissy Spacek, David Lynch's *Wild At Heart* in 1990, Dominic Sena's *Kalifornia* (1993) starring Brad Pitt and Juliette Lewis, and Oliver Stone's *Natural Born Killers* (1994) starring Woody Harrelson and (again) Juliette Lewis.

Springsteen wrote "Nebraska" from Starkweather's perspective. The story unfolds without judgment. Springsteen sings in such a flat, neutral voice, a voice void of emotion that he may as well be reading from a grocery list but underneath lie layers of moral ambiguity and violent impulses. The song itself sounds timeless, as if it were written in another century. It is sung in the modal starkness redolent of traditional Appalachian music but without a hint of sentiment. What's more, there is a quiet stillness to "Nebraska," a quality that Dave Marsh associates with the Library of Congress folk recordings of the 1930s and 1940s.

In the opening stanza, the Starkweather character sees a young girl—Fugate was 14 at the time of the killings—standing on her front lawn, twirling her baton, an image that Springsteen borrowed from the opening scenes of *Badlands*. Things move swiftly along for in the next line he confesses that he and her went for a ride "and 10 innocent people died." Beginning in Lincoln, Nebraska, and on through the badlands of Wyoming, the couple continues on their lethal journey.

Charles Starkweather was born in Lincoln, Nebraska, on November 24, 1938, the third of seven children of Guy and Helen Starkweather, and grew up the byproduct of a poor, uneducated but hardworking and respectable family. Although of average intelligence, Starkweather had a minor speech impediment and was considered a slow learner. He was often the butt of jokes. Perhaps to compensate for his perceived shortcomings, he soon earned a reputation as being cruel and tough. Starkweather's hero was James Dean, and he emulated the movie star by copying Dean's clothes (tight jeans and cowboy boots) and hairstyle (swept up, away from his forehead). Starkweather quit high school at the age of 16 and found work loading and unloading trucks for a paper company. But it was short-lived and before long he got another job as a garbage collector (in *Badlands,* when we meet the Starkweather alter ego, Kit, he is collecting garbage). He felt trapped and isolated with little prospect of leaving behind the working-class life. The only way to escape the poverty that seemed to be his fate—the only way he could get the respect he so desperately craved—he reasoned, was to choose a life of crime. Robbery would be his way out.

Empty stools. (Theresa Albini)

In *Roads: Driving America's Great Highways,* Larry McMurtry's fascinating meditation on the road and its impact on the American psyche, McMurtry wonders if the Midwest is a breeding ground for killers because of the monotony of the terrain. "It may be," he writes, "that the Midwest produces a distinct kind of disappointment, which, in some, becomes murderous resentment. I think this disappointment has to do with glamour—or rather, with the lack of it. After all, if the American media promises us anything, it's glamour." This could certainly apply to Starkweather.

The murder spree began on the afternoon of January 21, 1958—although Starkweather claimed his first victim more than a month earlier with the fatal shooting of a 21-year-old gas station attendant. After it was all done—the spree lasted a total of eight days—10 people died before Starkweather was caught during a shootout and high-speed chase in rural Wyoming and brought back to Lincoln to face trial.

The trial began four months later on May 5, 1958. Against the wishes of the Starkweather family (apparently, the stigma attached to a mental illness was worse than being a cold-blooded murderer), his lawyers entered a plea of innocent by reason of insanity. But the jury wasn't buying any of it. It didn't take long for the jury to reach a verdict—they found Starkweather guilty of first degree murder. But then again there wasn't much anyone could say in his defense. One of the psychiatrists at his trial testified that "the act of killing meant to him no more than stepping on a bug."

Starkweather was executed on June 25, 1959. Meanwhile, Caril Fugate was found guilty of murder on November 28, 1958. Because she was underage, though, she received a life sentence and was sent to the Nebraska Center for Women. She was paroled in June 1976.

As portrayed by Martin Sheen and Sissy Spacek in *Badlands,* the characters of Kit and Holly are vacant, morally challenged empty vessels, ready to soak up any kind of experience they can. When we first see Kit he is wearing his James Dean outfit: tight jeans, a white shirt, blue denim jacket, and cowboy boots. Holly can't miss the Dean-like resemblance.

As the voice-over narrator, Holly speaks in a flat, clinically detached monotone (Malick used this same device in an earlier movie, *Days Of Heaven*). Kit has a bit more of a personality but not much. As with all of Malick's films, the visuals are gorgeous: never-ending vistas under bright blue skies. When we first meet Holly she is twirling her baton in the street outside her house; the music is dreamy, innocent, almost childlike. In a departure from the historical truth, Kit is a bit older, 25, than Starkweather was at the time; Holly is 15. And in another departure, the setting has been moved from Nebraska to South Dakota (Holly herself has come up north from Texas).

After committing his first murder (of Holly's father), the couple hide out in the wilderness living a pre-Edenic existence, as if they are pioneers or, perhaps, the back to the land hippies of a later era, and dance to "Love Is Strange." It is a surreal, idyllic moment—pure Malick. Later on, Holly observes, "The world was like a far away planet from which I can never return."

After he is captured and the police officers ask him why he did what he did, Kit shrugs and replies with a simple, "I don't know. I always wanted to be in trouble, I guess." He is polite to a fault and the officers, perhaps in awe of being in the company of such a famous outlaw, gladly shake his hand. For better or worse, Starkweather may not have been the first criminal to capture the popular imagination—Jesse James, Bonnie and Clyde, Pretty Boy Floyd all came before him, an in another time and place, Robin Hood and Johnny Armstrong—but he was the first criminal of the television generation, certainly the first American teenage serial killer.

Significantly, Springsteen saw *Badlands* not in the theater during its initial release but on television. And yet he approached the writing of *Nebraska* as if he were a novelist or a short story writer although cinematic images also filled his head, especially John Huston's *Wise Blood* (based on the Flannery O'Connor novel), *True Confessions*, and John Ford's *The Grapes Of Wrath*. But *Badlands*, in particular, stuck in his mind. Intrigued by the story, he did some research on the Starkweather murders, which led him to the book *Caril* by journalist Ninette Beaver. He tracked her down. According to Dave Marsh, they talked for a half-hour about Starkweather. And when he played in Lincoln, Nebraska, during the 1984 tour, he dedicated the song "Nebraska" to Beaver, who was sitting in the audience as his guest.

Much of *Nebraska* was written at a time when Springsteen himself felt isolated, cut off from the world and listening to such quintessentially American singers as Hank Williams and Robert Johnson. Both were familiar with despair and it is this palpable sense of trepidation and aloneness that imbues their songs and, for that matter, Springsteen's *Nebraska*. Hank Williams' biographer Colin Escott, for one, describes lonesomeness as being the core of Williams' finest work. It is significant, I think, that Williams, who was brought up in the Fundamentalist Baptist tradition, appealed to Springsteen at a time when he was at his most vulnerable.

Springsteen had something else in common with Williams—the blues. During this period Springsteen was also listening to blues, not only Robert

Johnson but also John Lee Hooker and others steeped in the blues tradition. Like many musicians who came of age before the fragmentation of music, Williams grew up listening to black musical styles. He was taught guitar by an African American street singer named Rufe Payne. Writes Escott, "[I]t is impossible to understand the approach Hank brought" to his songs "without reference to the blues."

If the songs of Williams and others like him, such as Roy Acuff, revolve around traditional Anglo-Celtic balladry themes such as death, unrequited love, and sinners with no hope of redemption, Springsteen is different if only because he has not given up entirely. "I'm a romantic," he told Robert Hilburn of the *Los Angeles Times*. "To me, the idea of a romantic is someone who sees the reality, lives the reality every day, but knows about the possibilities too. You can't lose sight of the dreams."

Flannery O'Connor had a profound influence on "Nebraska" as well—both the song and the album. "Her stories reminded me of the unknowability of God and contained a dark spirituality that resonated with my own feelings at the time," Springsteen has said. Like O'Connor, Springsteen's characters are confused and tormented by the world around them and occasionally turn to violence to relieve their pain. And with titles like "The Lame Shall Enter First," "Revelation," or "Judgement Day" and Old Testament themes and imagery, it is easy to find a common ground between O'Connor the Catholic writer from the Deep South who took her faith so literally and Springsteen the lapsed Catholic with the soul of a frustrated seeker.

In O'Connor's remarkable short story, "A Good Man Is Hard to Find," one of the characters is a violent miscreant known as The Misfit, who has escaped from jail and shows no remorse for the crimes he has committed. The last line of "Nebraska" echoes the closing paragraphs of O'Connor's story as The Misfit discusses the tenets of his faith before shooting his victim, a chatty grandmother, three times in the chest:

> Jesus was the only One that ever raised the dead and He shouldn't have done it. He thown everything off balance. If He did what He said, then it's nothing for you to do but thow away everything and follow Him, and if He didn't, then it's nothing for you to do but enjoy the few minutes you got left the best way you can—by killing somebody or burning down his house or doing some other meanness to him. No pleasure but meanness.

Yet another influence on Springsteen during the recording of *Nebraska* was photographer Robert Frank's classic work, *The Americans,* a collection of stark black and white photographs that was published in 1958. In the late Fifties Frank traveled across the country in an old used car, capturing images of the America that he saw: haunting snapshots of an America in transition. Among the most Springsteen-esque images in the collection is a photo of a parked car with a "Christ Died for Our Sins" sticker on the rear window. What's more, the album cover of *Nebraska* reportedly was chosen because of its similarity to Frank's "U.S. 285, New Mexico," an evocative photo of a two-lane blacktop with one car in the distance driving away from an endless horizon.

Is *Nebraska* an immoral recording, as some have charged, or an even-handed portrait of evil?

When asked once why he writes so much about killers and if it were necessary to have actually met one, Springsteen responded with a thoughtful, "No, you're not trying to recreate the experience, you're trying to recreate the emotions and the things that went into the action being taken. Those are things that everyone understands, those are things that everyone has within them. The action is the symptom, that's what happened, but the things that caused that action to happen, that's what everyone knows about—you know about it, I know about it. It's inside of every human being."

A terrific alternate version of "Nebraska" appears on *Bruce Springsteen & The E Street Band Live/1975–85.* It offers a fuller arrangement—Max Weinberg's sinewy drumming truly captures the menace in the song—and boasts a particularly powerful Springsteen vocal.

THE STARKWEATHER VICTIMS

The Starkweather murder spree left 10 people dead:

• January 21, 1958: Marion Barlett, his wife Velda, and their two-year-old daughter Betty Jean;

• January 27, 1958: August Meyer, 70, on his farm on Route 43, two miles east of Bennet, Nebraska;

• January 27, 1958: Highschool sweethearts Robert Jensen and Carol King were slain in an old schoolhouse a mile and a hale from the Meyer farm;

• January 28, 1958: Businessman C. Lauer Wood, his wife, and their housekeeper, Lillian Fenel, were killed in their home at 2843 South 24th Street in Lincoln;

• January 29, 1958: Great Falls, Montana, shoe salesman Merle Collison was slain on U.S. 20, ten miles west of Douglas, Wyoming.

"Atlantic City"

from *Nebraska*
(Columbia, 1982)

One of the livelier numbers on *Nebraska,* "Atlantic City" depicts a young couple, desperately in debt, trying to make ends meet in the gambling capital of the East Coast, set against a background of mob violence and civic corruption.

"Atlantic City" is about death and moral decay. It opens with the demise of mob boss Philip "Chicken Man" Testa who was murdered in a bomb blast outside his Philadelphia home on March 15, 1981. The Philadelphia mob had strong ties to the steel and concrete companies that would later help with the construction of the casinos along the boardwalk (the New Jersey legislature approved gambling in Atlantic City on November 2, 1976). But the feeling of malaise that engulfs the song applies not only to the decadence of Atlantic City itself but also to the lost and confused young lovers who are the song's centerpiece. The narrator is so hard pressed for money—"I got debts that no honest man can pay" (a line that also appears in "Johnny 99")—that he withdraws his life savings from the local bank and buys two bus tickets for himself and his sweetheart so they can start all over again in Atlantic City, hoping against hope that lady luck will look fondly on them for once. Although their love for each other has diminished, he still promises to stay with her forever (of course, he has nowhere else to turn). And he still holds out for a better future. "Everything dies baby that's a fact," he tells his lover, "but maybe everything that dies some day comes back," he tentatively adds. Like the petty thief in Springsteen's earlier "Meeting Across The River," he is so desperate he is ready to try anything, even one last score.

"Atlantic City" was Springsteen's first video although you would never confuse it with the music videos of the MTV heyday (or, for that matter, Springsteen's own *Dancing In The Dark* video a few years later). In keeping with the bleakness of the subject matter, it was shot using black and white footage of Atlantic City from inside a moving car. Springsteen's Atlantic City ignores the town's glitzy, touristy image; instead, he presents the other Atlantic City, the Atlantic City of boarded-up windows and people loitering aimlessly on street corners. To my ears, it is reminiscent of Dylan's "Hurricane," with Springsteen's guitar and harmonica adding to its subtle power. (Things haven't changed that much. In early 2006, nearly half of the city's households were low-income while the crime rate was more than three times the national average.)

Springsteen songs can be a challenge for other singers to interpret—what does one do with all those words? One of the best covers, however, is of "Atlantic City" on *Badlands: A Tribute To Bruce Springsteen's* Nebraska by alt-country singer Hank III; that's right, Hank Williams' grandson.

Hank turns the first half of the song into a jaunty, good 'ol boy country romp but halfway through he drastically changes gears and, in a brilliant and inventively subversive move, borrows the distinctive riff from his grandfather's seminal "Ramblin' Man" and transforms the last section of the song into a dark and mournful dirge. It's something to hear.

"Mansion On The Hill"
from *Nebraska*
(Columbia, 1982)

> *"Tonight down here in the valley*
> *I'm lonesome and O how I feel*
> *As I sit here alone in my cabin*
> *I can see your Mansion On The Hill"*
> —Hank Williams, "A Mansion On The Hill"

On October 21, 1984 at the Oakland Coliseum, while on tour with the E Street Band, Springsteen recalled a childhood memory: "When I was a kid, I remember there used to be this house that stood on kinda this hill out on the edge of town, and I remember when I was young, I don't remember any real sense of having more money or less than the next person, somehow you just knew, I guess." He then sang "Mansion On The Hill." Years later, in 1996 at a benefit concert for a Hispanic community center in his hometown of Freehold, New Jersey, he introduced it as a song "set right here in town."

Springsteen borrowed the title from the 1947 Hank Williams song, "A Mansion On The Hill," a song that despite its jaunty melody is about the end of a relationship. An upper-class girl rejects the love of a poor suitor who lives in a cabin. Like Williams, Springsteen preserves the class consciousness theme.

Autobiographical in nature, Springsteen's song is written from a child's point of view. A mansion sits high on a hill, like a medieval fortress from another century, rising above both factories and fields. Children play not outside the mansion—steel gates completely surround it—but on the road that leads to it. At night, a father and his young son drive through the streets of the town, park along a back road, and look up at the mansion. During the summer, parties are held inside, while the young narrator and his sister hide out "in the tall corn fields," listening from afar. Historian Bryan K. Garman has commented on the economic disparity that exists in the song between the laborers who work in the mill and the owners of the mill who acquired their wealth from the sweat of these very workers. "As the fruits of their labor are transformed into the ornaments of wealth which segregate them from the comfort and success the mansion represents," writes Garman, "Springsteen suggests that labor does not deliver workers to the American dream, but rather isolates them from it."

"Mansion On The Hill" is accompanied only by harmonica and guitar. In the directness of its arrangement, it echoes the simple life of its characters as well as their place in society as outsiders perpetually looking in.

"Johnny 99"
from *Nebraska*
(Columbia, 1982)

> *"Ain't been here before, give 99 years, come back no more."*
> —Julius Daniels, "99 Year Blues"

> *"This song has it all . . . crime, punishment, drama, mama, and a one way ticket to hell."*
> —John Hiatt, on covering "Johnny 99," *One Step Up/Two Steps Back: The Songs of Bruce Springsteen,* 1997

"Johnny 99" begins with an eerie, melancholy wail that sounds like a primordial cry from beyond the grave. It is a nod to the songwriting of Woody Guthrie, to the spirit of Robert Johnson, and to the many artists that comprise Harry Smith's seminal *Anthology Of American Folk Music,* a major influence on Springsteen. Essentially, "Johnny 99" is about a deeply troubled man committing a violent act out of sheer desperation.

"Johnny 99" tells the story of a young autoworker named Ralph from Mahwah, New Jersey. He has just lost his job—the auto plant where he worked shut down. Unable to find work, he gets "too drunk" on a potent mixture of Tanqueray and wine. He tires of struggling and takes to a life of crime. He feels isolated from his job, from his family, from his friends, from his entire community (echoes of

Charles Starkweather). Frustrated and enraged at his own impotence, he shoots and kills a night clerk. Driving around in a part of town "when you hit a red light you don't stop," Ralph is arrested by an off-duty police officer in front of the Club Tip Top, a working-class bar. (Details are very important in a Springsteen song, adding particularity to an oftentimes universal story.)

The city supplies a public defender and Ralph's trial begins in the courthouse of "Mean John Brown," who has very little sympathy for the criminal kind. Ralph is sentenced to 98 and a year (hence his "Johnny 99" nickname). A fistfight breaks out in the courtroom, Ralph's girlfriend is dragged away, and his mother pleas for mercy. Ralph is asked if he wants to make a statement before he is taken away. He confesses that he has debts "no honest man could pay" (a similar lyric appears in "Atlantic City"). He tells the judge that the bank threatened to repossess his house. He admits that all of these unfortunate circumstances do not make him an innocent man—he does not deny his guilt—but the combustible combination of unemployment, alcohol abuse, a profound sense of displacement, and easy access to firearms lead to a tragic conclusion. He even requests his own execution.

The song is set to a shuffling, rockabilly beat, the harmonica and guitar nicely playing off each other. Jim Cullen places the melancholy wail that begins the song in the heart of the great working-class musical tradition, calling it "an act of musical homage," that echoes not only the ghost of Jimmie Rodgers, the Singing Brakeman of Mississippi, as he rightly suggests, but also the figure of another seminal Southerner, Hank Williams.

Springsteen uses a real-life incident as the background to the story. In June 1980 the Ford Motor Company closed its assembly plant in Mahwah, New Jersey, a facility that had been part of the community since 1955, and was replaced by the North American headquarters of a large Japanese corporation as well as a hotel and an office complex. Nearly 250,000 autoworkers lost their jobs in the early 1980s. To the autoworkers of Mahwah, then, Ronald Reagan's cheery "Morning in America" motto rang hollow; it was nothing more, in fact, than a cruel joke foisted on a community as it helplessly watched its local economy fall to Great Depression-era depths. Nationwide, the unemployment rate reached as high as 11 percent by 1982, the year *Nebraska* was released; while the industrial cities of the north further deteriorated and homelessness increased.

The *Anthology of American Folk Music,* released by Folkways in 1952 and edited by a West Coast artist, filmmaker, discographer, collector, literary editor, and all-around eccentric named Harry Smith, was a major influence on Springsteen. Long considered the bible of the American folk movement, or, as author Greil Marcus calls it, "the founding document of the American folk revival," essentially, it represents the music of the poor, the isolated, the marginalized, and the uneducated...an eclectic mix of hillbilly songs, traditional ballads, blues, and Cajun music. When it came out, Smith's *Anthology* stimulated a new wave of amateur interest in traditional music. During the 1960s, folk revival performers recorded their favorite versions of its songs, many of which entered the contemporary folk repertoires.

Springsteen came to the *Anthology* much later than his peers, not until he began writing the songs that would make up *Nebraska*, some 30 years after its release. Essentially, he conflated two songs from the collection, Julius Daniels's "99 Year Blues" (1927) and the Carter Family's "John Hardy Was a Desperate Little Man" (1930). Both songs provided the narrative and thematic structure for "Johnny 99" but Springsteen sets them in the economically depressed New Jersey of the 1980s.

"99 Year Blues" is about a young black man who is arrested for basically being poor and black. The judge sentences him to serve 99 years in "Joe Brown's coal mine." The protagonist is so enraged by the injustice of it all that he expresses a desire to "kill everybody" in town. "John Hardy," based on a real-life incident, is a ballad of African-American origin that was popular around the turn of the Twentieth century. Hardy worked for a West Virginia coal company. One night he kills a man in a crap game over a mere 25 cents and is scheduled to be executed by hanging on January 19, 1894. In a plot twist worthy of a Springsteen ballad, on the eve of his death, he confesses his sins and spends the rest of his life repenting his sins and singing hymns. What's more, a white Baptist preacher takes him down to the river and gives him an adult baptism. He is born again.

The ghost of Woody Guthrie also hovers over "Johnny 99." Shortly after reading Joe Klein's biography of Guthrie, *Woody Guthrie: A Life*, Springsteen began to offer his own interpretation of Guthrie's "This Land Is Your Land," the unofficial American national anthem. He continued to sing the song during both *The River* and the *Born In The U.S.A.* tours (Springsteen did not tour for *Nebraska*). Thematically, then, if not quite musically, "Johnny 99" is written in the tradition of Woody Guthrie.

"Highway Patrolman"
from *Nebraska*
(Columbia, 1982)

The longest cut on *Nebraska*, "Highway Patrolman," is a narrative ballad, an Abel and Cain story-song about the importance of family connections, of "blood on blood." The characters here are brothers: one good (Joe Roberts) and one bad (Frankie Roberts). Joe is a sergeant whose motto is to do an honest day's work, "as honest as I could." Frankie, on the other hand, is a perennial troublemaker. Springsteen once described the song as about "the conflict between what your heart tells you to do and what you do with it."

In true narrative fashion, Springsteen tells us Joe and Frankie's back story. Frankie joined the army in 1965; Joe received a farm deferment and married a local girl named Maria. But the wheat prices plummeted and, to make ends meet, Joe became a state trooper.

One night Joe receives a call regarding an altercation in a roadhouse "out on the Michigan line." It's a familiar story—an argument, a brief spurt of violence, blood on the floor, a young woman crying—all because of Frankie. Joe does what he has to do—up to a point. He races down the county roads before finally seeing Frankie at a crossroads—a nice reference to the Robert Johnson myth—and then follows him until he reaches the Canadian border. He pulls over to the side of the highway and watches "his taillights disappear."

The chorus of the song recalls better times, when Joe and Frankie— "laughin' and drinkin,'"—took turns dancing with Maria to "Night Of The Johnstown Flood." Significantly, the song they dance to is about one of the most devastating disasters in American history, the Johnstown Flood, when, on May 31, 1889, a poorly constructed dam burst and killed some 2,209 people. At the time, Johnstown, Pennsylvania, was a booming coal-and-steel town, a diverse community of mainly German, Welsh, Irish, Scotch-Irish, and Cornish workers. In the mountains above Johnstown, though, an old earth dam had been hastily rebuilt to create a lake that the industrial tycoons Andrew Carnegie, Henry Clay Frick, and Andrew Mellon used as a summer resort. The water that came tumbling down in torrents on the people of Johnstown sounded like the rush of an oncoming train, followed by the shattering of glass, and the ripping apart of houses. The small city of 30,000 people was devastated—and it took all of 10 minutes. Songs were written about the disaster, some with maudlin titles like "Her Last Message" or "That Valley Of Tears," and sermons were delivered on the meaning of the flood. The Johnstown Flood entered the realm of legend, its story passed down from generation to generation. But unless you are from the region or are an astute student of American history, it is likely that you never heard of Johnstown or the flood.

"Highway Patrolman" is a guitar-based song, quiet and introspective; a sturdy piece of writing that captures the weariness of the lead character. It is about the familial ties that bind one family member to another, of shared loyalty, and of the inner turmoil that results when the outside world makes expectations of us that we cannot possibly fulfill.

In 1991, Sean Penn wrote and directed *The Indian Runner,* a film that was inspired by "Highway Patrolman," starring Viggo Mortensen (very much pre-*Lord Of The Rings*), David Morse, and Patricia Arquette. A clumsy and uneven effort whose narrative veers considerably from the song, it failed to capture the humanity and essence of Springsteen's poignant lyrics.

JOHNSTOWN FLOOD

Johnstown Flood. (Author collection)

The Johnstown Flood was one of the most devastating disasters in nineteenth-century America. At the time of the disaster in 1889, Johnstown had 30,000 residents; today, the population is just under 24,000. The Johnstown Flood was the Katrina of its day. Consider the statistics:

- 2,209 people died;
- 99 entire families were wiped out;
- 396 children under 10 perished;
- 1600 homes and 280 businesses were destroyed;
- bodies were found as far away as Cincinnati and as late as 1911;
- the crest of a flood wave rose as high as 937 feet when it entered downtown Johnstown while the most destructive wave measured nearly 40 feet high and hit Johnstown at 40 miles per hour;
- dozens of books were written about the Flood, the first appearing just 7 days after the disaster

"State Trooper"
from *Nebraska*
(Columbia, 1982)

"I dreamed this one up comin' back from New York one night," Springsteen once recalled. It's an edgy little number, a stark, tightly wound doom-laced tale of fear and paranoia, accompanied only by an increasingly ominous electric guitar. The narrator is driving on the New Jersey Turnpike without a license or proper registration (although he does have a clear conscience "'bout the things that I done") and desperately hopes that the state trooper doesn't stop him. We aren't sure if he has in fact done anything wrong or if he is just trying to escape from something or someone. But, in his agitated state of mind, we suspect that he is just about capable of anything.

We feel his growing frustration. The radio talk shows with their endless and inane chatter signify his own inability to communicate with the people around him. He is looking for some kind of deliverance—and peace of mind—that will probably never come. And then he asks a rhetorical question—Is there anybody out there?—followed by a desperate plea, "deliver me from nowhere." It is a crucial line that also appears on "Open All Night" and "Living On The Edge Of The World," the latter being an early version of the song that appears on *Tracks*. And then, from the darkness, out come a whoop and a wail that's enough to send a shiver up anyone's spine. This man has been to hell and we're not quite sure if he can get himself out of it.

The imagery itself is harrowing and straight out of an urban nightmare—a smelly concentration of chemical plants, refinery towers, and relay towers. If Charles Dickens wrote about the satanic mills of England, then Springsteen is writing here about the industrial wasteland of the Garden State along a portion of the much-maligned New Jersey Turnpike.

During his acoustic *Devils & Dust* tour, Springsteen performed a revamped version of "State Trooper," turning an already-nasty song into the musical equivalent of the dark night of the soul.

"Open All Night"

from *Nebraska*
(Columbia, 1982)

"Open All Night" is *Nebraska's* only flat-out rocker, an infectious tale set to a driving rockabilly beat and accompanied by Springsteen's potent guitar playing and mile-a-minute lyrics. It shares several lines with other songs (most notably, "in the wee hours your mind gets hazy" and "deliver me from nowhere") as well as a few lyrical similarities. The glow of the refinery towers also appears in "State Trooper," but whereas on "State Trooper" the radio is "jammed up" with talk show stations, on "Open All Night" Springsteen changes it to gospel stations and adds a chilling coda—now lost souls are calling out for "long distance salvation."

In the song, Springsteen refers to New Jersey in the morning hours looking like a lunar landscape. He isn't the only artist who has compared the Garden State to the moon. The late American humorist and radio personality Jan Shepherd once described the Jersey Turnpike, particularly along exits 12 and 13, this way: "You see nothing but what looks like the moon—lunar landscape, that is dotted with what seems to be wretched, burned-out hulks of old tractor-trailer trucks and belching furnaces. Purple smoke rises to the horizon."

But it's not all bleak. Actually, "Open All Night" is one of the more life affirming of Springsteen songs, certainly it is the most bracing cut on *Nebraska*. It also boasts some striking imagery and delicious details such as when the narrator describes his girlfriend, Wanda, who works behind the counter at Bob's Big Boy. He recalls sitting in the front seat, Wanda on his lap, as they eat fried chicken and wipe their greasy fingers on "a Texaco road map."

"Open All Night" also shares similar lyrics with "Living On The Edge Of The World," an intense little rocker about trying to connect that appears on the *Tracks* CD and sounds one part rockabilly, one part The Clash. Indeed, one could easily imagine The Clash's lead singer, the late Joe Strummer, singing along.

"Open All Night" has often been compared to Chuck Berry's "You Can't Catch Me" but others, like Springsteen biographer Dave Marsh, hears the proto-rockabilly sound of Harmonica Frank Floyd and Hank Mizell, two fairly obscure figures who blended black and white elements in their music. A marvelous slowed-down country rendition of "Open All Night" by country rock band Son Volt appears on *Badlands: A Tribute to Bruce Springsteen's* Nebraska. During the Seeger Sessions tour in 2006, Springsteen offered a completely revamped interpretation—rendering the song unrecognizable—and transforming it into a marvelous mélange of swing, jazz, big band, and Louis Armstrong-meets-New Jersey-style boogie. It was, in other words, a joyous noise.

Open all night. (Theresa Albini)

"My Father's House"
from *Nebraska*
(Columbia, 1982)

Another of Springsteen's father and son relationship songs, "My Father's House" is probably the most poignant of the bunch. It has a simple yet stately melody and its lyrics recall both Hank Williams and traditional balladry with its combination of bucolic imagery—pines, forests, fields, branches, and brambles—and its primordial and elemental emotions. But it also has the nightmarish and unpredictable quality of a Grimm fairy tale.

It begins with a dream. In the dream, the narrator is a child trying to make it home through the forest "before the darkness falls." He hears the wind rustling through the trees and "ghostly voices" coming from the fields. In an image Springsteen culled from a Robert Johnson song, his narrator runs toward the sound, "the devil snappin' at my heels," breaks through the trees, and sees in the distance his father's house, "shining hard and bright," like a celestial city on a hill.

A harmonica breaks the spell. The narrator awakes but can't shake the vision. He gets dressed and drives to the house that he saw in his dreams. And now Springsteen turns methodical in his details. The narrator walks up the steps of the house and stands on the porch. A woman comes to the door—he doesn't recognize her—and, refusing to open the door (she apparently doesn't recognize the narrator either), speaks to him through a chain. He tells her about the dream and confesses that he has come to see his father. In a twist worthy of a Child ballad, the woman apologizes to him and says "no one by that name lives here anymore."

A lonesome harmonica cues up again, and Springsteen cloaks the song in biblical imagery as it reaches its denouement. The son who came to make amends to his estranged father leaves the house of his childhood feeling empty and alone. Where once lived a familiar face now resides a stranger. The reconciliation that he had longed for will not happen.

Written from a child's point of view, "My Father's House" is one of Springsteen's most autobiographical songs. It remains an eerie fable, complete with archetypal imagery, that evokes dark times and the sadness of broken relationships. Springsteen has said he wanted the songs on *Nebraska* to feel like "a waking dream." But more than this, he wanted the songs to feel "destined and fateful."

"My Father's House" does just that—in spades.

"Reason To Believe"
from *Nebraska*
(Columbia, 1982)

- A man stands over a dead dog that is lying by the highway in a ditch. He looks down at the dead animal with a puzzled look and pokes the dog, as if he stood there long enough the dog would get up and run.

- Mary Lou meets Johnny and, in a storytelling twist, she is the one who tells him that she will work hard every day and bring home the money. One day, Johnny just leaves her. Ever since then, Mary Lou stands patiently at the end of a dirt road, waiting for Johnny to return.

- A baby named Kyle Williams is baptized in a river as his family tries to wash away his sins.

- In a shotgun shack, an old man passes away. His body is taken to a graveyard and over his coffin, the well-wishers pray to the Lord, asking him, what does it all mean?

- A congregation gathers at the riverside. A preacher stands with a Bible while the groom stands waiting for his bride. By the time the sun sets, the congregation has left, but the groom still remains, standing alone and silently watching the river flow. He wonders where his bride can be.

Despite the darkness, despite the despair, despite no proof to the contrary, every character in these brief sketches still believes in something or someone. Such a notion strikes the narrator as "kinda funny." But at the end of the day— dead dogs, abandonment, or funerals aside (the stark imagery is worthy of a Sam Peckinpah movie)—some people will still find a Reason To Believe. A cynic, of course, may say it's just wishful thinking. But the narrator seems willing to give them the benefit of the doubt and also to grant them a modicum of respect for at least being able to get on with their lives.

And so "Reason To Believe," the last cut on *Nebraska,* is quirky and darkly humorous, as well as oddly touching, for it is, after all, the only truly hopeful song on the album.

Born In The U.S.A.
(Columbia, 1984)

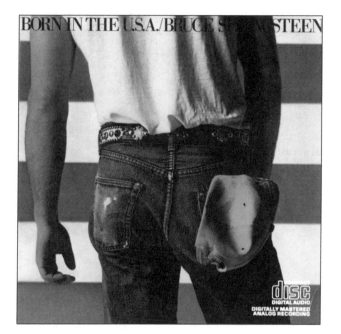

S pringsteen's most successful album to date, *Born In The U.S.A.* sold more than 30 million copies worldwide and stayed at the top of the American charts for seven weeks. Although most of the songs were lyrically bleak, the music carried the day with at least one critic calling it the most "tuneful album" of Springsteen's career. It was both a celebration and a grim portrait of the elusiveness of the American Dream.

Musicians:

Bruce Springsteen: lead vocals, guitar

Roy Bittan: synthesizer, piano, background vocals

Clarence Clemons: saxophone, percussion, background vocals

Danny Federici: organ, glockenspiel, piano

Garry Tallent: bass, background vocals

Steve Van Zandt: acoustic guitar, mandolin, harmony vocals

Max Weinberg: drums, background vocals

Additional musicians:

La Bamba: background vocals

Ruth Jackson: background vocals

Producers: Bruce Springsteen, Jon Landau, Chuck Plotkin, and Steve Van Zandt

Recorded at: Power Station and Hit Factory (New York)

Tracks:

"Born In The U.S.A." (4:39)

"Cover Me" (3:26)

"Darlington County" (4:48)

"Working On The Highway" (3:11)

"Downbound Train" (3:35)

"I'm On Fire" (2:36)

"No Surrender" (4:00)

"Bobby Jean" (3:46)

"I'm Goin' Down" (3:29)

"Glory Days" (4:15)

"Dancing In The Dark" (4:01)

"My Hometown" (4:33)

Running time: 44:19

"Born In The U.S.A."
from *Born In The U.S.A.*
(Columbia, 1984)

"I have not a clue about Springsteen's politics, if any, but flags get waved at his concerts while he sings songs about hard times. He is no whiner, and the recitation of closed factories and other problems always seems punctuated by a grand, cheerful affirmation: 'Born In The U.S.A.!'"
—Syndicated columnist George F. Will, after attending a Springsteen concert at the Capitol Center, in Landover, Maryland, August 1984

"America's future rests in a thousand dreams inside our hearts. It rests in the message of hope so many young people admire: New Jersey's own Bruce Springsteen. And helping you make those dreams come true is what this job of mine is all about."
—Ronald Reagan, at a campaign stop in Hammonton, New Jersey, September 19, 1984, during the 1984 presidential campaign

"Clearly the key to the enormous explosion of Bruce's popularity is the misunderstanding [of "Born In The U.S.A."]. He is a tribute to the fact that people hear what they want."
—Music critic Greil Marcus during the peak of Springsteen's popularity

"I'm a long gone daddy I don't need you anyhow."
—Hank Williams, "I'm a Long Gone Daddy" (1948)

Probably the most misinterpreted song in the Springsteen canon (although "American Skin" comes close) is the explosive rocker "Born In The U.S.A." The song is about a Vietnam veteran—who lost his brother in the war and seeks help from the Veterans Administration but is turned down by a public official— as he struggles to survive and make sense of his life after returning home. During the 1984 presidential campaign, Ronald Reagan tried to co-opt the song but was famously rebuffed by Springsteen himself.

Aside from the incendiary lyrics, the other most distinguishing feature about the anthemic song is the drumming of Max Weinberg—the drums sound as if they are being played in an enormous airplane hangar. The combination of Weinberg's snare drums (insistent, merciless, absolutely devastating) and the song's riff, as memorable and as instantly recognizable as any in rock 'n' roll, as well as Springsteen's ferocious vocals—snarling at the top of his lungs—creates a searing portrait of pain and anguish. The rhythm is martial, which lends a nice ironic quality for an inherently anti-war song. Springsteen writes in concrete, sturdy language ("born down," "first kick," "end up"), with the words chopped off to create a palpable tension.

The protagonist is a small-town boy—we get the impression that nothing has come easy to him nor has anything of any real consequence ever happened to him—who gets in "a hometown jam," is drafted, and ends up in Vietnam where he learns how to become an effective killing machine. He returns home to continue where he left off. But his job at the refinery has been replaced and he has no place to go. His hometown may give the character his sense of identity but, in the end, there is nothing left to return to. We learn that he had a brother, also presumably drafted, who fell in love with a Vietnamese woman in Saigon and fought at the disastrous battle of Khe Sahn. As a memento, the narrator keeps a photograph of the brother and his girlfriend.

It is significant that Springsteen chose to highlight Khe Sanh in the song. The siege of Khe Sahn began on January 21, 1968, when the North Vietnamese launched a full-scale attack on American forces. Considered a major tactical error, the siege not only distracted Pentagon top brass while the Viet Cong planned a bigger and deadlier assault, it also led to the death of 205 Marines. It was an unmitigated disaster and symptomatic of the futility of the entire war. The brother may have perished at Khe Sahn but the narrator continues to soldier on until at the end of the song, in a defiant declaration of pride and anger—a stubborn and perhaps guilty pride in being a survivor—he chants "Born In The U.S.A." and then adds a coda, paraphrasing a line from a Hank Williams song, "I'm a cool rocking daddy in the U.S.A."

The origin of "Born In The U.S.A." can be traced back to multiple sources, most notably Ron Kovic's book *Born On The Fourth Of July* (made into a critically acclaimed movie of the same title starring Tom Cruise in 1989). Springsteen's friendship with Vietnam veteran Bobby Muller, which led to an August 1981 benefit gig in Los Angeles, was also crucial. Another influence may have been the music of Jamaican singer Jimmy Cliff. According to *Backstreets* editor Christopher Phillips, Springsteen purchased a best of Jimmy Cliff tape, which included the song "Vietnam," at an airport gift shop during the 1981 E Street Band European tour. "Springsteen used a bit of Cliff's melody and his title as a starting point for a song about a Vietnam vet," adds Phillips.

Still another important influence was film director Paul Schrader. Schrader asked Springsteen to write some original music for a new film about a

Cleveland rock band he was working on. The screenplay sat on Springsteen's table until one day, he noted, "I was singing a new song I was writing called 'Vietnam.' I looked over and sang off the top of Paul's cover page, 'I was Born In The U.S.A.'" (Springsteen did finally get around to writing a song for Schrader, "Just Around the Corner To The Light Of Day" which became the film *Light Of Day* starring Michael J. Fox and Joan Jett.)

More than a few critics were deeply touched by the song. "Born In The U.S.A.," writes music critic Anthony DeCurtis, is the story of a Vietnam veteran "whose birthright...becomes a psychological death sentence, the song honors the forgotten life of its subject with a keyboard line reminiscent in its majestic majesty of Aaron Copland and drumming that slams home the singer's gripping fear and despair."

"Born In The U.S.A." took shape during the *Nebraska* sessions, but it didn't quite fit. Landau recalled how the *Nebraska* version of "Born In The U.S.A." just wasn't working. As an acoustic piece, he didn't think it was a particularly good song. "[I]t sounded alien." According to Dave Marsh, the melody was different—and much faster.

On the 1995 *Tom Joad* tour, Springsteen reclaimed the misinterpreted song by performing an acoustic arrangement closer to his original *Nebraska* version (at times during the *Joad* tour he even offered a fiery Delta-blues reworking, almost apocalyptic in tone, his voice a raspy holler, and using a slashing slide guitar). The slow-burning acoustic version sounded uncannily like a piece of classic country blues. In *Songs*, Springsteen placed the misunderstanding of the song on par with Woody Guthrie's "This Land Is Your Land," which had also been grossly misinterpreted. "But that didn't make me feel any better," he added.

"You put your music out and it comes back to you in a variety of different ways through your audience," he told Gavin Martin of the *New Musical Express* during the *Joad* tour. "But a songwriter always has the opportunity to go out and reclarify or reclaim his work; it pushes you to be inventive. I think the version I have now...for me, at least, it's the best version I've done of the song, I suppose it's the truest, y'know. It's got it all—everything it needs to be understood at the moment."

Although Springsteen admitted that the *Joad* version could not be misconstrued, he still preferred the original hard-rocking version, where, he believed, the song was at its most powerful. The electric arrangement made more sense to him, too; it worked better. The first time he played the finished version was for Bobby Muller, a Vietnam veteran and, at the time, the president of the Vietnam Veterans of America.

The *Born In The U.S.A.* tour was so popular and the song itself came to mean so many different things to different people that the advertising world came calling—but to no avail. According to Marsh, Chrysler made an offer estimated to be worth $12 million to Springsteen if he would sing in one of their 60-second commercials. Springsteen rejected the offer. Since they couldn't snare Springsteen himself, they did the next best thing—built an advertising campaign, which they called "The Pride Is Back"—built around him, or at least his public persona, and the spirit of his music. The "Pride Is Back" jingle was sung by Kenny Rogers and Sandy Farina.

SPRINGSTEEN ON WAR

Springsteen has sung about war and its aftermaths frequently throughout his career. The profane, some would say blasphemous, "Lost In The Flood," often considered an anti-war precursor to "Born in the U.S.A.," is steeped in Old Testament imagery. Vietnam veterans regularly appear as characters in his songs—"Frankie," "A Good Man Is Hard to Find (Pittsburgh)," "Shut Out The Light," "Brothers Under The Bridge," and, most famously, in "Born In The U.S.A." Other war veterans from different eras have surfaced too, including World War II ("Youngstown"), the Gulf War ("Souls Of The Departed"), and the Iraq War ("Devils & Dust"). During the *Born In The U.S.A.* tour he offered a fierce rendition of Edwin Starr's classic "War." Before introducing the song, he told the crowd, "Blind faith in your leaders, or in anything, will get you killed."

Springsteen did indeed seem everywhere that summer of 1984. *Born In The U.S.A.* forms the soundtrack to Bobbie Ann Mason's popular novel *In Country* (it was later adapted into a movie starring Bruce Willis and Emily Lloyd). One of the characters in the novel, teenager Samantha Hughes, looks at Springsteen the singer as a father figure. "Did you know the title song's about a vet?" the Hughes character asks a friend. "It's a great song." Later on, she dreamily confesses that there is something about Springsteen's songs that deeply affect her; they hold "a secret knowledge...as though he knew exactly what she was feeling."

As with many a song, the interpretation of "Born In The U.S.A." depended on the listener. Each individual brought to it their own baggage, their own personal history, their own political point of view from syndicated columnist George F. Will to the president of the United States. Where some heard exultation (especially in the inspirational chorus), others heard fury and anger. The America that Springsteen sang about in "Born In The U.S.A." had little, if anything, to do with Reagan's so-called new patriotism. Several nights after Reagan famously dropped Springsteen's name in a campaign stop in New Jersey, Springsteen himself responded. Following a particularly stirring rendition of "Atlantic City" in Pittsburgh, he remarked, "The president was mentioning my name the other day and I kinda got to wondering what his favorite album might have been. I don't think it was the *Nebraska* album. I don't think it was this one." He then offered an acoustic version of "Johnny 99."

Two months later, Reagan was re-elected in a landslide victory.

Springsteen considers "Born In The U.S.A." among his best work ("probably one of my five or six best songs," he says). Whatever your interpretation, it remains a potent rocker and a fiery piece of political songwriting.

"Working On The Highway"
from *Born In The U.S.A.*
(Columbia, 1984)

With its dark subject matter and rockabilly feel, "Working On The Highway" has *Nebraska* written all over it.

The narrator has little control over his future. He works for the county, holding up a "red flag" and watching as the traffic rushes by him. He is passive in other ways too. He daydreams about his girlfriend and living a better life than what he has now. But his judgment is cloudy. He meets the girl at a union hall dance, but since she is underage, she is accompanied by her brothers who don't seem to be pleased to see him. Determined, the narrator saves what he can and approaches her father, essentially asking for the girl's hand. But the father isn't impressed. "Son, can't you see," he asks, "that she's just a little girl?" (How young she is Springsteen doesn't say, but it is significant that the original title of the song was "Child Bride.")

This minor obstacle doesn't stop the narrator though. He takes her with him down to Florida ("we got along all right," he sings) before her brothers follow them to the Sunshine State and rescue her from his clutches. He in turn is arrested and sent to jail. Thus, it is only toward the end of the song that we realize that the narrator is in fact a prisoner working for the state as part of a highway chain gang. Initially, his woeful tale of lost love does seem sympathetic until, notes Jimmy Guterman, "you realize he's a pedophile." Ouch.

Despite the subject matter, it is a terrific song, at times both obliquely funny (even joyful) and penetratingly sad. Handclaps keep the rhythm going while the swirl of the organ lends it an extra layer of bliss. Maybe it represents Springsteen's Irish side—the coming together of ecstasy and sorrow. It's not surprising that country rocker Joe Ely chose to cover "Working On The Highway" when asked to contribute to the Springsteen tribute album, *Light Of Day*.

"Downbound Train"
from *Born In The U.S.A.*
(Columbia, 1984)

You can hear the pain in Springsteen's anguished, heavy, weight-of-the-world vocals in this dense and rich tale of a life gone irrevocably wrong.

Straightaway, we know this guy (his name is Joe) has lost everything—his job, his girl, his future. At first he works in a lumberyard. When he gets laid off, his relationship sours and then he finds work at a car wash "where all it ever does is rain" (a classic Springsteen line). Like a good country song about a love gone badly, Springsteen uses the admittedly shopworn (but here effective) device of the whistle of a train to indicate the end of a relationship. It's a tradition laid down by Hank Williams, Jimmie Rodgers, and Woody Guthrie and continued through the songwriting of Merle Haggard, Steve Earle, and countless others; in this way it connects Springsteen to the road and train songs of country and folk music, as well as hobo drifter songs and even cowboy songs. But Springsteen upends the train tradition. Historically, hopping a train personified freedom and the open-ended possibilities of a life lived on the road. In "Downbound Train," though, the train signifies oppression and a huge dose of pessimism. This train is going nowhere fast. Springsteen pushes the railroad metaphor even further at the end of the song when we learn that Joe is swinging a sledgehammer as part of a railroad chain gang. Not only has he lost everything that he once had, he has even lost his freedom.

One suspects an entire book could be written on the use of dreams and dream imagery in Springsteen songs. In "Downbound Train," Joe dreams that his girlfriend still loves him. She waits for him at home. Like the narrator in "My Father's House," Joe runs through the woods. When he reaches a clearing beyond the highway, he sees in the moonlight their wedding house. He rushes through the yard, bursts through the front door and, with his head pounding, climbs up the stairs only to find the room dark and their bed empty. And then, in the distance, he hears, once again, the lone whistle of a passing train.

Not everyone loved "Downbound Train" (Dave Marsh, for one, called it the weakest song Springsteen had released since *The Wild, The Innocent & The E Street Shuffle* as well as "incredibly sloppy"). To these ears, though, it remains one of Springsteen's best songs, a sad (okay, bleak) yet exceedingly moving tale of lost dreams that is worthy of a Sam Shepard play or a John Sayles film—and a memorable melody to boot. It is the kind of song that sticks with you, weeks, months, even years after first hearing it.

"I'm On Fire"
from *Born In The U.S.A.*
(Columbia, 1984)

Springsteen has said that this scary little piece of writing—intense and fraught with a slow-burning need—came to him in the studio one night while he was experimenting with a Johnny Cash and the Tennessee Three rhythm. It's short—2:36—yet powerful and very, very effective.

Is the narrator any good? Not sure. He comes across as a dangerous character, not someone you would want to mess with. In the song, he lusts for another man's wife. The imagery is violent (a knife, "edgy and dull"), and the atmosphere reeks of loneliness and desperation. We're not sure what this guy is capable of—or maybe we just don't want to know. At the end he lets out a whoop worthy of an outtake from *Nebraska*. Writes Debby Bull in a *Rolling Stone* review, "The way the band's turned down to just a light rattle of drums, faint organ and quiet, staccato guitar notes makes his lust seem ominous: You picture some pockmarked Harry Dean Stanton-type, lying, too wired to sleep, in a motel room."

It's not surprising that Johnny Cash liked it so much that he covered it as a bonus track on *Badlands: A Tribute To Bruce Springsteen's* Nebraska. A bit more surprising is that Springsteen's version reached Number Six on the *Billboard* charts when it was released as a single.

"No Surrender"
from *Born In The U.S.A.*
(Columbia, 1984)

It took Steve Van Zandt's considerable pull to convince Springsteen to include the uplifting "No Surrender" on *Born In The U.S.A.* Springsteen felt uncomfortable with it. It was, he thought, too black and white—too triumphant—in a world of grays. Fortunately, Springsteen changed his mind. It is a rousing portrait of friendship and the inspirational power that can come from a three-minute song. Years later, it even became the anthem of John Kerry's failed 2004 presidential campaign.

In "No Surrender," a middle-aged man remembers with great fondness the times he once shared with a childhood friend. One of Springsteen's more anthemic songs, it incorporates military imagery (soldiers vowing never to retreat) and the camaraderie of friendship ("blood brothers") to tell a story about two pals, soul mates, who saw in their love of three-minute rock 'n' roll songs that they also could have a future or at least a distinctive place in the world—perhaps with drums and guitars—that they could call their own. And in one of the song's most hopeful lines, the narrator sings that he is ready "to grow young again."

In the closing stanza, a bit of reality sets in. The narrator sits in his room as a war rages outside ("a war," he sings, that "ain't ours anymore to win") and yet he still hasn't given up entirely. Friendships too have given way to mature relationships. Thus, he wants to sleep "beneath peaceful skies" in his lover's bed with his head full of the visions of a "wide open country." He wants to live, in other words, in the America of his dreams. It is a vision that Springsteen would return to again and again, that of a better America than the one he currently lives in. (For comparison, contrast the ballad treatment the song receives on the *Live 1975-85* album.)

Inspirational and wildly romantic, "No Surrender" is Springsteen the dreamer at his idealistic best.

"I'm Goin' Down"
from *Born In The U.S.A.*
(Columbia, 1984)

It may be a song about the end of a relationship, about sexual frustration, about not getting what you want, but it sure sounds great—it has an infectious beat, buoyed by the wild drumming of Max Weinberg and the tight piano playing of Roy Bittan.

The song is wired and full of tension. While sitting in a car, the narrator tries to make a move on his girlfriend, but she lets out a "bored sigh." They get dressed up for a night on the town only to come home early to wage a terrible fight. The feeling that was once there is now gone. All this couple does is fight, bicker, and lob insults at each other.

But it sounds downright giddy. *They* may be miserable, but *we* are having a grand old time.

"I'm Goin' Down" reached Number Nine on the *Billboard* charts—the sixth Top 10 hit from *Born In The U.S.A.*

"Dancing In The Dark"
from *Born In The U.S.A.*
(Columbia, 1984)

"His jeans were as tight as rubber gloves, and he danced like a revved-up sports car about to take off."
—Samantha Hughes, the teenage protagonist of Bobbie Ann Mason's novel
In Country on watching the *Dancing In The Dark* video

Anyone who thinks "Dancing In The Dark" is just a happy dance song never bothered to listen to the lyrics. As exuberant as it may sound, it is not as simple as it may appear on first listen. As in many popular songs, a palpable tension exists between despair and joy. The character of Emmett in Bobbie Ann Mason's *In Country* perhaps sums it up best, "Rock 'n' roll," he says, "is happy songs about sad stuff."

"Dancing In The Dark" is also a happy song about a character trapped in a sad situation that he can't or doesn't know how to change. He gets up in the evening (not, significantly, the morning—he works the night shift) and has nothing to say. (In "Angel From Montgomery," Midwestern troubadour John

Prine echoed similar thoughts when he asked, "How the hell can a person go to work in the morning / And come home in the evening and have nothing to say"—one of the best couplets in all of rock.) He returns home in the morning and nothing much has changed. He is tired and bored with himself. Like Rod Stewart in "Every Picture Tells A Story," who combs his hair "a thousand ways" and ends up looking just the same, the narrator wants to change everything about himself too—his clothes, his hair, even his appearance. He says he lives in a dump and he just knows there is something better somewhere else, somewhere out there. And yet he is strangely passive. He *waits* for something to happen. All he needs is a little help, a little push. Dave Marsh has called "Dancing In The Dark" "a protest song worth keeping—a marching song against boredom, a battle cry against loneliness, and an accounting of the price the loner pays."

"Dancing In The Dark" was famous for several things: It was not only Springsteen's third single to top the charts, it also came with a music video directed by filmmaker Brian DePalma. DePalma concocted a plot line involving three girls. They arrive late to Springsteen's St. Paul show—the *Born In The U.S.A.* tour kicked off in St. Paul—and forget their tickets in the process. They manage to sweet talk their way into the hall and find themselves among the fortunate few—sitting in the front row. When Springsteen sings "Dancing In The Dark," he points at one of them and gestures for her to come up to the stage to dance with him. As everyone now knows, future *Friends* star actress Courteney Cox played the lucky concertgoer. What also made this video unusual—at least for Springsteen—is that the performance of "Dancing In The Dark" was lip-synced.

Springsteen didn't like the lip-syncing but explained the decision to go ahead with it this way, "...I think the best thing our band does is address the moment. And we go for authentic emotion and that gets all knocked out of whack when you're singing to something you recorded a long time ago. It was," he said, "kind of an experiment."

Not surprisingly, the video was roundly condemned as synthetic, artificial, and just plain phony. Also, the image—a smiling Springsteen dancing without seemingly a care in the world—clashed with the darkness of the lyrics. On the same day that the *Born In The U.S.A.* tour began, Columbia issued a dance mix of "Dancing In The Dark," produced by Arthur Baker, as a 12-inch disc. The experiment was a well-meaning but unsuccessful attempt to appeal to African-American listeners. To his credit, Baker did a terrific job, overdubbing tom-toms, dulcimer, glockenspiel, background vocals, bass, and horns into a potent mix, a radical restructuring of both its sound and mood. Marsh called it "a monumental achievement, making a great record even greater." However, black audiences stayed away in droves—and still do. The racial divide remains strong, perhaps as insurmountable as when Greg Tate wrote about the issue in the *Village Voice* in the late 1990s. After attending his first E Street Band concert, Tate looked around him at the sea of white faces and asked, "Where are all my Negroes at? Why aren't there more black people out here screaming Bruuuuce like Dolly Earshatterer to the rear of my right lobe?"

Regardless, with its synthesizer-based sound and the crash and boom drumming of Max Weinberg, "Dancing In The Dark" is a considerable achievement, whether you dance to it or just simply listen to it.

"My Hometown"
from *Born In The U.S.A.*
(Columbia, 1984)

> *"I was born right here on Randolph Street in Freehold."*
> —Bruce Springsteen, "In Freehold"

On May 19, 1969, the city fathers of Freehold, New Jersey, canceled a black unity parade because ostensibly they did not want it to compete with the town's traditional Memorial Day parade. By this time, though, racial tensions were already running high. The decision was a fateful and regrettable one for it triggered a rampage by frustrated black youths who stormed through the downtown area, throwing rocks at store windows and generally raising havoc. Later that night a carload of white youths pulled alongside a car of black teens and fired a shotgun blast to the backseat. The victims, Dean Lewis and Leroy Kinsey, Jr., suffered wounds to the face and neck. Although none of the injuries were fatal, Lewis did lose an eye.

The semi-autobiographical "My Hometown" does, of course, refer to Freehold, a no-nonsense working-class city of 10,000 situated in the heart of New Jersey. The song itself chronicles some of the hardships that Freehold experienced while Springsteen was growing up: the racial tensions, the closing of the A&M Karagheusian rug mill that left more than a thousand people out of work, and the flight of downtown merchants to suburban shopping malls, something that plagued towns and cities throughout the country, particularly during the Reagan era.

The story begins with a young man driving through the streets of the town where he was born and reminiscing about its fate. He recalls being eight years old, running to the bus stop to pick up a newspaper for his father. He sits in his father's lap as they drive around in a "big old Buick." He mourns the death of a way of life, the closing of the town's major source of income, a textile mill, and the subsequent vacant stores and boarded-up windows that dot the town's Main Street. The song ends the same way it began—with a father driving his son around town in a car only this time, it is the narrator—he is now 35—who is the father. He and his wife, Kate, had discussed the possibility of leaving ("maybe heading south") but he seems resigned to his fate; this is where he was born and this is where he will inevitably die. It is a quiet song, sung in a mellow voice, and gently punctuated with synthesizer and unobtrusive drums.

When Springsteen grew up there, Freehold was a town of two-family houses, with neat yards and very few expectations. "In Freehold," wrote Joseph Dalton in *Rolling Stone,* "you're expected to go to work instead of college, to make Scotch tape for 3M or instant coffee for Nescafe, and you weren't expected to make a lot of noise about it. Which is what Douglas Springsteen did, coming home from jobs as a factory worker or prison guard or bus driver to sit in his kitchen and think about the world."

The part of town where Springsteen grew up was called Texas because it was populated by Southerners who had moved north to work in the rug factory. When they left, they were replaced by Italians and then blacks. When Springsteen lived there, the rug mill mentioned in the song employed some 1,600 people—"half the jobholders in Freehold," writes Springsteen historian Bob Crane. The mill was the pride of Freehold—the Supreme Court building in Washington, D.C. and Radio City Music Hall in New York were both clients. By the time Springsteen was about to graduate from high school, though, the mill was experiencing irreversible economic woes.

Over the years, Springsteen has acted as Freehold's secular patron saint. In 1996, he played a benefit concert in the 1,300-seat gymnasium of his alma mater, St. Rose of Lima. At $30 per person, the tickets were available to Freehold residents only; the proceeds went to a parish center being built to serve the city's growing Hispanic population. He debuted a song there called, appropriately enough, "In Freehold."

The town has done its best to respect the privacy of its most famous son, rejecting efforts, for example, to erect a Springsteen statue in front of its city hall and renaming South Street, a main thoroughfare, to Bruce Springsteen Boulevard, as some have suggested. To honor him with a street name, to put a public face on a private relationship, notes Freehold historian Kevin Coyne, would be to miss the point entirely regarding the bond between Springsteen and Freehold: "they would memorialize it as something dead and distant...rather than the deep and complicated thing it really is, alive and near." In case there was any doubt, Coyne spells it out, "The reason we don't have any public acknowledgment of Springsteen in Freehold isn't because we don't love him here, but because we do."

Which is not to say that Freehold is entirely devoid of any form of public recognition of the Boss; it's just subtle. A local fire truck, for example, has stenciled on its side, "Born To Run" as a quiet thank you to Springsteen for contributing a $100,000 gift to the department. And as you leave Freehold, a sign thanks you for visiting "our hometown."

"My Hometown" is the unofficial anthem of Freehold. "I used to think that once I got out of town, I was never going to come back," Springsteen once said. "But as I got older, I'd come home off the road and drive back into town and still see some of my old friends and see what their lives were like and what they were doing. I realized that I would always carry a part of that town with me no matter where I went or what I did."

He wrote about the places he knew, and he knew Freehold better than just about anyone.

St. Rose of Lima Elementary School, Freehold, NJ. (Theresa Albini)

Tunnel Of Love
(Columbia, 1987)

*T*unnel Of Love is one of Springsteen's quieter albums (although not as quiet as *Nebraska* or *The Ghost Of Tom Joad*). He wrote the songs in quick succession and recorded them at home but, unlike *Nebraska*, this time he used a full 24-track digital recording studio located on his property. Although the E Street Band got credit, the album pretty much belongs to Springsteen (he recorded the basic tracks himself and then the band members overdubbed their parts).

The subtext of the songs is the passing of time. "The struggle to uncover who you are," writes Springsteen, "and to reach that moment and hold on to it, along with the destructive desire to leave it in ruins..." He wrote about his inner life, "not literally autobiographical" but something that he thought the audience would understand. They, like him, were presumably also moving on with their lives.

The reviews were uniformly excellent. Jay Cocks of *Time* magazine said *Tunnel Of Love* "is not about exaltation or passion but about the doubt and fear, longing and uncertainty that shadow every deep feeling, every tender gesture." The *Seattle Times* called it "one of the most truthful LPs in rock history..." while to Steve Pond of *Rolling Stone* it was an "unsettled and unsettling collection of hard looks at the perils of commitment."

Musicians:

Bruce Springsteen: vocals

Max Weinberg: percussion, drums

Danny Federici: organ

Garry Tallent: bass

James Wood: harmonica

Roy Bittan: synthesizers, piano

Nils Lofgren: guitar, vocals

Patti Scialfa: vocals

Clarence Clemons: vocals

Additional Musicians:

The Schiffer family: Roller coaster (Pt. Pleasant Beach, NJ)

Producers: Bruce Springsteen, Jon Landau, and Chuck Plotkin

Recorded at: A&M Studios and Kren Studio (Los Angeles), the Hit Factory (New York)

Tracks:

"Ain't Got You" (2:07)

"Tougher Than The Rest" (4:34)

"All That Heaven Will Allow" (2:38)

"Spare Parts" (3:39)

"Cautious Man" (3:56)

"Walk Like A Man" (3:36)

"Tunnel Of Love" (5:10)

"Two Faces" (3:01)

"Brilliant Disguise" (4:15)

"One Step Up" (4:21)

"When You're Alone" (3:21)

"Valentine's Day" (5:13)

Running time: 43:91

"Tougher Than The Rest"
from *Tunnel Of Love*
(Columbia, 1987)

Once again, the cavernous sound of Max Weinberg's drum kit sets the mood—moody, masculine, and slightly ominous. There's no real story to tell here. "Tougher Than The Rest" is all about atmosphere and attitude. The attitude Springsteen employs is that of a loner who is ready to commit to a relationship—his commitment is so complete, in fact, that it appears almost frightening.

Most love songs emphasize the gentle side of love. Not this one. The narrator is no sweet talker—he is direct and to the point—nor is he particularly handsome and, he admits, he has been around "a time or two." What's more, Springsteen turns on its head traditional attitudes toward masculinity. Springsteen's definition of manhood is an expansive one that involves commitment and community, as well as family and responsibility. The narrator—Springsteen?—knows just how tough and messy love can be and he's more than ready for it—ready to work at it and ready for any disappointments that may come his way. But in order to play the game, his female partner has to be just as tough and just as willing to take chances. The stern guitar solo and the lonesome harmonica add to the sober, austere mood.

Originally, "Tougher Than The Rest" was written as a rockabilly song, but the slower and more methodical rhythm of the final version makes more artistic sense. It remains one of the more underrated songs in the Springsteen canon.

"Spare Parts"
from *Tunnel Of Love*
(Columbia, 1987)

> *"'Take your son, your only son Isaac, whom you love, and go to the land of Moriah, and offer him there as a burnt-offering on one of the mountains that I shall show you.'"*
>
> —Genesis 22:2

> *"When they came to the place that God had shown him, Abraham built an altar there and laid the wood in order. He bound his son Isaac, and laid him on the altar, on top of the wood. Then Abraham reached out his hand and took the knife to call his son. But the angel of the*

Lord called to him from heaven, and said, 'Abraham, Abraham!' And he said, 'Here I am.' He said, 'Do not lay your hand on the boy or do anything to him; for now I know that you fear God, since you have not withheld your son, your only son, from me.'"

—Genesis 22:9–12

"Now a man from the house of Levi went and married a Levite woman. The woman conceived and bore a son; and when she saw that he was a fine baby, she hid him for three months. When she could hide him no longer she got a papyrus basket for him, and plastered it with bitumen and pitch; she put the child in it and placed it among the reeds on the bank of the river.

—Exodus 2:1–3

"The daughter of Pharaoh came down to bathe at the river, while her attendants walked beside the river. She saw the basket among the reeds and sent her maid to bring it. When she opened it, she saw the child. He was crying, and she took pity on him, 'This must be one of the Hebrews' children,' she said."

—Exodus 2:5–6

"She named him Moses, 'because,' she said, 'I drew him out of the water.'"

—Exodus 2:10

Janey, a young unwed mother, is abandoned by her boyfriend Bobby, a layabout who gave her nothing except empty promises. Forced to support a child by herself, she hears a story of a young mother who has committed infanticide. She considers doing the same, but instead chooses to bring her son back home.

This brief description fails to do justice to "Spare Parts," a harrowing song—abrasive, bleak, and tough-minded—of male irresponsibility and broken promises. "Spare Parts" is a remarkable piece of songwriting for another reason too. Springsteen is able to get into the mind of a young mother, suggesting in a few lines her hopes and dreams. Yes, she considers drowning her infant son in the river but then reconsiders, gets down on her knees and "cried till she prayed." In other words, Janey recognizes that, despite being cast off by her lover, she is responsible for another life. In this context, she alone makes the final decision as to whether this infant lives or dies. Instead of drowning her child, she baptizes him—"held her son down at the river side" in waist-deep water—and indeed herself into a new life. Water flows on as a symbol of rebirth. With one simple but significant act—an act that recalls both Abraham's near sacrifice of Isaac and the circumstances surrounding the birth of Moses when the king ordered all newborn Hebrew boys be killed—she changes her life.

"Religion is more explicitly expressed in *Tunnel Of Love*," writes sociologist/novelist Father Andrew Greeley, "than in any previous Springsteen album." The story that Springsteen describes in "Spare Parts" not only sounds biblical (is the shining sun that greets Janey as she enters the river meant to suggest the face of Jesus Christ himself?) but Greeley goes one step farther by suggesting that it is in itself a baptismal image. "How could it be anything else?" he asks. Even though Springsteen has gone on record as admitting to being a lapsed Catholic, Greeley seems to be saying that once a Catholic, always a Catholic. "[H]e is using in Catholic fashion these profoundly Catholic symbols of his youth: He is using light and water as symbols of rebirth."

But also, in its potent images, "Spare Parts" recalls two traditional Child ballads, "The Cruel Mother" and "Mary Hamilton," both about infanticide. Each is a tale of the longings of a young woman who finds herself trapped in a life that she did not plan and most certainly does not want. The traditional ballads never flinched from the darker side of human nature; their language is stark and straightforward. Thus, in "The Cruel Mother," the mother gives birth to two babies, and then she makes her decision:

> *She took from her ribbon-belt*
> *And there she bound them hand and foot.*

> *She took out her wee pen-knife*
> *And there she ended both babes' life.*

In "Mary Hamilton," the mother ties her infant up in her apron and throws it out to sea, sighing, "Sink ye, swim ye, bonny wee babe, Ye'll get no more of me." But she feels guilty for committing the deed.

"Spare Parts," on the other hand, reads more like a short story. After Bobby gets cold feet and runs away from their marriage plans, Janey moves in with her mother and confesses that "sometimes my whole life feels like one big mistake." She misses the life that she could have had—the parties she won't attend, the fun that now seems to be a thing of the past. Bobby works in the oil fields of South Texas, hears about the birth of his son, but refuses to accept responsibility for his actions, swearing instead that he will never go back. Meanwhile, Janey, uncertain and vulnerable, has been hearing stories about a woman in a place called Calverton (which sounds mysteriously like Calvary) who "put[s] her baby in the river" and "let[s] the river roll on." It is at this point in the song that Janey considers doing the same. But Janey not only changes her mind, she ties her wedding ring and wedding dress in a sash—shades of "Mary Hamilton"—and sells them both at the local pawnshop; thus, Janey's salvation comes in the form of "some good cold cash."

"Cautious Man"
from *Tunnel Of Love*
(Columbia, 1987)

Bill Horton, the protagonist with an almost pathological aversion to commitment in "Cautious Man," has LOVE tattooed on one hand and FEAR tattooed on the other. Not quite sure what to expect from life, he lives by his own code of behavior, but he remains forever fretful and always looking over his shoulder.

Bill falls in love with a young girl—during the month of May, of course—and throws all caution to the wind, laughing in the process at his own temerity. When Indian summer comes around, he marries and, with his own hands, builds "a great house" down by the archetypal riverside. (The building of a house with one's own hands appears in other Springsteen songs, most notably in "Across The Border.")

Although Bill is described as an honest man, he feels like a fraud and is haunted by doubt and restlessness. He considers leaving his wife, to flee from the responsibilities marriage has brought. In the darkness he gets down on his knees and prays for guidance and for strength. One night he dreams a terrible dream. He calls his wife's name but she does not answer. He gets dressed in the moonlight and goes down to the highway but all he sees is a stretch of open road and he's not sure where it leads. A younger Springsteen would have looked at this open road as a challenge and would have risen to it; now an older Springsteen only sees it as a cop-out, a cowardly excuse to flee an uncomfortable situation. At first, Bill feels a coldness rise within him and he realizes he will always be torn between the two words tattooed on his hands. Like Janey in "Spare Parts," though, he makes a moral decision and returns home. Looking at his sleeping wife, he gently brushes her hair aside as the glow from the moon fills the room with "the beauty of God's fallen light."

"Cautious Man" is the most *Nebraska*-like song on *Tunnel Of Love*, similar in delivery and tone to "Highway Patrolman"—quiet, measured, and hushed with a simple guitar-based melody. And like the character Joe Roberts in that song, "Cautious Man" follows one person's life, his feelings, and his mixed emotions.

Like many of Springsteen's songs, "Cautious Man" is written in what can be called the American noir tradition of songwriting. Josh Olson, the screenwriter of *A History of Violence* and a huge Springsteen fan aptly and hilariously calls it Springsteen noir (Olson wrote, as it turns out, *History* while listening to *Darkness On The Edge Of Town*). Springsteen, a great admirer of film noir, has admitted lifting the idea of the LOVE and FEAR tattoo from the film *The Night Of The Hunter* (1955) directed by Charles Laughton, a chilling movie shot in shadows and steeped in the biblical themes of greed, innocence, sin, and corruption, and starring the quintessential bad boy of moviedom, Robert Mitchum. In it, Mitchum plays a Jekyll and Hyde character—self-appointed "preacher" by day, murderer by night—who has LOVE and HATE tattooed on his knuckles. Laughton, who used a stark, expressionistic black-and-white cinematography to great advantage, called it "a nightmarish sort of Mother Goose tale."

Based on a novel of the same name by Davis Grubb, the movie was inspired by actual events. The Mitchum character was modeled after Harry Powers, who gained notoriety as West Virginia's most famous mass murderer. Hanged on March 18, 1932, at the West Virginia Penitentiary in Moundsville, Powers was convicted of killing a widow and her three children and another widow in the early 1930s.

"Walk Like A Man"
from *Tunnel Of Love*
(Columbia, 1987)

Another father-and-son song, "Walk Like A Man" is arguably the most moving song on *Tunnel Of Love*, certainly the most personal, as a man on his wedding day reminisces about the meaning of his father's life and, by extension, his own. It has a lovely, unobtrusive melody that feels as if the singer is speaking, perhaps confessing, directly to the listener.

Although the narrator mentions his bride, it is the father whose larger-than-life presence fills every moment of its lyrics. He recalls, as a boy, how rough his father's hands felt in his and remembers a particularly vivid memory of being five years old, following behind him at the beach and trying valiantly to walk in his footprints in the wet sand.

The groom recalls living near a church—as usual, Springsteen is specific here, giving the church a name, Our Lady of the Roses—and the time his mother dragged him and his sister to see a wedding in progress. He watches the "handsome groom and his bride" step into "that long black limousine." But there is something ominous about this image. In a strange and unsettling way, the long black limousine conjures up memories of "Mystery Train," that portentous blues classic that Elvis made so famous. In both "Mystery Train" and "Walk Like A Man" there are hints that something is about to go wrong or, at the very least, that things won't quite turn out as planned. Is it mere coincidence, for example, that Springsteen calls the journey in the limousine to presumably the couples' honeymoon site a "mystery ride"? Is the limousine in the song really a hearse in disguise?

The final verse looks back as the son admires all the hard work that went into being a father—prior to his wedding day, he had no clue what it required. And yet still he feels that he comes up short, that he can't quite fill the footsteps of the person who came before him. There were so many steps he had to learn on his own, he confesses. Where was the father that he admired so much during these times? Apparently, he was, like Springsteen's own father, beaten down by daily living and ready to give up ("I saw your best steps stolen away from you").

"Walk Like A Man" reveals a level of maturity—warm, insightful, compassionate, and completely guileless—in Springsteen's songwriting that is simply breathtaking.

"Tunnel Of Love"
from *Tunnel Of Love*
(Columbia, 1987)

> *"...if you can't fix it you got a stand it."*
> —Ennis del Mar, in Annie Proulx's "Brokeback Mountain"

For the title cut of *Tunnel Of Love* Springsteen uses a funhouse metaphor with its hall of mirrors to explore the deceit and delusion that comprises relational breakdowns.

The relationship Springsteen describes here consists of three parts: the couple themselves and "all that stuff we're so scared of." Thus, the roller coaster relationship echoes the real roller coaster the couple finds themselves on.

Springsteen here acknowledges the complexities that entail a mature relationship. On the surface, he admits, it should be simple ("man meets a woman and they fall in love") but along the way, the "house is haunted" and the "ride gets rough." Every stop along this carnival ride is certainly scary and bumpy. It is for this and other reasons that music critic Anthony DeCurtis has called the album "a *Nebraska* of the heart."

The narrator on "Tunnel Of Love" acknowledges that there are some things "you can't rise above"—you either have to learn to live with them or you resign yourself to a fate that is not of your liking. Looking at themselves through the crazy mirrors, the characters in the song laugh at each other. But as the shadows in the room turn dark, are they laughing out of humor or out of derision? Out of love or out of hate (if not hate then something close to it)? As the narrator admits, playing off the funhouse metaphor, it's easy "for two people to lose each other."

"Tunnel Of Love" is the most musically complex song on the album. It has a modern synthesizer sound, accompanied by layers of sound effects, including the noise and laughter of an actual family riding on a roller coaster in Pt. Pleasant Beach, New Jersey.

Palace Amusements, Asbury Park, NJ. (June Sawyers)

The amusement park metaphor of *Tunnel* revisits the Asbury Park milieu that Springsteen wrote so evocatively about in his early albums. Of course, the Springsteen that emerges on *Tunnel Of Love*—pensive, doubtful, uncertain, and struggling with the consequences of life's decisions—is vastly different from the immature, street poet of *Greetings From Asbury Park, N.J.* and *The Wild, The Innocent & The E Street Shuffle* who fought tooth and nail to escape responsibility. And yet Springsteen did co-opt one aspect of Asbury Park for the 1988 *Tunnel Of Love* tour: the face of Tillie the clown—Tillie, after all, had come to personify Asbury Park—splashed across the tour T-shirts. Tillie's Cheshire-grin graced the façade of Palace Amusements, the part fun house, part penny arcade building that was such a crucial part of the cultural landscape of Asbury Park until it was closed in 1988 and then finally demolished in 2004. One of the Tillie faces was removed from the building walls and placed on a flatbed truck to a storage area as more than 200 spectators and the watchful eye of the media looked on.

The iconic face of Tillie, Asbury Park, NJ. (June Sawyers)

"Two Faces"
from *Tunnel Of Love*
(Columbia, 1987)

Springsteen continues the theme of deception in this dark but ostensibly cheerful song with its beguiling Beatlesque melody. The narrator meets and runs away with a girl and promises to make her happy. But their happy life soon disintegrates before their eyes.

The narrator projects a Jekyll and Hyde persona: sunny one moment, dark the next; laughter is followed by tears, hello means goodbye. He doesn't understand the things that he does and so in the evening he gets down on his knees to pray that this "other man"—this side of himself that he abhors and finds revolting—will leave. It is a chilling thought in a chilling song. He is his own worst enemy, and he's not sure what to do about it.

In the final verse, Springsteen employs one of the most romantic images in the popular song tradition—kissing your love beneath a willow tree—but, once again, he comes face to face with the other and this other, this doppelganger— what Robert Louis Stevenson, who knew a thing or two about parallel lives, called a double—insists that the life they are leading is a lie. In the last line, though, the song turns cautiously but defiantly optimistic as the narrator goads his other, darker half to "go ahead and let him try."

"Brilliant Disguise"
from *Tunnel Of Love*
(Columbia, 1987)

The centerpiece of *Tunnel Of Love* is "Brilliant Disguise," a chilling song of quiet power that builds slowly, adding layer upon layer of doubt and deception. Secrets remain hidden. Words are whispered just as someone turns away, their meaning gone forever. The narrator sees his wife on the edge of town and seems startled. Why is she there? He would love to read her mind. If he asked, would she tell him the truth? He wonders too about himself. What does she see in him?

The narrator struggles to do everything right but things fall apart anyway. He doesn't trust his wife but neither does he trust himself. And yet they go along with their lives, pretending everything is fine and playing their respective roles—she "the loving woman," he "the faithful man." They both wear masks, each for their own reasons and each as a coping mechanism to get through daily life. In the last few lines of the song, the narrator, wracked with self-doubt, turns to God, asking for mercy and, perhaps, some kind of understanding and a measure of relief.

"Brilliant Disguise" is a disturbing portrait of a couple who had something special but lost it somewhere along the way. It is a song that raises plenty of questions—questions about individual motives, questions about the life decisions we all make, and, ultimately questions about identity (who am I?)—without supplying the answers.

In *Songs*, Springsteen explained the motivations behind *Tunnel Of Love*. As he indicates, it was an album that he was not ready to make until he was further along in his own emotional development. "I wanted to write a different kind of romantic song," he said, "one that took in the different types of emotional experiences of any relationship where you are really engaging with that other person and not involved in a narcissistic romantic fantasy or intoxication or whatever...I wanted to make a record about what I felt about really letting another person in your life and trying to be a part of someone else's life. That's a frightening thing," he admits, "something that's always filled with shadows and doubts and also wonderful things and beautiful things...I couldn't have written any of those songs at any other point in my career. I wouldn't have had the knowledge or the insight or the experience to do it."

In the end, it all comes down to trust, Springsteen concludes. "Trust is a fragile thing. [I]t requires allowing others to see as much of ourselves as we have the courage to reveal."

The video of the song is especially effective. Springsteen strums a guitar, sitting precariously on the edge of a chair, apparently in his own kitchen, looking uncomfortable (or is it that we feel uncomfortable looking at him?). He looks straight into the camera, never flinching, even for a moment, as he sings the lyrics about what it means to trust someone. It is quite a performance—direct, candid, and bracing. At times, it's almost too painful, too personal, to watch but, alas, it's impossible to avert our eyes.

"One Step Up"
from *Tunnel Of Love*
(Columbia, 1987)

Several years ago I was staying at a bed and breakfast in the Pennsylvania Amish country. At one point during the evening I began talking about music to a woman I had just met. Eventually Bruce Springsteen came up. When I asked her—she was middle-aged—which Springsteen song was her favorite, she answered "One Step Up." I was a bit taken aback. I had expected the usual suspects—"Thunder Road" or "Born To Run" came immediately to mind—so I was pleasantly surprised that she chose a lesser-known song from the Springsteen catalogue. "That song was my life," she sighed.

The best Springsteen songs are like that. Within the span of two or three minutes, they lay out your entire history. The secret is in the details. That's where the story of our lives lie and that's where the power of a song begins.

"One Step Up" is a quiet ballad. Despite its reassuring melody—it feels solid and sturdy—it is about a relationship gone sour, about not facing up to our responsibilities. It's much easier to flee.

IN THE VAULTS
Springsteen has officially released more than 250 songs but countless more have not been released. They include "It's The Little Things That Count," "Sell It And They Will Come," "Losin' Kind," "On The Prowl," "Another Thin Line" (with Joe Grushecky), "I'm A Coward," "When The Lights Go Out," "Sugarland," and "Pilgrim In The Temple Of Love."

It begins with a broken furnace and an engine that won't start, and that pretty much sums the song up and serves as a metaphor for the characters' unstable lives. The couple have been together long enough that they should have picked up a few lessons from their sad-sack experiences but "we ain't learnin'." Instead, they fling accusations at each other, slam a few doors, and continue the battle that has become their "dirty little war." Neither one is blameless. Looking at himself in the mirror, the narrator doesn't like what he sees.

Springsteen lists a litany of small moments that say a lot: the bird outside the narrator's motel room is silent; church bells don't ring for a young girl dressed in white for her June wedding day. The narrator sits in a bar, considering whether or not to hook up with a girl who seems interested, all the while dreaming of dancing with his wife back home.

In an interview he did with *Newsweek* around the time that the album was released, Springsteen said that he wanted the record to be about honesty and about the search for the truth. "...we live in a society that wants us to buy illusion every day," he said. "There's the will to pretend everything is OK. That I'm OK, and you're OK. People are sold this every day: You're gonna live happily ever after. So when you do begin to feel conflict—the natural human conflict that comes with any human relationship—people have a tendency to repress it, make believe it's not there, or feel guilty and ashamed about it.

"I wanted the record to be against that."

He more than succeeded.

"Valentine's Day"
from *Tunnel Of Love*
(Columbia, 1987)

"Valentine's Day," a pensive guitar-based ballad with the soft swirls of a synthesizer, gained a certain notoriety as being the only song from the *Tunnel Of Love* album that was never played live—until the 2005 *Devils & Dust* tour when Springsteen performed it—on piano—in Atlanta.

"Valentine's Day" is haunted by the possibility of loss. The narrator is driving home one night on a dark highway—"driving a big lazy car"—and thinks about a conversation he had with a friend who recently became a father (the song was written before Springsteen himself became a father). Everything in the song appears heightened, everything in life and in nature is connected and intertwined. Indeed, throughout the song Springsteen writes rhapsodically about the wonder of nature, "of the skies," "the rivers," even "the timberwolf in the pines." They say, adds the narrator, the person who travels fastest travels alone—but he doesn't agree. (Springsteen used an almost identical line in "Lucky Man.") Instead, he would rather be at home with his girl. Even something as innocuous as the sound of blowing leaves makes him jumpy as he drives home on "this spooky old highway." But what scares him most is losing the thing, the person, that he loves most.

More than a few people—no less than Father Andrew Greeley—have commented about the religious imagery in the song. Greeley has called "Valentine's Day" the most "liturgical" of the songs that appear on *Tunnel Of*

Love. In the final verse, the narrator wakes from a nightmare, scared and breathing hard but also "born anew." He recalls the feeling of dread that he felt in the dream—the "cold river bottom" that rushed over him, the bitterness that engulfed him, the wind in the "gray fields" that swept through his arms. But what made him wake from his dark reverie was "God's light that came shinin' on through" and the love of his partner lying next to him.

Greeley calls it "Catholicism, pure and simple."

Is it not significant that Springsteen evokes the figure of St. Valentine, the patron saint of romantic love in the song? There are several legends about the origin of St. Valentine's Day. According to one account, Valentine (or Valentinus) was a priest in Third Century Rome. The emperor, Claudius II, forbade young men to marry—single men, he reasoned, would be more battle ready. Undaunted, Valentine conducted secret marriages anyway and for this he was arrested and sent to prison. He not only denied the authority of Rome he also refused to abandon his Christian faith. Eventually, he was executed for his transgressions. While awaiting his execution, though, he restored the sight of a young girl, supposedly the daughter of the judge who presided over his case.

But there is more. Before being beheaded on—yes—February 14 in the year 296 A.D., Valentine is said to have written a farewell note to the young girl he cured. He signed it, "from your Valentine." A pink almond tree bloomed at his gravesite, becoming the symbol of eternal love. In 498, Pope Gelasius named February 14 as St. Valentine's Day.

Who knows whether a priest named Valentine really existed. But the story—and a nice story it is—lives on in tradition, in custom, and, of course, in the words of many songs, including a Springsteen song. Significantly, the title does not appear in the song but Springsteen does ask his beloved to be his "lonely valentine."

Human Touch
(Columbia, 1992)

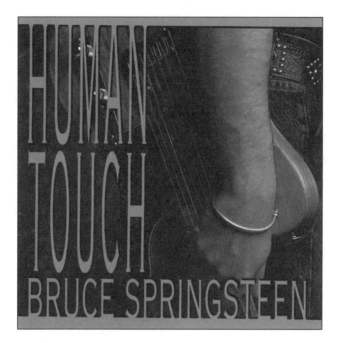

Generally speaking, the critics have not been kind to *Human Touch*. Most consider it Springsteen's weakest album. Among the harshest critics is Jimmy Guterman who calls it "a boring record…[i]ts sound shiny, its lyrics generic, its songs are often as clichéd as their titles…" Other critics, though, were more generous in their assessments. Anthony DeCurtis in *Rolling Stone* described the title cut as "pulsing…which stands among Springsteen's best work…" *Human Touch* was released simultaneously with *Lucky Town*.

Musicians:

Bruce Springsteen: guitar, vocals

Roy Bittan: keyboards

Randy Jackson: bass

Jeff Porcaro: drums, percussion

Patti Scialfa: harmony vocals

Michael Fisher: percussion

Sam Moore: harmony vocals, vocals

Tim Pierce: second guitar

David Sancious: Hammond organ

Bobby King: backing vocals, vocals

Bobby Hatfield: harmony vocals

Ian McLagan: piano

Producers: Bruce Springsteen, Jon Landau, Chuck Plotkin, and Roy Bittan

Recorded at: A&M Studios (Los Angeles)

Tracks:

"Human Touch" (6:28)

"Soul Driver" (4:36)

"57 Channels (And Nothin' On)" (2:25)

"Cross My Heart" (3:49)

"Gloria's Eyes" (3:42)

"With Every Wish" (4:35)

"Roll Of The Dice" (4:15)

"Real World" (5:24)

"All Or Nothin' At All" (3:19)

"Man's Job" (4:35)

"I Wish I Were Blind" (4:46)

"The Long Goodbye" (3:26)

"Real Man" (4:29)

"Pony Boy" (2:13)

Running time: 55:22

"Human Touch"
from *Human Touch*
(Columbia, 1992)

Springsteen described the making of *Human Touch* as an "an exercise" to get himself "back into writing and recording." In it, he works in a variety of musical genres from rock and pop to soul (Sam Moore of Sam & Dave fame contributes vocals on "Soul Driver" and "Man's Job") and R&B. *Human Touch* is also the first time Springsteen worked with musicians other than the E Street Band. "I felt I needed to see what other people brought with them into the studio and how my music would be affected by collaborating with different talents and personalities," he recalls in *Songs*.

The writing did not come easy. The common thread on the album is the need for connection, whether emotional or physical or a combination of both.

"A lot of the music is about pursuing what defines my manhood: what are my commitments and how to try and stick by them in a world where we can't really know anybody else or even really know yourself," he told David Hepworth of *Q* magazine.

"For me," he continued, "this music is about trying to get closer…"

The title song, a long mid-tempo ballad, is about second chances, about allowing things to slip away. The narrator is a realist—he's not looking for prayers or pity, he confesses—just for someone to talk to and, if possible, something tangible to hold onto.

Again, Springsteen uses religious imagery to get his point across. In "Thunder Road," he makes clear he is no hero or savior. Similarly, in "Human Touch," he expects neither mercy nor "bread from heavenly skies," nor "wine" from his blood to rescue anyone from their particular fate. The woman in the song may be yearning for a sense of safety but the narrator warns her that it comes "with a hard hard price." In other words, everything requires some kind of risk and pain.

"Human Touch" was the first and only single released from the album.

"All Or Nothin' At All"
from *Human Touch*
(Columbia, 1992)

There isn't much to say about some songs. Sometimes less truly is more. "All Or Nothin' At All" falls under that category. But in three minutes or so, it condenses Springsteen's philosophy of life into a nutshell: "I want it All Or Nothin' At All." If Mick Jagger and company can't always get what they want, Springsteen goes a step further. There's no in between with him, no middle ground. The song also just sounds terrific: an irresistible slice of combustible rock 'n' roll with a catchy chorus that, once you hear it, you simply can't get out of your head.

"I Wish I Were Blind"
from *Human Touch*
(Columbia, 1992)

This often-overlooked beauty of a song is a heartfelt plunge into despair. The lyrics are simple and straightforward, the images bucolic (cottonwoods and bluebirds in the spring) that veer just this side of cliché (although some may think Springsteen crosses the line). But the emotion—of seeing someone you love with another man—is real and painful enough. The lovely keyboards and gorgeous harmony vocals of ex-Righteous Brother Bobby Hatfield add to the atmosphere.

The message that Springsteen conveys—the beauty of the world hidden under a veil of pain—is also bittersweet. And once again, Springsteen filters the images through a religious prism as the narrator acknowledges the grace and loveliness all around him while admitting that his anguish prevents him from fully appreciating it.

On the *Devils & Dust* tour, Springsteen performed "I Wish I Were Blind" accompanying himself on a piano, which accentuated its inherent loneliness and brought out the essential pathos of the song.

Lucky Town
(Columbia, 1992)

*L*ucky Town is the better half of *Human Touch*. Although an underrated album and unjustly ignored, *Lucky Town* contains some of the strongest songwriting of Springsteen's career: Good-natured rockers, hard luck tales, and sweet ballads. Springsteen wrote and recorded *Lucky Town* in just three weeks.

Musicians:

Bruce Springsteen: vocals, bass

Randy Jackson: bass

Lisa Lowell: backing vocals

Patti Scialfa: backing vocals

Soozie Tyrell: backing vocals

Roy Bittan: keyboards, keyboard bass

Ian McLagan: Hammond organ

Producers: Bruce Springsteen, Jon Landau, Chuck Plotkin, and Roy Bittan

Recorded at: Thrill Hill Recording (Los Angeles)

Tracks:

"Better Days" (3:59)

"Lucky Town" (3:24)

"Local Hero" (4:02)

"If I Should Fall Behind" (2:55)

"Leap Of Faith" (3:22)

"The Big Muddy" (4:03)

"Living Proof" (4:44)

"Book Of Dreams" (4:20)

"Souls Of The Departed" (4:15)

"My Beautiful Reward" (3:54)

Running time: 36:98

"Better Days"
from *Lucky Town*
(Columbia, 1992)

It's not often that a happy state of mind translates into a good song but the rousing "Better Days" falls into that fortunate category. The Springsteen on this record relishes his new-found happiness, waxing not in nostalgia but in the sense of fulfillment that permeates the present. He is not only in love, but he also happens to have a woman who he can call his friend.

"Better Days" also boasts one of Springsteen's most self-deprecating lyrics. When he refers to being "a rich man in a poor man's shirt," you just know that he doesn't take himself too seriously.

"Better Days" opens *Lucky Town* with a burst of energy and an irresistible optimism that makes it almost impossible to dislike.

"If I Should Fall Behind"
from *Lucky Town*
(Columbia, 1992)

During the 1999 *Rising* tour, the penultimate song was invariably "If I Should Fall Behind," the touching ballad from *Lucky Town*. On the concert stage, Springsteen and members of the E Street Band took solo turns, until all the vocalists—five of them—congregate around a single microphone. Perhaps music critic Greg Kot described it best: "a doo-wop group on a dimly lit street corner lifting a prayer wrapped in harmony."

With its gorgeous melody and timeless lyrics, 'If I Should Fall Behind" sounds like an instant classic. It's also one of Springsteen's most unabashedly romantic songs. It is a song of commitment; of staying together "come what may." It is also a song that acknowledges the differences that exist among couples—the tension—as well as the uncertainty of the world.

Like "My Beautiful Reward," also from *Lucky Town*, it closes with pastoral imagery (rivers and valleys and oak trees) that evokes a reassuring, overall sense of equanimity. All may not be well with the world, but in this song, at least, the world certainly appears a bit less menacing.

"The Big Muddy"
from *Lucky Town*
(Columbia, 1992)

"The Big Muddy" is a brooding country-blues ballad, augmented by a mean acoustic slide guitar riff. It's about many things—infidelity, moral compromise, and greed. Everyone is guilty of something, the narrator sings, tainted by some kind of questionable behavior. "There ain't no one leavin' this world, buddy," he insists, without getting their hands at least a little bit dirty. No one is completely innocent. Although Springsteen includes pastoral images in the song (the beautiful river that flows, the birds that sing), he contrasts the innocence of nature with the "messier" denizens of humanity who give the world a darker hue. Once again, Springsteen wallows in grayness. In the Springsteen universe, there is no black and white, just layer after layer of moral uncertainty.

It is significant, I think, that Springsteen quotes directly from Pete Dexter's critically acclaimed novel *Paris Trout*. "You watch what you do / poison snake bites you and you're poison too." (He uses a similar line in "Gave It A Name.") In the novel, which won the 1988 National Book Award, a murder takes place in the small Georgia town of Cotton Point just after World War II. The subsequent trial reveals race and class wounds that run wide and deep.

Paris Trout is a storekeeper who is accused of shooting a young black girl. He harbors no feeling of guilt. Indeed, he assumes that the system will probably work in his favor and the hypocritical townspeople will look the other way. Trout lives by his own rules all the while flaunting societal customs and mores when it is convenient. He sells used cars—the rust is well hidden under a new coat of paint—and subjects the local black community into repaying loans with high interest. When a customer, a local African-American youth, refuses to pay for one of Trout's damaged cars, Trout shoots to death the young man's mother and a young black girl. Much to his surprise—he felt the shooting was justified because the customer owned him money—Trout is brought to trial.

Poison is one of the symbols that Dexter uses in the novel, and it is this ravenous toxin that consumes and eats apart the entire town. Everyone knows Trout is guilty but few want to pursue the matter, hoping it will just go away.

One can see why *Paris Trout* resonated so deeply with Springsteen. It is set in a morally ambiguous world and its themes—racism, injustice, and hypocrisy—are subjects that he has written about extensively. *Paris Trout* has been described as a neo-gothic novel by some, and with its Southern setting and grotesque characters, it recalls the work of Flannery O'Connor, a major influence on

Springsteen. Indeed, novelist William Styron compared it to the best of O'Connor. (Dexter's novel is based on a true story about that took place in Milledgeville, Georgia, O'Connor's hometown.)

In 1991, Pete Dexter adapted *Paris Trout* into a movie for HBO starring Dennis Hopper, Barbara Hershey, and Ed Harris.

And it is surely no accident that the chorus of the song appropriates the title of Pete Seeger's 1967 allegorical anti-Vietnam War anthem, "Waist Deep in the Big Muddy" in which an ineffectual officer ("and the big fool said to push on") orders his platoon to ford a muddy river and hence blindly leads them into quicksand.

"The Big Muddy" ends with one of Springsteen's patented whoops, as the singer himself sounds as if he is stuck between what he wants to do and what he should do. "Waist deep," in other words, in a moral quagmire.

"Living Proof"
from *Lucky Town*
(Columbia, 1992)

"The night my son was born," Springsteen told *Q* magazine in August 1992, "I got close to a feeling of real, pure, unconditional love with all the walls down. All of a sudden, what was happening was so immense that it just stomped all the fear away for a little while and I remember feeling overwhelmed. My music over the last five years has dealt with those almost primitive issues; it's about somebody walking through that world of fear so that he can live in the world of love."

"Living Proof" is a father's musical homage to his newborn son. "In his mother's arms it was all the beauty I could take," Springsteen sings. But it is also a song about second chances, about renewing oneself. For a goodly amount of time—perhaps a big chunk of his adult life—Springsteen kept an emotional distance, or as he puts it, placing his "heart and soul" out of arm's length on a shelf. "I was real *good* at music," he once said, "and real *bad* at everything else." He had lost faith in himself. In an attempt to regain a semblance of humanity (in an earlier song, he would say he was trying to "get his hands clean"), he uses a biblical metaphor in "Living Proof" to describe the feeling of being reborn—he goes "down into the desert city" to shed his old skin only to emerge from a cavernous darkness into the brightness of a new day.

In the next verse, he sings about finding someone who saw through his anger and rage but who saw as well a frightened man who relied on far too many old behavioral crutches to get by. By the end of the song, all the singer knows is that life is built on a house of cards, its foundation "as fragile as each and every breath." One thing he is certain of though is the love that he feels for his son. He closes by referring to his family as "a band of happy thieves," another biblical image. Freely admitting that his life has been "a long, long drought," he gleefully sings about a joyful rain that pours down on their roof and the mercy of God that it brings.

"Living Proof" was originally recorded for *Human Touch* until Springsteen decided that it belonged on a separate album. As it turns out, "Living Proof" served as the creative impetus for the rest of the songs that appear on *Lucky Town*.

Writing "Living Proof," said Springsteen "was a big moment...that was where I wanted to be. I'd spent a lot of my life writing about my past, real and imagined, in some fashion. But with *Lucky Town*, I felt like that's where I am. This is who I am. This is what I have to say. These are the stories I have to tell. This is what's important in my life right now."

"Book Of Dreams"
from *Lucky Town*
(Columbia, 1992)

This sweet, guitar-based ballad begins with the narrator, a man about to be married, as he stands in a backyard "drinkin' in the forgiveness" of life while listening to a party going on inside. He seems slightly adrift though, as if he is looking at his own life from an outsider's perspective.

In the second verse, he watches his bride through a window—a simple pane of glass separates him from his beloved—as she socializes with her girlfriends from "back home." She shows off her dress. There is laughter and a toast and then the narrator, beaming with pride, refers to her as "the prettiest bride" he's ever seen.

A veil of darkness envelops the third verse as we find the couple together for the first time. But then something unusual happens—some have even called it mystical. Suddenly the narrator imagines himself "way up high." He holds her closely to him as moonlight streams through the window. He seems to be having an out-of-body experience, dissociating himself from the earthly realm.

In the last verse, the actual wedding ceremony beings—"the ritual," as Springsteen calls it. They dance beneath the heavens and the "ancient light" of the stars lighten the "darkening trees." They are in awe of each other, and undoubtedly frightened, by the traditions they promised to carry on, and in the love that deepens their very being.

In these few lines, Springsteen captures the essence of love—its "mystery and danger"—but it is the uncertainty of human relationships that makes this song so moving and so poignant.

But there is something else going on, too, something that transcends time. Jim Cullen finds in the chorus—"Oh won't you baby, be in my Book Of Dreams"—an adolescent quality. "It sounds like a line a girl group like The Ronettes might have sung in the early Sixties," he writes. "A wise man, Springsteen seems to be saying, always retain the wonder of a child."

One suspects it is this innocent quality that Dion found so appealing. On *Light Of Day: A Tribute To Bruce Springsteen,* the Fifties icon offers a doo-wop version. "'Book Of Dreams' is a great song," he writes in the album's liner notes. "It reminded me of my wedding day 40 years ago."

One suspects that many couples have played "Book Of Dreams" at their own weddings.

"My Beautiful Reward"
from *Lucky Town*
(Columbia, 1992)

A metaphor on life and love, "My Beautiful Reward" ends *Lucky Town* on a mystical note, as the narrator searches for that elusive something—be it gold and diamond rings or a love interest—that remains forever out of reach.

In the second verse, Springsteen describes a "sacred light" that emanates from a house on a hill. He walks through the house's rooms—echoes of "Mansion On The Hill"—down empty and silent hallways, but he realizes that nothing in the house belongs to him. It's all a materialistic mirage, a sham.

In the last verse, the song turns into a dreamlike fantasy. The narrator looks back on his life and, now transformed into a black bird, soars over gray fields, following the river's edge but still searching, still seeking. Lyrics notwithstanding, Ian McLagen's Hammond organ accentuates the song's already strong religious dimension.

It is a lovely song—one of Springsteen's most elegiac ballads—full of a quiet simplicity and an understated elegance.

The Ghost Of Tom Joad
(Columbia, 1995)

*T*he Ghost Of Tom Joad is a largely acoustic album (the musical equivalent of a short story collection) that owes a great deal of its subtle power to the sensibility and storytelling tradition of Woody Guthrie, the Carter Family, and traditional balladry in general. Its stories are populated by ex-cons, border patrol officers, undocumented immigrants, and other people just (barely) getting by. Quiet and somber, it's a collection of dark lamentations, and the first overtly social commentary since *Born In The U.S.A.* Mikal Gilmore of *Rolling Stone* called *The Ghost Of Tom Joad* "among the bravest work that anyone has given us" during the Nineties. "I wanted to make a record," says Springsteen, "where I didn't have to play by any rules." Although its sensibility is modern, its language can be traced back to folk and blues. "In some ways," he noted, "I've been going a little more backwards..."

Musicians:

Bruce Springsteen: vocals, guitar, harmonica, keyboard

Danny Federici: keyboard, accordion

Marty Rifkin: pedal steel guitar

Garry Tallent: bass

Jim Hanson: bass

Gary Mallaber: drums, percussion

Soozie Tyrell: violin, backing vocal

Chuck Plotkin: keyboard

Jennifer Condos: bass

Lisa Lowell: backing vocal

Patti Scialfa: backing vocal

Producers: Bruce Springsteen and Chuck Plotkin

Recorded at: Thrill Hill (Los Angeles)

Tracks:

"The Ghost Of Tom Joad" (4:23)

"Straight Time" (3:25)

"Highway 29" (3:39)

"Youngstown" (3:52)

"Sinaloa Cowboys" (3:51)

"The Line" (5:14)

"Balboa Park" (3:19)

"Dry Lightning" (3:30)

"The New Timer" (5:45)

"Across The Border" (5:25)

"Galveston Bay" (5:04)

"My Best Was Never Good Enough" (2:00)

Running time: 47:27

"The Ghost Of Tom Joad"
from *The Ghost Of Tom Joad*
(Columbia, 1995)

"I'll be around in the dark. I'll be everywhere. Wherever there's a fight so hungry people can eat, I'll be there. Wherever there's a cop beatin' a guy, I'll be there. I'll be in the way guys yell when they're mad; I'll be in the way kids laugh when they know supper's ready. And when the people are eatin' the stuff they raise, and livin' in the houses they build, I'll be there, too."

—as quoted by Henry Fonda as Tom Joad in John Ford's *The Grapes Of Wrath*

"They stood on a Mountain and they looked to the West
And it looked like the promised land.
That bright green valley with a river running through it,
There was work for every single hand, they thought,
There was work for every single hand....

Wherever little children are hungry and cry
Wherever people ain't free.
Wherever men are fightin' for their rights
That's where I'm gonna be, Ma.
That's where I'm gonna be."

—Woody Guthrie, "Tom Joad"

Pete Seeger recalled the night in 1940 that Woody Guthrie wrote "Tom Joad." He told Seeger that Victor Records suggested that he write a song about the Tom Joad character that appeared in John Steinbeck's *The Grapes Of Wrath*—the novel had just been published the previous year. At the time, Guthrie was recording a number of songs that would come to be known as the *Dust Bowl Ballads*. John Ford's movie version had just come out, and the record company—in an early version of movie tie-ins—wanted to link the song with the popular film. But Guthrie needed a typewriter and asked his friend Seeger if he knew anyone who had one.

"Well, I'm staying with someone who has one," he said. When Seeger asked why, Guthrie responded, "Well I gotta write a ballad. I don't usually write ballads to order but Victor wants me to do a whole album of Dust Bowl songs and they say they want one about Tom Joad, the character in the movie *The Grapes Of Wrath*."

"Have you read the book?" asked Seeger.

"No," replied Guthrie, "but I went and saw the movie, great movie…"

By the end of the evening, fueled by a half-gallon jug of wine, Guthrie had finished his masterpiece. He set the melody to the classic folk song "John Henry." (Coincidentally, Springsteen offers his rendition of "John Henry" on *We Shall Overcome: The Seeger Sessions*, a collection of traditional American ballads.) Like Guthrie, then, it was Ford's movie, not Steinbeck's novel that served as Springsteen's inspiration for the song. Springsteen first saw *The Grapes Of Wrath* in 1975 when he was 26. "It had a tremendous effect," he said. "It resonated in the rest of my life in some fashion."

In 1936 George West, an editor at the *San Francisco News*, commissioned John Steinbeck to write a series of articles on the Dust Bowl migration that was then sweeping across California. A combination of poverty, drought, and foreclosure led scores of people, mostly farmers, to leave their parched homes and travel to the presumably greener pastures—the promised land—of California in search of work. From 1935 to 1938 between 300,000 to 500,000 "Okies," as they were pejoratively called, left. Not all were from Oklahoma, though; others came from Texas, Arkansas, and Missouri.

That summer of 1936 Steinbeck began touring California in an old bakery truck. The articles—seven of them—eventually ran in the *News* from October 5 to 12, 1936. Tom Collins, the manager of a federal migrant labor camp in California's Central Valley, was an invaluable resource for Steinbeck. Collins first met the author at the federal government's Resettlement Administration's Weedpatch Camp at Arvin, in Kern County, California, and traveled with him to farms and migrant settlements. Collins also served as the role model for the fictional Jim Rawley, manager of the Wheatpatch Camp in Steinbeck's novel.

More than just a dry journalistic exercise, though, Steinbeck's articles took a stand and demanded a call to action, recommending, for example, an expansion of the federal camp program, advocating establishment of a state agricultural labor board to protect and promote the migrants' rights to organize unions, and urging both federal and state authorities to a program of resettling the migrants on small family farms, perhaps even on public land.

In the articles, Steinbeck described the migrant workers as a "shifting group of nomadic, poverty-stricken harvesters driven by hunger and the threat of hunger from crop to crop, from harvest to harvest, up and down the state and into Oregon to some extent, and into Washington a little." California took in the majority of them though. The state's highways were filled "with open rattletrap cars loaded with children and with dirty bedding, with fire-blackened cooking utensils." Along side roads and near the rivers, the migrants lived in filthy squatters' camps, a no man's land of dirty rags and scrap iron and houses built of corrugated paper with dirt floors.

In 1938 the Simon J. Lubin Society published the *News* articles in pamphlet form, calling it *Their Blood Is Strong.* The following year, Steinbeck's Depression novel, *The Grapes Of Wrath,* was published. It was an instant success and soon spawned a major motion picture directed by John Ford and starring Henry Fonda as Tom Joad. Tom Collins was hired as the film's technical adviser. Much of the filming was actually shot at the Weedpatch Camp and in the area around Arvin.

In 1988, the Berkeley-based Heyday Books reprinted the collection as *The Harvest Gypsies: On The Road To The Grapes Of Wrath,* with a new and insightful introduction by Charles Wollenberg along with 22 evocative black-and-white photographs by Dorothea Lange and others.

Although it is hard to believe, "The Ghost Of Tom Joad"—a modern rendition of a traditional narrative folk ballad—started out as a rock song. Originally, Springsteen intended to include it on his *Greatest Hits* album, but "it didn't feel right," he said. Setting it aside, he revisited it several months later. By that time, he had a sense of the direction he wanted to take. "The Ghost Of Tom Joad," like the rest of the songs on the album, would be a largely acoustic affair with sparse instrumentation and feature lyrics about the people left behind in what President George H.W. Bush called the "new world order," referring to his vision of the world following the first Gulf War.

Tom Joad, of course, is the main character in Steinbeck's famous Great Depression-era novel, about a family driven from their Oklahoma farm and forced to eke out a living in the migrant labor camps of California. Joad has become an almost mythic figure in popular American iconography, representing the dignity and inner strength of the working man. The character of Tom Joad almost transcends time (is it a coincidence that the name recalls Job of the Bible?). Springsteen takes the character and updates it, giving it a multicultural dimension. In "The Ghost Of Tom Joad," Springsteen follows a new wave of migrants, in this case, a migrant describing life in a box underneath a freeway, as he tries to survive in late Eighties, early Nineties America.

"The Ghost Of Tom Joad" opens with an image of men walking along the railroad tracks. They do not know exactly where they are going but they know wherever it is, there is no turning back. In "Born To Run," the highway offered the promise of escape. In "The Ghost Of Tom Joad," though, no one is pretending that better days exist beyond the horizon. This time around, the highway may be "alive tonight," but "where it's headed everybody knows," Springsteen sings. Commenting later about the meaning of the line, he adds, "I don't think there is any such thing as an innocent man; there is collective responsibility." Just as Preacher Jim Casy in Guthrie's "Tom Joad" emphasized a collectivist vision ("Everybody might be just one big soul / Well it looks that a-way to me"), so too does Springsteen but in "The Ghost Of Tom Joad" there is a difference—whereas Guthrie's Casy tries to organize working people into one "big soul," Springsteen's unnamed preacher sits in a cardboard box, like his fellow hoboes, waiting passively "for when the last shall be first and the first shall be last." Meanwhile, highway patrol helicopters hover overhead as the men eat a modest meal of soup heated by a campfire under a bridge. At night, they sleep on "a pillow of hard rock," hunger in their belly, and a gun their hand.

Playing his harmonica and accompanied by Garry Tallent's haunting bass, Springsteen summarizes the conditions that many of the marginalized people he sings about find themselves in. Shelter lines stretch around corners while throughout the Southwest families sleep in their cars, as their prized—and often only—possession serves as both a method of transportation as well as their home. The character in the song is visited by an apparition, the Joad character from Steinbeck's novel, and it is here that Springsteen paraphrases the famous monologue that appears in both the Ford movie and Guthrie's song although he updates it by being more inclusive ("Wherever somebody's strugglin' to be free / Look in their eyes, Mom, you'll see me").

The influence of country, folk, and blues is everywhere in *The Ghost Of Tom Joad*. Springsteen's exploration of country music began in earnest in the late Seventies and continued into the early Eighties. Listening to the music of Hank Williams led Springsteen to Dylan's protest song era (*The Freewheelin' Bob Dylan* of 1963, *The Times They Are A-Changin'* of 1964, and *Another Side Of Bob Dylan* in 1964), and then on to Guthrie himself. He read Joe Klein's biography, *Woody Guthrie: A Life* and listened to Guthrie's *Dust Bowl Ballads*. What particularly impressed Springsteen about Guthrie was that he said so much with so few words and with sparse instrumentation. What's more, he told such great stories. "I was tremendously moved with his sense of community," Springsteen said. "He worked his way into the souls of people and examined what they were thinking and feeling about themselves and the world around them. And he did this better than anyone I had ever heard before." Guthrie believed that music could change the world for the better. "Guthrie was one of the few songwriters at the time," Springsteen told Will Percy, "who was aware of the political implications of the music he was writing."

Some critics have condemned *The Ghost Of Tom Joad* for lacking authenticity (one critic, in particular, found "nothing less than shameful" Springsteen's mispronunciation of Spanish words and misspelling of Spanish names on the lyric sheet). How could a millionaire (albeit a self-made one) write about illegal immigrants, drug runners, and boy prostitutes? What gives him the right, they seemed to be saying, to compose songs about topics that are presumably outside his own purview? It is a common complaint launched against songwriters in particular but not, curiously, novelists or short story writers or filmmakers. According to this warped theory, songwriters, especially rock stars, should not write songs with a social bent. Of course, these are exactly the kind of songs that mean so much to Springsteen. Springsteen's music is about facing consequences. It is about asking the hard questions. It's about how you go on with your life *after* you've reached adulthood. "He's a guy," Dave Marsh once said, "who lives with his eyes open."

During interviews supporting the album, Springsteen tried to answer his critics. "I don't have some big idea," he told Gavin Martin of the *New Musical Express.* "I don't feel like I have some enormous political message I'm trying to deliver. I think my work has come from the inside." He insisted that he was not trying to preach, but rather just tell a story. "I don't like the soap-box thing," he said, "so I begin internally with things that matter to me personally and maybe were part of my life in some fashion.

"I lived in a house where there was a lot of struggle to find work," he continues, "where the results of not being able to find your place in society manifested themselves with the resulting lack of self-worth, with anger, with violence. And as I grew up, I said, 'Hey, that's my song,' because, I don't know, maybe that was my experience at a very important moment in my life."

Around the same time, he told David Corn in *Mother Jones* magazine, "I believe that your politics are emotionally and psychologically determined by your early experiences. My mother worked the same job her whole life, every day, never sick, never stayed home, never cried. My dad had a very difficult life, a hard struggle all the time at work. I've always felt like I'm seeking his revenge.

"My memory is of my father trying to find work, what that does to you, and how that affects your image of your manhood, as a provider. The loss of that role is devastating. I wrote coming from that spot—the spot of disaffection, of loners, outsiders. But not outlaws," he emphasizes. "It's about people trying to find their way in, but somebody won't let them in. That pretty much obsesses me to this day—and probably will the rest of my life."

"Youngstown"
from *The Ghost Of Tom Joad*
(Columbia, 1995)

At its simplest level, "Youngstown" is about the collapse of a steel town. But it is also about lost dreams and lost pride and about never being able to make a livelihood or to live the kind of life you had grown accustomed to in your hometown ever again. The origin of the song, though, begins with journalist Dale Maharidge and photographer Michael Williamson.

In 1982, Bill Moore, city editor of the *Sacramento Bee,* had just returned from a downtown bar where he encountered an aging hobo. The hobo regaled him with fascinating stories about unemployed middle-class people who, desperate for work, were riding the rails just as they did during the Great Depression. Moore couldn't believe his ears—he knew a good story when he heard it. He told Maharidge, a reporter on the paper at the time, to find out for himself what it was like for this new generation of homeless men and women—formerly middle-class people—to be drifting from place to place. Recruiting Williamson as his photographer, Maharidge hopped a northbound train and for one week rode the rails up and down the length of California. They extended their research, traveling around the country for three months by car, by rail, by thumb, and on foot. The fruit of their research coalesced into *Journey To Nowhere: The Saga Of The New Underclass,* which was first published in 1985. (Together Maharidge and Williams explored other sides of contemporary American society, including *And Their Children After Them: The Legacy of Let Us Now Praise Famous Men* (1990), a portrait of the surviving members and descendants of the tenant families first brought to the public consciousness by writer James Agee and photographer Walker Evans in 1936 and for which they shared the Pulitzer Prize; *Homeland* (2004), a glimpse of the country before and after the September 11 attacks; and, most recently, *Denison, Iowa: Searching For The Soul Of America Through The Secrets Of A Midwest Town* (2005), a chronicle of the socioeconomic and seismic demographic shift in Middle America.)

Springsteen didn't actually read *Journey To Nowhere* until some ten years later when, during a sleepless night, he found the stories that Maharidge described both disturbing and frightening. He could not get them out of his mind. The portraits of dying steel towns and contemporary boxcar hoboes inspired Springsteen to write "Youngstown," as well as "The New Timer." In fact, he was so impressed by Maharidge and Williamson's work that he wrote the introduction to the revised 1996 edition. "Dale Maharidge and Michael Williamson," Springsteen wrote, "put real lives, names, and faces on statistics we'd all been hearing about throughout the Eighties."

In 1802, according to the account laid down by Maharidge in *Journey To Nowhere,* businessmen James and Daniel Heaton discovered iron ore on the banks of Yellow Creek, just south of Youngstown, Ohio. They hastily built a blast furnace and with it came the makings of the modern steel-making industry. During the Civil War, the factories manufactured such necessities as cannonballs. Later, around the turn of the century, steel was in great demand. America was growing and it needed steel for its bridges and ships and, eventually, cars. Youngstown was chosen as a site for the mills; Bessemer converters replaced the smaller furnaces.

The steel manufactured in Youngstown made its way around the world—it was used in the gates of the Panama Canal and the metal for the tanks of both world wars as well as the wars in Korea and Vietnam. "At one time," writes Maharidge, "28 blast furnaces churned out molten iron, and more steel was made in Youngstown than in any other city in the nation."

The population boomed, nearly doubling between 1870 and 1880. During World War II, Youngstown Steel and Tube, owner of the Jeanette Blast Furnace—the Jenny mentioned in Springsteen's song—developed a particular type of steel used for the manufacture of machine gun belts. After the war, though, increased shipping costs and fierce competition throughout the industry took its toll. On September 19, 1977, more than 4,000 workers of the Campbell Works suddenly lost their jobs. Soon thereafter, conditions only worsened. Owners of other mills decided either to relocate or were forced to close because of their reliance on outdated open-hearth furnaces. And in a symbolic blow to the already devastated community, Youngstown Sheet and Tube shut down the 500-ton Jeanette furnace in 1977. Although the Jeanette Blast Furnace Preservation Association fought valiantly to save the furnace, the Jenny was demolished in January 1997.

"Youngstown" is a magnificent song, defiant and compassionate, a rock ballad full of fiery conviction. Many consider it the best song on the album. Following the historical chronology laid out by Maharidge, Springsteen sings about the early days of the steel industry in Youngstown, accompanied at first only by his guitar before the band—Jim Hanson on bass, Gary Mallaber on drums and percussion, Chuck Plotkin on keyboard, Marty Rifkin on pedal steel guitar, and Soozie Tyrell on violin—comes to life in the second verse. The narrator's father worked in the furnaces "and kept 'em hotter than hell." A generation later, the son returns home from yet another war—this time

Vietnam—and works his way up the chain to be a scarfer, a difficult and poorly compensated job that required cutting off the steel's molten metal; that is, torching the steel to remove any inperfections. It is a job, he sings, that would "suit the devil as well." But it pays enough to feed his children and keep the creditors at bay.

In the third verse, the steel yard has turned into scrap and rubble; industry changes and the forces of the marketplace did "what Hitler couldn't do," laments the father, as the steel industry is brought to its knees. An industry that built the materiel for the country's wars is now reduced to ruin and the narrator wonders what all those wartime deaths meant. The workers made the Carnegies and Fricks of the world rich, but now they don't even have the decency—or vision—sings Springsteen, to keep the mills open…whether in the Monongahela Valley, the Mesabi iron range in Minnesota, or the coal mines of Appalachia.

In the end, the son prays that "the devil comes and takes me to stand in the fiery furnaces of hell." Heaven, for him, just won't do. Soozie Tyrell's plaintive violin underscores the poignancy of the material.

When asked his emotional motivation behind the song, Springsteen told BBC Radio, "My connection to it was probably through my own kids and my own job, in the sense that the thought of being told after 30 years or so, that what you're doing isn't useful anymore, or has no place, or that the world has changed and that's the way it is. And you're 50 and gotta find something else to do. That's almost impossible…I don't know what I would do in that circumstance."

The Boss. (Kreg Yingst)

"Sinaloa Cowboys"

from *The Ghost Of Tom Joad*
(Columbia, 1995)

"Once the domain of outlaw biker gangs, the nation's meth trade has been taken over by Mexican drug families in the rural belt from San Diego County to Redding. Operating from Sinaloa and other states deep inside Mexico, these families oversee teams of cookers dispatched to orchards, cotton fields, chicken ranches, and abandoned diaries north of the border."

—Mark Arax and Tom Gorman, *Los Angeles Times,* March 13, 1995

Sinaloa, a state in Mexico, is located along the Gulf of California that extends from the foothills of the western Sierra Madre mountain range to the Pacific Coast. From bases in Sinaloa and elsewhere throughout Mexico, Mexican drug families operate a vast network of contacts, their tentacles spread out across California, which allows them to produce methamphetamine (known as crack or speed) in mass quantities with alarming speed and distribute it across the United States in a matter of days. A *Los Angeles Times* article on the issue, "California's Illicit Farm Belt Export," which ran in early 1995, inspired Springsteen to write "Sinaloa Cowboys." Written by reporters Mark Arax and Tom Gorman, it examined the illicit drug trade among illegal Mexicans in the rural San Joaquin Valley, where pound after pound of methamphetamine has become, in the words of the reporters, "California's newest crop export." Inside the makeshift labs that are scattered throughout the state and usually housed in inconspicuous farmhouses with chickens in coops and children innocently playing outside, teams of "cookers" make hundreds of pounds of methamphetamine as a cheaper substitute for the more expensive cocaine. The demand is insatiable.

After the story ran, Gorman reportedly received a telephone call from a member of Springsteen's staff. Springsteen not only wanted to know about the manufacturing of methamphetamines but more particularly about the Mexican farm workers who "cook" the drug. He wanted to gather enough details in order to personalize the story, to flesh out the emotions behind the facts, and to make his characters recognizably human.

In "Sinaloa Cowboys," two undocumented immigrants, brothers Miguel and Luis Rosales, cross the border from northern Mexico to California to find work in the orchard fields of the Central Valley, roughly the same area that the members of the fictional Joad family worked. But before they leave, their father utters a prophetic warning, "everything the North gives," he says, "it exacts a price in return."

Soon, word spreads that the men from Sinaloa—according to Arax and Gorman, the so-called Sinaloa cowboys cut a sartorial figure, with their beaver hats, boots, and ostrich-skin belts—are looking for some help. The Rosales' brothers accept the offer, and here Springsteen's research is used to great effect. The two brothers can make as much money in one ten-hour shift in the drug trade as they do toiling in the orchards as migrant farmers. But if they should make a mistake, they will pay the price—hydriodic acid not only can burn through skin but breathing in its toxic fumes can cause chemical pneumonia that, as Springsteen sings, would "leave you spittin' up blood in the desert."

In a small tin shack on a deserted chicken ranch on the edge of a ravine, the brothers begin cooking their deadly substance. Early one evening, while Luis works inside the shack, there is an explosion. Miguel carries his fatally injured brother to the creek side, where he dies amid the tall grass. He lifts his brother's lifeless body into a truck and then drives to a eucalyptus grove. Miguel buries Luis and takes the $10,000 dollars—the loot they earned from their illicit activities—they had hidden beneath the ground. And then the song, like Luis' life, is over. In death and in life, Luis, like so many other faceless immigrants who cross the border, leaves this world without fanfare; indeed, without anyone taking particular notice.

"The border story is something that I hadn't heard much of in the music that's out there," Springsteen told David Corn in *Mother Jones*. "It's a big story. It's the story of what this country is going to be: a big, multicultural place."

"Sinaloa Cowboys" is a chilling tale and the arrangement is appropriately muted as Springsteen accompanies himself on guitar and keyboards.

At a concert in Fresno, California, Springsteen introduced the song by summoning the memory of John Steinbeck, "Sixty years after John Steinbeck wrote *The Grapes Of Wrath*, people are working under conditions in the Central Valley that as Americans we really shouldn't tolerate."

"The Line"
from *The Ghost Of Tom Joad*
(Columbia, 1995)

An American soldier turned border patrol officer turns the other way, allowing a Mexican woman and her family to cross the border.

It reads like the synopsis of a short story, or a screenplay, rather than a five-minute song.

After being discharged from the military, Carl, the protagonist of "The Line," doesn't know what to do with himself. A lonely widower, he feels lost and anchorless in this strange new world and yearns for something—or someone. He accepts a new position as a California border patrol officer for the INS. It is familiar territory and retains some of the same military cachet.

Carl befriends Bobby Ramirez, a 10-year veteran of "the line," whose family hails from Guanajuato, Mexico. For him, the job is different; it's personal. He tells Carl that the illegal immigrants risk death just trying to make it across the border and then they give all their hard-earned savings to the smugglers. "We send 'em home and they come right back again." The cycle never ends. "Carl," he adds, "hunger is a powerful thing."

Carl takes pride in his work, keeping his uniform neatly pressed and freshly clean. At night he tries to prevent the would-be immigrants—which includes not only drug runners but also farmers and their families, young women with children—from crossing the line. During their off hours, Bobby and Carl relax and throw back a few drinks in a bar in Tijuana where they see the same people they had sent back the day before.

The first time Carl sees Luisa is in a holding pen. Their eyes fleetingly meet and they look away. Carl is smitten. "Her eyes reminded me of what I'd lost," he thinks to himself. In her arms, she holds a crying child. Later, they dance in the same Tijuana bar that Carl and Bobby frequent in their off-hours, when Luisa tells him that she has family in California. He agrees to help her, her child, and her young brother get across. But the plan turns complicated when Bobby arrives one night just in time to see Luisa running through the ravines, on her way to a new life in the American West. He lets her go.

Bobby never brings up the incident again. Six months later, Carl leaves the line. He moves to the Central Valley, taking odd jobs and searching at night in the local bars and in the migrant towns for his Luisa "with the black hair fallin' down."

"The Line" is a lovely song, the gentle melody accentuating its poignant tale of love lost, love sought, and love tantalizingly out of reach.

WHAT'S IN A NAME?

Springsteen's songs are interspersed with all kinds of names—nicknames, first names, full names, even the names of historical figures.

First Names

Mary
"Mary Queen Of Arkansas,"
  "Thunder Road," "The River,"
  "Mary's Place," "The Rising"

Scott
"Blinded By The Light"

Rex
"Does This Bus Stop At 82nd
  Street?"

Mary Lou
"Does This Bus Stop At 82nd
  Street?," "Reason To Believe"

Sandy
"Fourth of July, Asbury Park
  (Sandy)"

Kitty
"Kitty's Back"

Rosalita
"Rosalita (Come Out Tonight)"

Billy
"New York City Serenade,"
  "The Big Muddy"

Terry
"Backstreets"

Wendy
"Born To Run"

Eddie
"Meeting Across The River"

Cherry
"Meeting Across The River"

Candy
"Candy's Room"

Sonny
"Racing In The Street"

Sherry
"Sherry Darling"

Ralph
"Johnny 99"

Frankie
"Highway Patrolman"

Maria
"Highway Patrolman"

Wanda
"Open All Night"

Johnny
"Reason To Believe," "When
  You're Alone"

Kyle William
"Reason To Believe"

Wayne
"Darlington County"

Joe
"Downbound Train"

Bobby Jean
"Bobby Jean"

Bobby
"Glory Days," "Spare Parts,"
  "With Every Wish"

Kate
"My Hometown"

Janey
"Spare Parts"

Gloria
"Gloria's Eyes"

Doreen
"With Every Wish"

Frank
"This Hard Land"

Charlie
"Straight Time"
Carl
"The Line"

Luisa
"The Line"

Frank
"The New Timer"

Charles
"American Skin (41 Shots)"

Joe
"Nothing Man"

Bobbie
"Devils & Dust"

Rosie
"Long Time Comin'"

Lynette
"Black Cowboys"

Maria
"Maria's Bed"

Leah
"Leah"

Nicknames
Broadway Mary
"Does This Bus Stop At 82nd
  Street?"

Jimmy the Saint "Lost In The Flood"	Cat "Kitty's Back"
Spanish Johnny "Incident on 57th Street"	Missy Bimbo "Wild Billy"
Puerto Rican Jane "Incident on 57th Street"	Margarita "Wild Billy's Circus Story"
go-cart Mozart "Blinded By The Light"	Sampson "Wild Billy's Circus Story"
Early-Pearly "Blinded By The Light"	Little Tiny Tim "Wild Billy"
Crazy Janey "Spirit In The Night"	Little Dynamite "Rosalita"
Hazy Davy "Spirit In The Night"	Little Gun "Rosalita"
Killer Joe "Spirit In The Night"	Jack the Rabbit "Rosalita"
Power Thirteen "The E Street Shuffle"	Weak Knees Willie "Rosalita"
Little Angel "The E Street Shuffle"	Sloppy Sue "Rosalita"
Big Pretty "Kitty's Back"	Big Bones Billy "Rosalita"
Jack Knife "Kitty's Back"	Diamond Jackie "New York City Serenade"

Bad Scooter
"Tenth Avenue Freeze-Out"

Magic Rat
"Jungleland"

Dirty Annie
"You Can Look (But You Better
  Not Touch)"

Little Spider
"Balboa Park"

Real People
In "In Freehold," which has
  never been recorded,
  Springsteen immortalizes
  Maria Espinoza, who gave the
  singer his first kiss.

Big Man (aka E Street Band
  saxophonist Clarence
  Clemons) "Tenth Avenue
  Freeze-Out"

Mean John Brown
"Johnny 99"

Elvis Presley
"57 Channels (And Nothing
  On)"

James Dean
"Cadillac Ranch"

Burt Reynolds
"Cadillac Ranch"

James and Dan Heaton
"Youngstown"

Jesus
"Wild Billy's Circus Story,"
  "It's Hard To Be A Saint In
  The City," "Leap Of Faith,"
  "The New Timer," "Jesus Was
  An Only Son"

Jack Thompson (1904–1946)
  World Welterweight Champion
  in 1930 and 1931 "The
  Hitter"

Surnames
Bill Horton
"Cautious Man"

Joe Roberts
"Highway Patrolman"

Lieutenant Jimmy Bly
"Souls Of The Departed"

Raphael Rodriguez
"Souls Of The Departed"

Tom Joad
"The Ghost Of Tom Joad"

Miguel Rosales
"Sinaloa Cowboys"

Luis Rosales
"Sinaloa Cowboys"

Bobby Ramirez	Rainey Williams
"The Line"	"Black Cowboys"
Billy Sutter	John McDowell
"Galveston Bay"	"The Hitter"

"Balboa Park"

from *The Ghost Of Tom Joad*
(Columbia, 1995)

"Balboa Park" is the second song on *The Ghost Of Tom Joad* that was inspired by a *Los Angeles Times* article. "Children Of The Border" by Sebastian Rotella, which ran April 3, 1993, describes the precarious existence of young illegal Mexican immigrants who survive on the streets of San Diego through prostitution and drugs. The homeless boys squat in Balboa Park, a 1,158-acre cultural and recreational center on the northeast edge of the San Diego business district. Wealthy men driving BMWs circle the area both day and night, like a swarm of ravenous buzzards, seeking out children and looking for easy drugs. According to Rotella, lunchtime and late afternoon are particularly busy.

The illegal youths, some as young as nine years old, sleep wrapped in blankets under freeway bridges. They come from Tijuana, Sinaloa, Mexico City, Guadalajara, and Honduras, and they sport nicknames like Batman, Squirrel, Little Dracula, Karate Kid, and The Russian.

This is the sordid nether world of "Balboa Park." Little Spider, Springsteen's protagonist, closely resembles Martin, the 14-year-old boy described in Rotella's article. Like Martin, he sleeps underneath the freeway. As the evening turns dark, he sniffs *toncho* from a Coke can, getting high on its toxic fumes. Toncho is a deadly substance, writes Rotella, that "bears a resemblance to fumes from a gas tank…" Although the vapors assuage cold and hunger, it also corrodes the lungs, kidneys, heart, and brain.

Exhilarated by the effects of the toncho, Little Spider heads with a swagger toward Balboa Park to service the wealthy men who drive by in their Mercedes. "He did what he had to for the money," sings Springsteen. Sometimes, he sends money back home, but mostly he spends the booty on high-top sneakers, more toncho, and expensive jeans. Like Martin, he grew up in the Zona Norte neighborhood near the Tijuana River, a gritty spot where migrants and smugglers, thieves, and drug users congregate. He is recruited as a rock cocaine runner in San Diego's Twelfth Street strip. One night, during an INS raid, a border patrol car inadvertently runs him over as he tries in vain to dodge in and out of traffic. He manages to reach his makeshift bed, his "home," that lies beneath a highway underpass, where, clutching his stomach, he closes his eyes and listens to the cars rushing above him, as his life slowly ebbs away.

"Balboa Park" doesn't pull any punches. Like the newspaper article that inspired it, the song simply tells a story without judgment, without commentary. Although Springsteen was criticized by some for writing about a milieu and a culture that was not his, "Balboa Park" actually is an extension of the type of songs that Springsteen has been writing about for most of his career, even down to use of nicknames (not only Little Spider but also X-man and Cochise). The characters and their surroundings are reminiscent of the earlier generation of youths who populated such songs as "Blinded By The Light," "Spirit In The Night," "The E Street Shuffle," "Incident On 57th Street," and "New York City Serenade." As he himself explained in *Songs*, both "Balboa Park" and "Sinaloa Cowboys" "traced the lineage of my earlier characters to the Mexican migrant experience in the New West. These songs completed a circle," he continued, "bringing me back to 1978 and the inspiration I'd gotten from Steinbeck's *The Grapes Of Wrath*. Their skin was darker and their language had changed, but these were people trapped by the same brutal circumstances."

"The New Timer"
from *The Ghost Of Tom Joad*
(Columbia, 1995)

Springsteen found inspiration for one of his great story-songs, "The New Timer" in Dale Maharidge and Michael Williamson's harrowing *Journey To Nowhere: The Saga Of The New Underclass*. Maharidge defines new timer as a "new breed of street person, forced to the bottom by economic hardship." What set these nouveau homeless apart from their fellow hoboes, was that they came from the middle class and so their fall from grace was especially painful.

In tone, atmosphere, and even melody, "The New Timer" is reminiscent of "Nebraska," but it is also as dark and bloody and disturbing as any traditional ballad. Both "The New Timer" and "Nebraska" offer bleak portraits of the underbelly of the American dream and both songs contain violence, but the protagonist in "The New Timer" is the victim rather than the aggressor.

The unnamed protagonist befriends an older man, a hobo named Frank, who has rode the rails since the Great Depression ("50 years out on the skids"). Frank plays the role of mentor as well as protector, a father figure who offers advice ("You don't cross nobody / You'll be all right out here, kid"), provides company and conversation, and generally shows him the ropes. We know that the younger man left his family in Pennsylvania, searching for work, before he met Frank in a freight yard in East Texas, but we don't know the circumstances that prompted his departure. He does odd jobs to get by, hoeing sugar beets, picking peaches, and, along with a hundred others, bunking in a barn "just like animals."

Come springtime, he and Frank go their separate ways. He never sees him again except for one rainy night when he catches a glimpse of him riding on a railcar (called a grainer), perched on one of its narrow ledges. Frank shouts his name and then, like a ghostly apparition, disappears in the rain and wind. It is a chilling image and a premonition of what is to come.

Frank is found dead outside of Stockton, California. Nothing was taken from him, Springsteen notes, "somebody killin' just to kill," which again in its cruelty recalls the serial killer in "Nebraska," who when asked why he did what he did offers a lame, "guess there's just a meanness in this world."

The old hobo, Frank, is modeled after Thomas Jefferson "Alabama" Glenn, who began riding the rails after the Great Depression. He was murdered, as is Springsteen's character, along with two other hoboes—his body repeatedly stabbed—sometime during the night when they huddled around a campfire. There was no sign of a struggle, nor was robbery a motive. Police suspected a fellow transient, someone who would "kill for the sake of killing."

After hearing about Frank's sudden death, the younger man daydreams about the home he left behind, about the wife and son he abandoned back in Pennsylvania. He imagines his wife making a meal in the kitchen and his son sitting at the table. He wonders whether his son misses him. Does he even wonder where he is?

That night, he picks a campsite with great care, fully aware of the dangers on the road. He gathers some wood for the fire and in the early darkness of winter, with the wind whistling all around him, he heats up some coffee and stares into the night, unable to sleep, with a machete at his side for protection. He prays to Jesus, asking for love and mercy, but only hatred and retribution fill his battered heart.

The young hobo in "The New Timer" bears a striking resemblance to *Journey To Nowhere's* Don, a small business owner whose life was turned upside down when the recession hit, his business went bankrupt, and he lost his house.

After looking for work for nine months, he bought a one-way Amtrak ticket in St. Louis and hit the road. He became, in other words, a new timer.

Like the best Springsteen story-songs, the emotionally wrenching "The New Timer" requires the listener's complete attention. It is full of precise details and subtle nuances—you can almost feel the fear of the hobo as he tries to sleep at night—as well as unexpected twists and turns. The melody is simple but memorable, the lyrics as concise as a tightly woven short story. What's more, Springsteen's confessional vocals draw the listener in, as this tragic tale of murder and deceit slowly and inexorably unfolds. During the *Devils & Dust* tour, Springsteen performed "The New Timer" on the autoharp, turning what was already an unsettling tale into an unforgettable journey into the abyss.

"Across The Border"
from *The Ghost Of Tom Joad*
(Columbia, 1995)

> *"The Lord is my shepherd, I shall not want.*
> *He makes me lie down in green pastures;*
> *he leads me beside still waters;*
> *he restores my life.*
> *He leads me in paths of righteousness*
> *for his name's sake.*
>
> *Even though I walk through the valley of the shadow of death*
> *I fear no evil;*
> *for you are with me;*
> *your rod and your staff—*
> *they comfort me.*
>
> *You prepare a table before me*
> *in the presence of my enemies;*
> *you anoint my head with oil;*
> *my cup overflows.*
> *Surely goodness and mercy shall follow me*
> *all the days of my life,*
> *and I shall dwell in the house of the Lord*
> *for my whole life long."*

—Psalm 23

Springsteen has described "Across The Border" as a beautiful dream. "It's the kind of dream you have before you fall asleep, where you live in a world where beauty is still possible. And in that possibility of beauty there is hope." For this reason alone, it is the most optimistic song—perhaps the only truly optimistic song—on *The Ghost Of Tom Joad,* a deeply spiritual meditation on what lies just beyond the horizon.

"Across The Border" plays like a campfire ballad of sorts. It has a fuller, more lilting sound than most of the songs on *Tom Joad.* E Street Band alumni Danny Federici's tasteful keyboard and accordion playing, Soozie Tyrell's subtle violin, Marty Rifkin's poignant pedal steel guitar, as well as the backing vocals of Patti Scialfa and Lisa Lowell and Springsteen's own delicate vocal phrasing all add texture and gradation to this wistful, waking dream of a song.

The protagonist packs his bags and walks across the railroad tracks that lead to the border. He looks forward to a tomorrow where, he envisions, his love and he will sleep beneath "auburn skies" in the land—the promised land?—across the river, leaving behind the pain and sadness that lies on the other side of the Rio Bravo. He promises to build a house for his beloved ("high upon a grassy hill") in their new home. Evoking the spirit of Psalm 23, he dreams of an earthly paradise of gold and green pastures that roll gently down into "cool clear waters."

The character prays that he will receive the blessing and grace of the saints so that he can safely cross to the other side, hoping too that someday they both will be able to drink from "God's blessed waters and eat the fruit from the vine." The music and, in particular, the choice of instrumentation—harmonica, violin, accordion, pedal steel guitar—create a warm, rustic glow.

During the *Tom Joad* tour, Springsteen introduced "Across The Border" by emphasizing its mystical qualities. "This song's about the mystery of human nature, human spirit. How people just keep going, keep going...We've been beat up pretty bad, but we keep going." "Across the Border," then, is almost a Southwestern version of *Nebraska's* "Reason To Believe," an equally optimistic-despite-the-odds song that refuses to surrender to the hopelessness of despair.

Springsteen biographer Dave Marsh suggests that "Across The Border" pays homage to Ry Cooder's "Across the Borderline," which appeared in the 1982 Jack Nicholson movie, *The Border.* Nicholson portrays an INS agent, much like the widowed Carl in Springsteen's "The Line," trapped in a dead-end relationship that is sympathetic to the plight of the illegal immigrants he must arrest every day.

In 2005, Springsteen released "Matamoros Banks," a gritty sequel to "Across the Border," on *Devils & Dust.* He continues the story of the hopeful young immigrant. Unfortunately, his fate is not a happy one.

"Galveston Bay"
from *The Ghost Of Tom Joad*
(Columbia, 1995)

The Vietnam War had a profound effect on the United States. In Texas, though, the war came home in ways that few had anticipated.

The war left millions of Vietnamese either dead, injured, or otherwise ruined. After the fall of Saigon in 1975, many of the South Vietnamese, allies of the United States, were pressured by the Communist government to leave the country. Between 1975 and 1983, thousands of refugees fled on unsafe boats bound for Indonesia, Malaysia, Thailand, Hong Kong, and the Philippines. Many died at sea. Alarmed by the growing humanitarian crisis, the United Nations held a conference in an effort to assist these so-called boat people. Consequently, several countries—the United States, Australia, Canada, and France—agreed to resettle nearly 700,000 of the Vietnamese refugees. But the United States decided to scatter the refugees across the country as not to have too many in one location. A considerable amount chose to go to Texas, a state that, prior to their arrival, had few Asians among its population. By 1980, about 30,000 Vietnamese were living there. Unable to speak the language and with little capital of their own, the Vietnamese gravitated toward the fairly accessible shrimping industry. Or as one immigrant explained, "We like the weather, we like the shrimping, we like a chance to start our own business."

But the residents, fearful of competition and resentful of their presence, pressured most of the local bait shops to boycott the Vietnamese. The immigrants responded by working longer and harder than their American counterparts. And they prospered. Racial tension continued to grow between the white fishermen and the Asian fishermen. The Texans accused the Vietnamese of over fishing as well as fishing out of season. Conditions came to a head between 1979 and 1981 when several Vietnamese shrimp boats were burned in the Galveston Bay area. One incident that occurred on August 3, 1979, was particularly tragic. In Seadrift, Texas, about 60 miles from Corpus Christi, not only were several Vietnamese boats burned, but also a Vietnamese house—fortunately, no one was inside—was firebombed. Tensions escalated further when a Vietnamese shrimper fatally shot Billy Joe Aplin, an American crabber. Two Vietnamese men were tried for murder but acquitted on the grounds of self-defense.

Outraged by the court's decision, white groups sought the assistance of Louis Beam, the Great Dragon of the Texas Knights of the Ku Klux Klan. On

February 14, 1981, a group of white fishermen organized a rally against the Vietnamese. Two months later, on April 16, 1981, civil rights activist and lawyer Morris Dees agreed to represent the Vietnamese Fishermen's Association, led by a former colonel in the South Vietnamese army named Nguyen Van Nam. Dees filed a lawsuit on behalf of the Vietnamese fishermen against the Klan in the federal district court of the Southern District of Texas, seeking a court order to prevent the Klan's ongoing campaign of intimidation and violence and citing violations of federal civil rights statues and antitrust statues. The judge assigned to the case was Gabrielle Kirk McDonald, the first African American in Texas and the third African American woman in the United States to serve in the federal judiciary. After a four-day trial, the court issued an injunction prohibiting the Klan from threatening, intimidating, or harassing the Vietnamese fishermen.

"Galveston Bay" was inspired by the Vietnamese lawsuit discussed by Dees in his memoir, *A Season For Justice.* Dees and his law partner Joseph J. Levin, Jr., along with fellow civil rights activist Julian Bond, founded the nonprofit Montgomery, Alabama-based Southern Poverty Law Center in 1979, essentially to combat all forms of bigotry. Dees is also the author of *Hate On Trial: The Case Against America's Most Dangerous Neo-Nazi* (1993), about the trial against white supremacist Tom Metzger and his White Aryan Resistance group and *Gathering Storm: America's Militia Threat* (1996), which discusses the dangers of domestic terrorist groups. In 1991, a television movie was made, *Line Of Fire: The Morris Dees Story,* starring Corbin Bernsen in the title role.

Springsteen brings all of this to life in "Galveston Bay." Le Bin Son represents Nguyen Van Nam. In Springsteen's version, though, Le is not a colonel but an ordinary Vietnamese soldier who fought the Communist North Viet Cong for 15 years alongside his American compatriots until the fall of Saigon in 1975. He leaves his native country and brings his family to "the promised land" of Seabrook, Texas. The Delta country, he thinks, resembles home. He works as a machinist and saves enough money to buy a shrimp boat with his cousin "and together they harvested Galveston Bay." Each morning before sunrise, a grateful Le kisses his sleeping daughter before going to work.

We next meet Billy Sutter. Sutter, also a Vietnam veteran, fought with Charlie Company in Quang Tri, a province in central Vietnam. Sutter was wounded on August 18, 1965, in the battle of Chu Lai, the first military operation of the war and considered a major victory for U.S. forces. He returns home in 1968, marries a local girl, and works the Gulf fishing grounds in a boat belonging to his father. Like Le Bin Son, he also kisses his child—in his case, a son—each morning before leaving for work.

Sutter watches the fall of Saigon on his television set and turns resentful toward the looming Vietnamese presence in his town. Members of the white community, growing increasingly agitated themselves, gather in the local bars and talk ominously about an "America for Americans." Soon, they ask the Texas Knights of the Ku Klux Klan for help. When three Klan members try to burn Le Bin Son's boat, Le shoots and kills two of them. Brought to trial, the jury acquits Le on the grounds of self-defense. Sutter vows vengeance. As Le emerges from the courthouse, Sutter confronts him on the steps and utters a threat, "My friend," he says, "you're a dead man."

One summer night, as Le smokes a cigarette by the waterside, Sutter stands in the shadows, holding a knife in his hand. But then he makes a moral decision. At this particular moment, in this particular place, Billy Sutter chooses not to go through with the murder; he chooses not to add to the violence and brutality of the world. He decides to allow the violent urges to wash over him and lets them pass, "for whatever reason," says Springsteen. "That's a miracle that can happen, that does happen. People get to a certain brink, and they make a good choice, instead of a deadly choice."

Come dawn, Billy returns home, this time to his sleeping wife, kisses her, and then returns to the waters of Galveston Bay, casting his net into the sea.

The Texan-Vietnamese incidents were also the subject of a movie, the critically panned *Alamo Bay* in 1985. Directed by Louis Malle from an original screenplay by Alice Arlen and starring Amy Madigan and Ed Harris, it was loosely based on the events in Texas. Residents of a Texas Gulf town accuse the newly arrived Vietnamese of invading their traditional fishing grounds. Harris plays the character of Shang, an angry, hard-drinking man who is afraid he won't be able to maintain the payments on his boat. He is having an affair with a local woman (Madigan) whose father (Donald Moffat) rents the boats to the Vietnamese. As in real life, the Klan gets involved, hoping to instigate violence against the Vietnamese.

From a musical perspective, "Galveston Bay" has been criticized as being barely there, so minimal is the melody, so imperceptible the instrumentation. To historian Jim Cullen, though, it is "less a song or even a poem than it is a sparse, vivid short story—one with a clearly etched setting, memorable characters, and an unpredictable plot that climaxes near the end of the song."

The Rising
(Columbia, 2002)

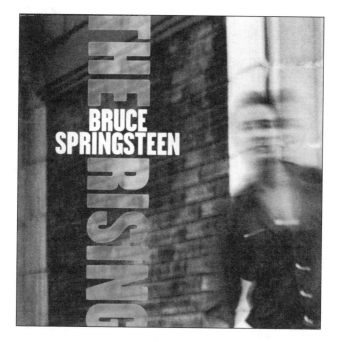

*T*he *Rising* is the first full album Springsteen made with the E Street Band since *Born In The U.S.A.* in 1984 as well as the first Springsteen recording ever produced by an outsider, in this case, Brendan O'Brien, producer of such bands as Pearl Jam and Rage Against the Machine. Springsteen completed the album in a speedy seven and a half weeks. Springsteen's response to September 11, the entire album can be interpreted as a thoughtful meditation on life and death, sin and redemption, grace and mercy, and the presence or absence of God.

Musicians:

Bruce Springsteen: lead guitar, vocals, acoustic guitar, baritone guitar, harmonica

Roy Bittan: keyboards, piano, mellotron, kurzweil, pump organ, korg M1, crumar

Clarence Clemons: saxophone, background vocals

Danny Federici: B3 organ, vox continental, farfisa

Nils Lofgren: electric guitar, dobor, slide guitar, banjo, background vocals

Patti Scialfa: vocals

Garry Tallent: bass

Steven Van Zandt: electric guitar, background vocals, mandolin

Max Weinberg: drums

Additional musicians:

Soozie Tyrell: violin, background vocals

Brendan O'Brien: hurdy gurdy, glockenspiel, orchestra bells

Larry Lemaster: cello

Jere Flint: cello

Jane Scarpantoni: cello

Mark Prender: trumpet

Mike Spengler: trumpet

Rich Rosenberg: trombone

Jerry Vivino: tenor saxophone

Ed Manion: baritone saxophone

Nashville String Machine: Carl Gorodetzky (contractor/concert master); Pam Sixfin; Lee Larrison; Conni Ellisor; Alan Umstead; Dave Davidson; Mary Kathryn Vanosdale; David Angell (Violins); Kris Wilkinson; Gary Vanosdale; Jim Grosjean; Monisa Angell (Viola); Bob Mason; Carol Rabinowitz; Julie Tanner; Lynn Peithman (Celli); Ricky Keller

Asif Ali Khan Group: Asif Ali Khan (lead singer); Manzoor Hussain Shibli; Sarfraz Hussain; Raza Hussain; Imtiaz Shibli; Shahnawaz Hussain Khan; Bakhat Fayyaz Hussain; Omerdraz Hussain Aftab; Karamat Ali Asad (harmonium player); Haji Nazir Afridi (tabla player); Waheed Hussain Mumtaz

Alliance Singers: Corinda Carford (also contractor); Tiffeny Andrews; Michelle Moore (choir solo); Antionette Moore; Antonio Lawrence; Jesse Moorer

Producer: Brendan O'Brien

Recorded at: Southern Tracks Recording (Atlanta)

Tracks:
"Lonesome Day" (4:05)
"Into The Fire" (5:01)
"Waitin' On A Sunny Day" (4:16)
"Nothing Man" (4:20)
"Countin' On A Miracle" (4:40)
"Empty Sky" (3:32)
"Worlds Apart" (6:02)
"Let's Be Friends (Skin To Skin)" (4:18)
"Further On (Up the Road)" (3:50)
"The Fuse" (5:36)
"Mary's Place" (5:59)
"You're Missing" (5:07)
"The Rising" (4:47)
"Paradise" (5:34)
"My City Of Ruins" (5:00)

Running time: 69:67

"Into The Fire"
from *The Rising*
(Columbia, 2002)

> *God is our refuge and our strength*
> *in straits a present aid:*
> *Therefore, although the earth remove,*
> *we will not be afraid.*

—Psalm 46

Springsteen had planned to write "Into The Fire" for the national *America: A Tribute to Heroes* telethon that ran after the September 11 attacks, but he didn't finish it in time so he performed "My City Of Ruins" instead, a song he had written a year earlier about Asbury Park.

But remnants of the song lingered with him. In particular, he couldn't let go of the image of firefighters and emergency workers climbing higher and higher up the stairs of the crumbling World Trade Center as terrified people rushed *down* the stairs to safety and solid ground. He was impressed by the workers' sense of duty. Many of them, of course, would make the ultimate sacrifice in their quest to help others. The religious notion of ascension comes into play too. But ascending into what? A higher level? The afterlife? Crossing the line from this world to the next is a crucial theme of the song.

Like many people in the days after September 11, Springsteen also read the obituaries that ran in the *New York Times*. "I found those to be very, very meaningful—incredibly powerful," he told *Time* magazine, and he couldn't help but notice how many times that the obituaries mentioned that "Thunder Road" or "Born In The U.S.A." were played at the memorial services. He needed to flesh out the details of the song with small narrative threads. So he did his customary research and talked to people directly affected by the terror attacks, including the spouses of firefighters. Their stories became the foundation for "Into The Fire," as well as "The Rising."

"Into The Fire" has the simplicity of a hymn. Springsteen has described the song as folk-blues with a gospel chorus. The chorus doubles as a prayer. As he told *Rolling Stone's* Mark Binelli, "…the first verse is the blues…country blues. I'm doubling my voice around a 12-string guitar, so when you hear the beginning…, you hear a spirit out of the past. Mandolins. Appalachian fiddles."

The verses describe the terror of the aftermath of the attacks—the sky streaked with blood, the darkness of a "smoky grave," but there is also a yearning human connection. Springsteen seeks to transcend hatred and replace it with something more permanent and universal.

What is perhaps most significant about the song, though, is how other people react to it and are affected by it. On the morning of the first anniversary of the September 11 attacks, Freehold's town historian Kevin Coyne attended an interfaith service at one of the local Protestant churches. The service was, as expected, solemn and respectful. The names of county residents who died that terrible day were called out. And then the chorus started to sing, without any commentary or introduction, a few lines from a song:

May your strength give us strength
May your faith give us faith
May your hope give us hope...

After the reading of Psalm 46, they sung the same few lines, "as if," recalls Coyne, "it were a psalm itself, a refrain that everyone everywhere is saying today, a prayer that dates back centuries rather than the chorus of a song that was released barely a month ago, Bruce Springsteen's 'Into The Fire.' Springsteen's name is never mentioned; his words are simply absorbed into the fabric of the day."

During the length of the song, Springsteen sings the prayer litany a total of nine times and ends with a single, hopeful line, "May your love bring us love."

"Empty Sky"
from *The Rising*
(Columbia, 2002)

It is no surprise that an important memorial to the September 11 attacks bear the name of a Springsteen song that offers a choice between good and evil.

In July 2004, "Empty Sky," a memorial by Frederic Schwartz, won the competition for New Jersey's September 11 memorial. As of this writing, it is supposed to be built directly across the Hudson River from ground zero at Liberty State Park in Jersey City. A unanimous choice, the Schwartz submission was selected from 320 proposals and represents the families of the more than 700 New Jersey victims of the terror attacks. "Empty Sky" consists of two walls of stainless steel with the names of each victim engraved on them. Each wall will be 30 feet high and 200 feet long. At the base of each wall will be a space for visitors to leave personal memorials to, and remembrances for, the dead.

"I look up from my desk out my window. It was filled with the World Trade Center, and now the sky is empty," said Schwartz, eerily echoing a line from "Empty Sky."

Frederic Schwartz Architects is also designing the Westchester County September 11 memorial, called "The Rising," at Kensico Dam Plaza, in Valhalla, an 80-foot hight stainless steel sculpture of 109 intertwining steel rods reaching skyward and honoring the 109 Westchester residents who died in the attacks.

"Empty Sky" was the last song Springsteen wrote for *The Rising*. The inspiration came from a photograph of a cloudless sky that his art director had sent him, and from that simple image Springsteen wrote in a matter of days one of the best songs on the album. With its understated melody and subtle elegance, "Empty Sky" is both graceful and heartbreaking. It also contains some of Springsteen's finest lyrics ("On the plains of Jordan, I cut my bow from the wood / Of this tree of evil, of this tree of good"), words that evoke the mysticism of a religious hymn, as well as the ordinary sense of loss that comes with losing someone close to you. Some words, though, were misconstrued. At the March 7, 2003, Atlantic City show during the *Rising* tour, Springsteen felt compelled to comment about the meaning of the song. Contrary to public conception, he said, "Empty Sky" was never intended to be "a call for blind revenge or bloodlust" (some people in the audience cheered, for example, when he sang, "I want an eye for an eye") rather he wrote the song, he said, as "an expression of the character's anger, and confusion, and grief."

"Worlds Apart"
from *The Rising*
(Columbia, 2002)

"I wanted other voices, other situations than just American ones. The eleventh was ultimately an international tragedy. I wanted Eastern voices, the presence of Allah," writes Springsteen in *Songs* about "Worlds Apart." And in an interview with Adam Sweeting in *Uncut* magazine, he discusses its origin. "I think," he says, "the song started when I saw a picture of the women in Afghanistan with the veils off a few days after they'd routed the Taliban out of Kabul, and their faces were so beautiful."

Musically, "Worlds Apart" doesn't sound like anything that Springsteen ever recorded before, more Peter Gabriel perhaps than classic Springsteen. The otherworldly chorus, sung by the Pakistani qawwali singer Asif Ali Khan (and which gives me goose bumps every time I hear it), counteracted the electric guitars and drums, also reflecting the musical gulf that exists among cultures (qawwali is the vocal music of the Sufi sect of Islam).

But the troubled lovers in "Worlds Apart"—one American, one Muslim— are separated by more than just a cultural divide. Geographical distance and a brutal war also separate them. The American may hold his lover in his arms, may "seek faith" as something as simple as a kiss, but when he looks into her eyes, they still remain worlds apart.

And yet, and yet…Springsteen, the cautious optimist, still yearns, more so than ever perhaps, to make a human connection. The song is a sincere and heartfelt wish to "let blood build a bridge" because what do we have to loose, he seems to be asking. The only other choice we have is more bloodshed. Ultimately, "Worlds Apart" is a tribute to the living, a call to (peaceful) arms, to those who refuse to surrender to their darker impulses. In that sense, it is a typical Springsteen song, but tempered with restraint, and boasting a gorgeous melody. A sense of urgency can be heard in his voice, as if time is running out not only for his lovers but for the rest of us.

After all is said and done, Springsteen is saying, all we really have left is the moment, "then it's all just dark and dust." It is best to make the most of it.

"You're Missing"
from *The Rising*
(Columbia, 2002)

One of the most frightening words in the English language is vanish. What do you do when someone disappears without saying goodbye?

A mournful cello opens "You're Missing," the perfect accompaniment for such a soulful lament. It is also lovely and touching and heartbreakingly sad and, oh, so delicate like the lives it honors. But more than anything, it is a song about absence.

In the days after the September 11 attack, New Yorkers hung posters of the missing all over town, as if to say, "You may not have known these people, but they did live, they were here, and their lives are worth remembering." The snapshots pasted onto city walls acted as testimonials, secular holy cards, to the memory of lives that should not be forgotten.

Similarly in "You're Missing," Springsteen catalogues the ordinary things that make up a life, mostly in the form of mundane household items: Shirts in the closet, coffee cups on the counter, jackets hanging over a chair, newspapers on the doorstep, pictures on the nightstand—all are associated with someone, and that someone is no longer there. It is the details that give the song, that give a life, meaning.

"Loss is about what you miss," Springsteen told *Time* magazine. "You miss a person's physical being—their skin, their hair, the way they smell, the way they make you feel. You miss their body. When my father died, my children wanted to touch him, to touch his body. And the kids got something out of it. The people in this situation, you know, they aren't going to get that."

Evening follows morning. Life may go on for most of us, but for many others, life will never be the same and no amount of comfort or well wishes can soothe a broken heart or console the inconsolable.

Evoking the anthrax scare of late 2001, Springsteen ends the song on a chilling note ("God's drifting in heaven, devil's in the mailbox"). The anguish, the uncertainty, continues.

"The Rising"
from *The Rising*
(Columbia, 2002)

The communities most deeply affected by the New York September 11 attacks were working-class neighborhoods; many of the victims were police officers and firefighters. Monmouth County, deep in the heart of Springsteen country, lost 158 people when the Twin Towers collapsed...more than any other county in New Jersey. And a goodly portion of the victims were Springsteen fans; in fact, their families played Springsteen songs at funeral services.

And so it makes perfectly good sense that "The Rising," the rousing title cut from the album of the same name, is written from the point of view of a New York City firefighter—Springsteen considers "The Rising" a bookend to "Into The Fire," the other firefighter song on *The Rising*—as he enters one of the Twin Towers, now engulfed in flames ("Can't see nothin' in front of me / Can't see nothin' coming up behind").

To flesh out the details of the story, to capture the essence of the narrative that he wanted to share, Springsteen interviewed survivors of the emergency workers who perished on that day, not to exploit their grief but to tell the stories of people who otherwise might have been forgotten and, ultimately, to immortalize them in song.

As the firefighter ascends a smoke-filled stairwell, he becomes disoriented, losing track of time—he doesn't know how far he's climbed nor does he how long he has been in the building. In fact, for him at least, time stands still. Eventually the song turns deeply spiritual as the religious image of ascension and the hope of an afterlife becomes a celebratory affirmation of life itself. Indeed, the song's bridge is a musical meditation on mortality. In the last verse, the firefighter speaks to his wife or is she, perhaps, a religious vision ("I see Mary in the garden")? She is surrounded by pictures of their children. Is the firefighter talking directly to God as he anticipates his demise? (more than a few think so) or is he talking to his wife in the afterlife? (as others have also suggested). Is "the rising" of the title, in fact, another word for the resurrection? Springsteen leaves it open to interpretation. Whatever its source, the firefighter carries the image with him before his own untimely death. He yearns to sustain some kind of physical intimacy as long as humanly possible, if only in his mind's eye.

And then Springsteen turns a song, ostensibly about destruction, into a triumphant avowal of renewal, repeating the mantra, "a dream of life." The firefighter is aware of what has been lost (the deaths of nearly 3,000 people) and what is about to be lost (his own life). And yet there is still hope. Springsteen has called "The Rising" his version, albeit a secular one, of the Stations of the Cross, with the firefighter portraying a latter-day Jesus.

"The Rising" affected many people in many ways and people reacted to it in many, sometimes rather surprising ways. In Asbury Park, a condominium waterfront project initially referred to a new planned development as "The Rising" until Springsteen, in a letter to the local *TriCity News*, requested that the name be dropped. "First," he wrote, "'The Rising' was written in the shadow of September 11th and should remain connected to the heartbreak and courage of that day....I respectfully ask the city fathers and developers to place both my and my song's names out of the running for any new buildings, streets, hot dog stands (well, maybe hot dog stands) as the city moves toward its exciting future." (Clearly, he retained a proper perspective, as well as a sense of humor, about it). Of course, the developer agreed to change it.

Others responded with their own artistic interpretations. Choreographer Bob Boross presented "empty sky...*The Rising*," a dance theater performance piece set to 11 songs from *The Rising*.

"The Rising" also happens to be a great rock song with a terrific and instantly memorable melody, and like any rock song worth its salt, it gets the blood pumping; in a concert setting, the crowd chants along. The song—indeed, the album—may be about horror and grief and rage, but it is also about resilience and redemption and salvation. "The Rising" is, in a word, cathartic; it is a salve to tortured souls in a troubled world.

"Paradise"
from *The Rising*
(Columbia, 2002)

The most beautiful song—fragile, delicate, and elusive—on *The Rising* is also the most haunting: two people from different worlds, with entirely different experiences, share a common bond. Beautifully written, the lyrics pack all the necessary information in a few lines. In the first verse, a young Palestinian suicide bomber contemplates his last moments on earth. In the second verse, a Navy wife longs for her husband who died in the attack on the Pentagon during the September 11 terrorist attacks. In the last verse, the character exists between worlds, confronting lost love, but even in the afterlife, there is little solace. The wife can see no peace in his eyes ("they're as empty as paradise"). And yet, in the real world, life goes on.

Springsteen wrote the verse involving the suicide bomber after reading a newspaper account about a teenage girl who blew herself up in Jerusalem in 2002, killing herself and several others. "I was looking for something kind of quiet," says Springsteen about the writing of "Paradise," "and I think it was the week there'd been the teenage girl suicide bombers. It was devastating, so the first verse came out of thinking about that, the loss of life and the false paradise."

The Virginia widow in the song was also loosely inspired by a real person. "Then I'd met a woman who had lost her husband at the Pentagon," says Springsteen, "and she came to Asbury one night, and they were just long time fans I guess. I think I was thinking of the woman when I wrote the song...I thought, 'What do you miss?' You miss the physicalness and the ability to touch somebody."

He calls the last verse a "survivor's verse."

"...I imagined someone who had been left," Springsteen told *USA Today*. "The person goes into the river and goes under—and comes back up. It's like saying, 'We're still here, and this is the only life we have.'"

"My City Of Ruins"
from *The Rising*
(Columbia, 2002)

After the terror attacks on September 11, Springsteen sang a new song about Asbury Park called "My City Of Ruins" and performed live for the first time at the *America: A Tribute To Heroes* telethon on September 21, 2001. Although Springsteen has called it "a sort of prayer," "My City Of Ruins" is open-ended enough to speak to other cities and apply to other equally dire circumstances, whether a stubborn poverty or war-time destruction.

Nearly 150 people from Springsteen's own Monmouth County died in the attacks. "People knew people. In the surrounding communities there were quite a few people affected. You knew this woman and her husband, someone else's son, someone else's brother.

"In the coming weeks, if you were driving towards the beach or something, if you drove to the Catholic church there was a funeral every day," Springsteen says. "Then people got together and there were some shows done and benefits and candlelight vigils and a wide variety of ways that people were trying to sort through what happened. I don't know what it was like in the middle of the country or on the West Coast, but here it was very real."

In ways both profound and superficial, the ruins of Asbury Park reflected the psychological state of the nation.

Ruins of the Casinos, Asbury Park, NJ. (June Sawyers)

A gorgeous piece of white gospel, "My City Of Ruins" has much in common with Curtis Mayfield's civil rights anthem "People Get Ready," both in its stately pace and melody, as well as in its elegant arrangement. It also contains a great lyric, evoking the despair of a place where there is little hope. The rain is falling down, the church doors are left open but the congregation is gone while young men stand on street corners "like scattered leaves," surrounded by boarded-up windows and empty streets. It could, in fact, be anyplace in urban America.

Here, Springsteen plays the role of Everyman, the nation's town crier. A city is destroyed by abject poverty and benign neglect, but Springsteen not only reports the situation, he does much more than this—he exhorts the crowd to actually do something about it. With a powerful refrain of "Rise up!," delivered with all the fervor of a latter-day preacher (albeit a secular rock 'n' roll one), Springsteen demands action. The notion of social justice—I am my brother's keeper—is a fundamental part of Catholicism and, as a lapsed Catholic with a strong social conscience, this aspect of his cradle faith would surely have appealed to him. But he is also realistic. Springsteen doesn't promise to take away the pain—no one can do that—but he does remind us that we are not alone in our suffering.

Convention hall, Asbury Park, NJ. (June Sawyers)

The chorus on "My City Of Ruins" serves as a prayer ("May your strength give us strength / May your hope give us hope…"), and, accompanied by the warmth of Danny Federici's organ, Springsteen sings with an increasing sense of urgency, praying for the strength to continue, for the faith to believe again, for the love to sustain him. Ultimately, "My City Of Ruins" is about learning to begin all over again—both in a physical place and in a relationship.

As for the city of Asbury Park, there is talk of renewal once again even though the city, at least portions of it, still looks like a ghost town—no, a war zone may be more accurate, with the scattered debris, crumbling and derelict buildings, unfinished high rises, and boarded-up storefront windows. For Lease and For Sale signs are everywhere.

And yet there is something majestic about the "ruins." The once-elegant Casino, a husk of its former self, stands at the southern end of the boardwalk, graffiti scrawled across its façade and the waters of the Atlantic lapping against its back. Palace Amusements, the old penny arcade affectionately known as Tillie that entertained generations of locals, is now gone.

Stone Pony, Asbury Park, NJ. (June Sawyers)

But Springsteen's presence is both palpable and reassuring. At night, as you drive down Sunset Avenue toward the ocean, the Convention Hall is lit up: GREETINGS FROM ASBURY PARK, it calls out. Springsteen saw his first concert here back in the Sixties when an unlikely combination of The Who, Herman's Hermits, and The Blues Magoos played—unbelievably, an obscure Sixties relic, the Blues Magoos, were the headliners.

Nowadays Asbury Park is being touted as the new gay haven. Many of the old Victorian houses are being gobbled up. A hotel along the shore, the Paradise, caters almost exclusively to this market.

Asbury has something else going for it, though. Unlike most faded resort towns, it is a rock 'n' roll landmark, a destination for rock fans. As of this writing, the Stone Pony, one of the most famous rock venues in the country, is still there, as is Madam Marie, sitting mysteriously on the boardwalk like a gypsy vision.

Will Asbury Park rise from the ruins? Only time will tell.

Devils & Dust
(Columbia, 2005)

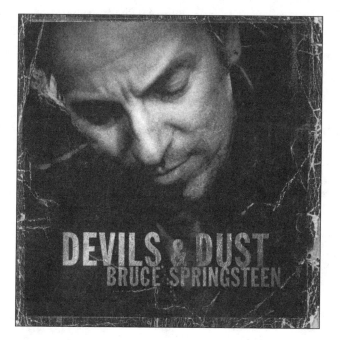

Springsteen wrote much of *Devils & Dust* during the *Tom Joad* tour. It debuted at #1 on the charts. A subdued, mostly acoustic collection of songs, the mood is somber, earnest, and apprehensive with the occasional swagger. The focus here is on telling other peoples stories—a soldier, a boxer, an immigrant, and even Jesus himself.

Musicians:
Bruce Springsteen: vocals, guitar, keyboards, percussion, tambourine, drums
Brendan O'Brien: bass, tambora, sitar, electric sarangi, hurdy gurdy
Steve Jordan: drums
Nashville string Machine: Strings
Susan Welty: horns
Thomas Witte: horns
Chuck Plotkin: piano
Marty Rifkin: steel guitar
Brice Andrus: horns
Donald Strand: horns
Dan Federici: keyboards
Soozie Tyrell: violin, background vocals
Patti Scialfa: background vocals
Lisa Lowell: background vocals
Mark Pender: trumpet

Producers: Brendan O'Brien, Bruce Springsteen, and Chuck Plotkin

Recorded at: Thrill Hill Recording (Los Angeles and New Jersey) and
Southern Tracks Recording (Atlanta)

Tracks:
"Devils & Dust" (4:58)
"All the Way Home" (3:38)
"Reno" (4:08)
"Long Time Comin'" (4:17)
"Black Cowboys" (4:08)
"Maria's Bed" (5:35)
"Silver Palomino" (3:22)
"Jesus Was An Only Son" (2:54)
"Leah" (3:31)
"The Hitter" (5:53)
"All I'm Thinkin' About" (4:22)
"Matamoros Banks" (4:20)

Running time: 48:66

"Devils & Dust"

from *Devils & Dust*
(Columbia, 2005)

Originally intended for the E Street Band, "Devils & Dust" was the last song written for the album. At one point, Springsteen considered turning it into an acoustic ballad, but producer Brendan O'Brien persuaded the singer that his original intention to explore a fuller, more fleshed-out approach using keyboards, bass, drums, strings, and horns in addition to the guitar would work better.

Written from a soldier's point of view and set during the Iraq war, "Devils & Dust" "is about being placed into a situation where your choices are untenable—and the price of that conflict is in blood and spirit," Springsteen told *Rolling Stone's* Brian Hiatt.

"Devils & Dust" forms the centerpiece of the album and its moral core. Springsteen asks, "What if what you do to survive kills the things you love?" The rest of the songs on the album pivot on that crucial question.

The soldier is doing his best to survive in a world of grave moral uncertainty and gross ambiguities. What is right? What is wrong? And how can one tell the difference? He is far away from home, both geographically and philosophically, and he doesn't know whom to trust. Initially, he believes he has God on his side—doesn't everyone?—but the terrible things that he witnesses and an all-encompassing fear threaten to consume him and turn a heart that was once good into a twitchy, black hole until faith "just ain't enough."

He dreams of a lost comrade dying in a field of dried blood and hard stone, and although he still wants to take a righteous stand—in this place, at this time, in this desert wilderness—he must rely instead on the trigger of a gun for protection rather than the "God-filled soul" that once claimed his heart. Springsteen sings with great conviction and a quiet fervor.

"Jesus Was An Only Son"
from *Devils & Dust*
(Columbia, 2005)

"My Father, if it is possible, let this cup pass from me; yet not what I want but what you want."

—Matthew 36:39

"I was raised Catholic so Jesus was my de facto homeboy."

—Bruce Springsteen, *Devils & Dust* tour, 2005

On the 2005 *Devils & Dust* tour, Springsteen prefaced "Jesus Was An Only Son" by referring to "the poetry, the mystery, and the terror" of religion. As a lapsed Catholic, Springsteen brings to Catholicism conflicting emotions: moved, on the one hand, by its transcendence as well as its pageantry, while on the other hand, repulsed by its authoritarianism and its emphasis on rules and dogma.

Leave it to Springsteen then to emphasize the simpler side of the story that resides within the heart of the divine. If one were to strip the story of Christ's Passion to its most fundamental elements, it concerns a son trying to console his mother about the choices he has made. Of course, things are a bit more complicated because the son here is Jesus and the mother is Mary, but Springsteen views it from a parent-child perspective. "[S]he was just losing her boy," he says.

"I was thinking of Jesus as someone's son and Mary as the mother. A funny thing happens, I think, when we turn things into icons: We sort of blow them up and diminish them, and at the same time, we forget the human side—that there was an actual life there all the time."

In "Jesus Was An Only Son," Springsteen reflects on what might have been if Jesus married and had lived long enough to have a family ("He prayed for the life he'd never live"). The lyrics are direct, the melody dignified, almost hymn-like in its stateliness. Jesus walks up Calvary Hill, with his mother Mary beside him, as his blood spills onto the ancient streets. Throughout the pain and suffering, his mother promises to stay by his side. In the garden at Gethsemane, a fearful Jesus prays for the strength to endure what he knows he must; he gradually accepts his fate.

In the powerful final verse, Jesus kisses his mother's hands and tries to comfort her with a particularly concise yet potent piece of writing, "For remember the soul of the universe willed a world and it appeared."

"Our choices gain their value by the things that we sacrifice," says Springsteen. "You choose something and you give up other things—that's what gives our choices value and meaning."

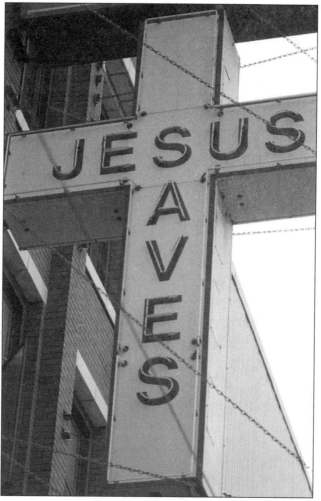

Jesus saves. (Theresa Albini)

"Matamoros Banks"
from *Devils & Dust*
(Columbia, 2005)

"Matamoros Banks" is a sequel to *The Ghost Of Tom Joad's* "Across the Border." In "Across The Border" a Mexican immigrant dreams of crossing the border, but he never quite makes it over; in "Matamoros Banks" Springsteen follows the same character as his ongoing search for a better life ends in tragedy.

Matamoros is a city in northeastern Mexico located near the mouth of the Rio Grande and directly across the river from Brownsville, Texas. In "Matamoros Banks," Springsteen plays with time, following the immigrant's journey in reverse. In the first verse, we learn the character's fate: He dies trying to cross the Rio Grande. After two days, his lifeless body rises to the surface of the river and floats past playgrounds and empty switching yards.

But in subsequent verses, we see him beginning his journey, as he walks in sandals made of twine across dry riverbeds under a pale moon. He dreams of his love across the river, and it is this love that sustains him. He can see the lights of Brownsville and, in the lovely chorus, he sweetly asks her to meet him on the Matamoros banks. Before his death, he graciously thanks God for her love.

The ghostly "Matamoros Banks" was written in the mid-Nineties shortly after Springsteen composed what could easily be called the Border Suite on *The Ghost Of Tom Joad*—four songs with a California/Mexican theme ("Sinaloa Cowboys," "The Line," "Balboa Park," and "Across The Border").

During the *Devils & Dust* tour, Springsteen made clear his low opinion about the American immigration policy, "[E]very year, hundreds of people die trying to get into the United States. They die in the rivers, they die in the mountains, crossing the deserts, and they die in the back of vans and trailers. Instead of vigilantes down along the border, we need a president with the guts to come up with a humane immigration policy."

Despite some particularly nightmarish images—specifically, turtles eating away the skin from the dead immigrant's eyes—"Matamoros Banks" is not all bleakness. It does suggest the promise of a better life, if not on this earth then somewhere else. Even in death, the narrator tries to preserve the values he cherishes and the people he adores. In Springsteen's universe, sometimes endless sorrow can turn into eternal hope.

WE SHALL OVERCOME: THE SEEGER SESSIONS
(Columbia)

Pete Seeger never sounded like this.

Springsteen's first fully fledged album of covers, *We Shall Overcome: The Seeger Sessions* is a rousing, joyous reinterpretation of classic American balladry associated with the legendary folk singer Pete Seeger—anti-war songs, Negro spirituals, work ballads, hymns, protest songs, and even a children's song with roots that date back to 1549 Scotland. Every cut on the CD was recorded live in the living room of Springsteen's New Jersey farmhouse in three one-day sessions with no rehearsals.

In the liner notes, Springsteen refers to the songs as "street corner music, parlor music, tavern music, wilderness music, circus music, church music, guitar music....It was a way back and forward to the informality, the freeness and the eclecticism of my earliest music and then some." In other words, Springsteen—who, after all, was originally labeled as a folkie—has come full circle. "He always was a folk singer," says Peter Yarrow of Peter, Paul, and Mary. "He always had it in his heart." But anyone who knows Springsteen's music really shouldn't be surprised at this turn in direction. Think about the eclecticism on *The Wild, the Innocent & the E Street Shuffle* (especially the genre-defying "Wild Billy's Circus Story") and his long-held admiration for traditional music. In that context, Springsteen's Seeger turn is not so surprising. The reviews were uniformly excellent. *The Seeger Sessions* were called "rambunctious," "unexpected, and liberating," and "jubilant." It reached #3 on the pop charts.

Musicians:

Bruce Springsteen: guitar, mandolin, B3 organ, piano, percussion, harmonica, tambourine, lead and backing vocals
Sam Bardfield: violin, backing vocals
Art Baron: tuba
Frank Bruno: guitar, backing vocals
Jeremy Chatzky: upright bass (bowed), backing vocals
Mark Clifford: banjo, backing vocals
Larry Eagle: drums and percussion, backing vocals
Charles Giordano: B3 organ, accordion, piano, pump organ
Lisa Lowell: backing vocals

Ed Manion: saxophone, backing vocals
Mark Pender: trumpet, backing vocals
Richie "La Bamba" Rosenberg: trombone, backing vocals
Patti Scialfa: backing vocals
Soozie Tyrell: violin, backing vocals

Producer: Bruce Springsteen

Recorded at Thrill Hill, Boxwood Studios (New Jersey)

Tracks:
Old Dan Tucker (2:31)
Jesse James (3:47)
Mrs. McGrath (4:19)
O Mary Don't You Weep (6:05)
John Henry (5:07)
Erie Canal (4:03)
Jacob's Ladder (4:28)
My Oklahoma Home (6:03)
Eyes on the Prize (5:16)
Shenandoah (4:52)
Pay Me My Money Down (4:32)
We Shall Overcome (4:53)
Froggie Went A Courtin' (4:33)

Running time: 58:29

Bonus tracks: (only available on DualDisc format)
Buffalo Gals
How Can I Keep from Singing

An expanded version of *We Shall Overcome* was released in late 2006. This *American Land Edition* included "American Land," studion versions of "How Can A Poor Man Stand Such Times And Live?" and "Bring 'Em Home (If You Love Your Uncle Sam)."

Going Round in Circles

"Ah, my God, what is this land of America?
So many people traveling there"
> —"He Lies In The American Land," Andrew Kovaly, circa 1900

"What is this land of America?
So many travel there, I'm goin' now while I'm still young"
> —"American Land," Bruce Springsteen, 2006

From Robert Burns to Woody Guthrie to Pete Seeger to Bob Dylan, artists have been adapting folk melodies and refashioning lyrics to reflect the times they live in for centuries. It's a common and hallowed custom within the folk tradition. To cite just one example, Guthrie wrote the lyrics to "Pittsburgh Town" (which Seeger covered in 1957), and set the melody to the old Scots song "Froggie Went A' Courtin.'" Dylan especially was a master at using older material as the blueprint for his own songs ("A Hard Rain's A-Gonna Fall" a reworking of the Child ballad "Lord Randal"; "Lord Franklin's Dream" led to "Bob Dylan's Dream"; "I Dreamed I Saw Joe Hill" spawned "I Dreamed I Saw St. Augustine"; Robert Burns' "My Heart's in the Highlands" is transformed into the mesmerizing sweep of the $16\frac{1}{2}$ minute "Highlands"), an act of musical thievery that historian Sean Wilentz calls "as American as apple pie, and cherry, pumpkin, and plum pie, too." The *New Yorker's* music critic Alex Ross refers to it as "the magpie mode of writing," which means taking a line or stanza from an older song and adding a verse or stanza of his own. Springsteen did a similar thing, carrying on the vaulted tradition, in *We Shall Overcome: The Seeger Sessions*, especially on the *American Land* expanded version, released six months later.

On June 22, 2006 at New York's Madison Square Garden, during the *We Shall Overcome* tour, Springsteen introduced "American Land," which he called "an immigrant song for New York City." Based on a song that Pete Seeger recorded in 1957, Springsteen's rendition had more of an Irish feel to it (*Backstreets* described its sound as the Pogues meet the Clancy Brothers and Tommy Makem). But it has much deeper roots. Written around 1900 by a Slovak steelworker named Andrew Kovaly, the lyrics were inspired by a tragic incident that occurred at a Bessemer mill in McKeesport, Pennsylvania, 15 miles north of Pittsburgh. A fellow Slovak, who also happened to be a friend and co-worker of Kovaly, had saved enough money to enable his family to come over from Slovakia. While the worker's wife and children were en route to America, the friend was killed while on the job. Kovaly broke the news to his colleague's family when they arrived at the train station. Then he wrote the song that would become "He Lies in the American Land." In 1947, after finishing a concert for the International Worker's Union near Pittsburgh, Seeger met Kovaly, who reportedly sang the song to him. Seeger later translated it into English and set it to music, giving it a subtle but altogether appropriate Eastern European musical cast. It appears on Seeger's *American Industrial Ballads* (Smithsonian Folkways, 1957). Springsteen's version, though, is more universal, almost epic-like in its scope; a survey of American immigration history from Ellis Island to the present day.

On the same tour, Springsteen offered his take on Seeger's anti-Vietnam War era anthem "Bring 'Em Home (If You Love Your Uncle Sam)" when he debuted the song in Paris. By adding several new verses and changing specific words (from Seeger's "It'll make our generals sad" to "It will make the politicians sad"), he brings the song into the present day. But more than this, he connects the song to an older and grander tradition of anti-war sentiments. When Springsteen sings "the church bells will ring with joy...to welcome our darlin' girls and boys," he is quoting almost verbatim from the Civil War era anti-war song "When Johnny Comes Marching Home" by Patrick Gilmore, himself an Irish emigrant ("the old church bells will peal with joy...to welcome home our darling boy") while slyly referring back to *We Shall Overcome*'s "Mrs. McGrath," another Irish anti-war song. Is it any surprise that Springsteen enthusiastically acknowledged the Irish influences on *We Shall Overcome* when performing in Dublin that summer? (Seeger himself updated the lyrics of "Bring 'Em Home" in 2003 to reflect the Iraq War. The alternate version, in which Seeger is accompanied by Billy Bragg, Ani DiFranco, and Steve Earle, appears on *Seeds: The Songs Of Pete Seeger, Vol. III*.)

Another song that Springsteen tinkered with is Blind Alfred Reed's "How Can a Poor Man Stand Such Times and Live?," which was written a month after the stock market crash of 1929. Springsteen first heard the song on Ry Cooder's 1970 debut album. On the *We Shall Overcome* tour he updated the lyrics to include references to Hurricane Katrina and the destruction of New Orleans. Springsteen retained only one verse though (the last one) and rewrote the rest, using graphic imagery to describe the storm's aftermath ("There's bodies floatin' on Canal and the levees gone to Hell"), making pointed commentary on George W. Bush's cavalier attitude ("He took a look around gave a little pep talk...then he took a walk"), acknowledging the dispersal of Katrina evacuees across the country ("from Texas all the way to Baltimore"), and even lifting a line from Woody Guthrie's "I Ain't Got No Home" ("And I ain't got no home in this world no more"). Guthrie wrote the song in 1938 while visiting one of the Dust Bowl era migrant camps as a parody of the Baptist hymn "This World Is Not My Home," made popular by the Carter Family. Guthrie biographer Joe Klein has called the song "a call to arms." With the reinventing of Reed's "Poor Man" nearly 70 years later, Springsteen offered his own attack on the perils of complacency, his own attempt to bear witness.

Just like Harry Smith compiled a democratic mix of widely disparate musical styles in his seminal 1952 *Anthology of American Folk Music*, Springsteen too has—in Smith-like fashion—created his own irresistible hodgepodge. *We Shall Overcome* is a pastiche of American music styles— blues, folk, spirituals, gospel, Cajun, funk, New Orleans R&B, Dixieland, Tex-Mex, swing, a swirl of Irish reels and a wee dash of Scots riddles and nonsense rhymes—with Springsteen in the role of the charismatic ringmaster presiding over a latter-day traveling salvation minstrel show. The narrator of "Wild Billy's Circus Story" has come full circle.

LIVE CONCERTS AND COMPILATIONS

Bruce Springsteen & The E Street Band Live/1975–85
(Columbia)

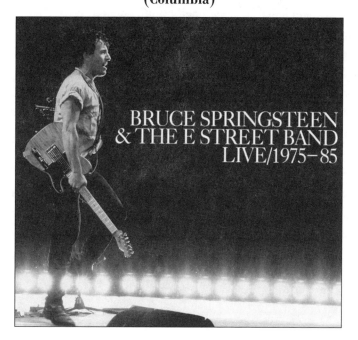

One of the greatest-selling rock albums of the rock era, the live album entered the *Billboard* charts at Number One...a remarkable achievement given its price ($25 at the time for the album, $40 for CD) and length (a five-record set).

Musicians:

Bruce Springsteen: vocals, guitar, harmonica

Roy Bittan: piano, synthesizer, background vocals

Clarence Clemons: saxophone, percussion, background vocals

Danny Federici: organ, accordion, glockenspiel, keyboards, background vocals

Nils Lofgren: guitars, background vocals

Patti Scialfa: synthesizer, background vocals

Steve Van Zandt: guitars, background vocals

Max Weinberg: drums

Additional musicians:

Flo and Eddie (Howard Kaylan and Mark Volman): backing vocals

The Miami Horns (Stan Harrison, tenor saxophone), Eddie Manion (baritone saxophone), Mark Pender (trumpet), Richie "La Bamba" Rosenberg (trombone)

Producers: Bruce Springsteen, Jon Landau, Chuck Plotkin

Tracks:

Disc One

"Thunder Road" (5:46)

   Recorded October 18, 1975 at the Roxy Theatre, Los Angeles

"Adam Raised A Cain" (5:26)

   Recorded July 7, 1978 at the Roxy, Los Angeles

"Spirit In The Night" (6:25)

   Recorded July 7, 1978 at the Roxy, Los Angeles

"4th of July, Asbury Park (Sandy)" (6.34)

   Recorded December 31, 1980 at the Nassau Coliseum, Long Island, New York

"Paradise By The C" (3:54)

   Recorded July 7, 1978 at the Roxy, Los Angeles

"Fire" (2:51)

   Recorded December 16, 1978 at the Winterland, San Francisco

"Growin' Up" (7:58)

   Recorded at July 7, 1978 at the Roxy, Los Angeles

"It's Hard To Be A Saint In The City" (4:39)

   Recorded July 7, 1978 at the Roxy, Los Angeles

"Backstreets" (7:35)

    Recorded July 7, 1978 at the Roxy, Los Angeles

"Rosalita (Come Out Tonight)" (10:08)

    Recorded July 7, 1978 at the Roxy, Los Angeles

"Raise Your Hand" (5:01)

    Recorded July 7, 1978 at the Roxy, Los Angeles

"Hungry Heart" (4:30)

    Recorded December 18, 1980 at the Nassau Coliseum, Long Island, New York

"Two Hearts" (3:06)

    Recorded July 8, 1981 at Brendan Byrne Arena, East Rutherford, New Jersey

Running time: 71.13

Disc Two

"Cadillac Ranch" (4:52)

    Recorded July 6, 1981 at Brendan Byrne Arena, East Rutherford, New Jersey

"You Can Look (But You Better Not Touch)" (3:58)

    Recorded December 29, 1980 at the Nassau Coliseum, Long Island, New York

"Independence Day" (5:08)

    Recorded July 6, 1981 at Brendan Byrne Arena, East Rutherford, New Jersey

"Badlands" (5:17)

    Recorded November 5, 1980 at Arizona State University, Phoenix

"Because the Night" (5:19)

    Recorded December 28, 1980 at the Nassau Coliseum, Long Island, New York

"Candy's Room" (3:19)

    Recorded July 8, 1981 at Brendan Byrne Arena, East Rutherford, New Jersey

"Darkness on the Edge of Town" (4:19)

    Recorded December 29, 1980 at the Nassau Coliseum, Long Island, New York

"Racing In The Street" (8:12)

    Recorded July 6, 1981 at Brendan Byrne Arena, East Rutherford, New Jersey

"This Land Is Your Land" (4:21)
> Recorded December 28, 1980 at the Nassau Coliseum, Long Island, New York

"Nebraska" (4:18)
> Recorded August 6, 1984 at Brendan Byrne Arena, East Rutherford, New Jersey

"Johnny 99" (4:24)
> Recorded August 18, 1985 at Giants Stadium, East Rutherford, New Jersey

"Reason to Believe" (5:19)
> Recorded August 18, 1984 at Brendan Byrne Arena, East Rutherford, New Jersey

"Born in the U.S.A." (6:10)
> Recorded September 30, 1985 at the Los Angeles Coliseum

"Seeds" (5:14)
> Recorded September 30, 1985 at the Los Angeles Coliseum

Running time: 68.10

Disc Three

"The River" (11:42)
> Recorded September 30, 1985 at the Los Angeles Coliseum

"War" (4:53)
> Recorded September 30, 1985 at the Los Angeles Coliseum

"Darlington County" (5:12)
> Recorded September 30, 1985 at the Los Angeles Coliseum

"Working on the Highway" (4:04)
> Recorded August 19, 1985 at Giants Stadium, East Rutherford, New Jersey

"The Promised Land" (5:36)
> Recorded September 30, 1985 at the Los Angeles Coliseum

"Cover Me" (6:57)
> Recorded September 30, 1985 at the Los Angeles Coliseum

"I'm on Fire" (4:26)
> Recorded August 19, 1984 at Brendan Byrne Arena, East Rutherford, New Jersey

"Bobby Jean" (4:30)
> Recorded August 21, 1984 at Brendan Byrne Arena, East Rutherford, New Jersey

"My Hometown" (5:13)

> Recorded September 30, 1985 at the Los Angeles Coliseum

"Born to Run" (5:03)

> Recorded August 19, 1985 at Giants Stadium, East Rutherford, New Jersey

"No Surrender" (4:41)

> Recorded August 6, 1984 at Brendan Byrne Arena, East Rutherford, New Jersey

"Tenth Avenue Freeze-Out" (4:21)

> Recorded August 20, 1984 at Brendan Byrne Arena, East Rutherford, New Jersey

"Jersey Girl" (6:30)

> Recorded July 9, 1981 at Brendan Byrne Arena, East Rutherford, New Jersey

Running time: 70:68

"Seeds"

from *Bruce Springsteen & The E Street Band Live/1975–85*
(Columbia, 1986)

Unable to find a job in his hometown, an angry unemployed oil worker moves his wife and children to Houston. They head down south from the industrial north with "just spit and a song," hoping for a better life. But the promise of work doesn't materialize. Jobs that were once so plentiful are now hard to come by. "Sorry, son," he is told, "it's gone, gone, gone."

In a modern version of Steinbeck's Okies, the father sees homeless men living by the railroad tracks and tents pitched along the highway. His situation is not much better and getting more desperate by the day. He doesn't know where he and his family will sleep tonight, he sings. So he parks his unheated car in the parking lot of a lumberyard, "freezin' our asses off." His children lie in the backseat, but they have a "graveyard cough"—it is details like this that make the song sing—while he and his wife sleep in the front. In the middle of the night, his troubled sleep is disrupted by the sound of a billy club rattling on the windshield. "Move along man," the officer says, echoing Tom Joad's predicament in *The Grapes Of Wrath*, "move along."

How many times, he wonders, can somebody get up after they've been hit? He cautions his fellow citizens up north to think twice about coming down south. "You're better off," he states ominously, "buyin' a shotgun dead off the rack."

"Seeds" seethes with righteous anger and the fiery clash of the guitars keeps up with Springsteen's own searing vocals, as he effectively captures the hopelessness of the ravaged father in the song. He is so poor that he can't even spare to part with his own spit when a shiny black limousine—the vehicle of choice of Springsteen's businessmen—passes through an oil field.

"Seeds" was recorded live on September 30, 1985, at the Los Angeles Coliseum during the *Born In The U.S.A.* tour. It was written during a time when Springsteen seriously began to explore the ramifications of Reaganomics (of course, he chronicled wasted lives and broken dreams several years earlier in *Nebraska*). Significantly, though, Springsteen performed "Seeds" during the same L.A. concert where he sang a particularly powerful rendition of Barrett Strong and Norman Whitfield's Motown classic "War" (Edwin Starr's version reached Number One in 1970). If the songs were not quite bookends, they did make clear Springsteen's position on war itself and American foreign policy, as well as American domestic policy.

He would continue to probe the rotten underbelly of the American dream in other songs, especially on *The Ghost Of Tom Joad;* but "Seeds" was a harbinger of what was to come.

BEST COVERS *BY* SPRINGSTEEN
"Jersey Girl" — Tom Waits (live)
Springsteen Live

The song Springsteen *should* have written. It has Springsteen's traits all over it—the organ music, the wildly romantic lyrics, even a reference to New Jersey itself. The fact that Tom Waits actually wrote it is one of the mysteries of the universe. It doesn't matter though because Springsteen makes it his own, giving one of his finest vocals in a voice absolutely drenched with deep emotion and utter passion.

"Chimes Of Freedom" — Bob Dylan (live)
Chimes of Freedom

It makes sense that Springsteen would sing one of Dylan's most powerful social protest songs, in which he lists a litany of the misunderstood and marginalized peoples of the world. Like Springsteen's own "Land Of Hope And Dreams," Dylan too is inclusive. The chimes of freedom toll for both the rebel and the rake. Appropriately, Springsteen performed a rousing version of the song with the E Street Band in 1988 on the Amnesty International tour commemorating the fortieth anniversary of the Declaration of Human Rights.

"Trapped!" — Jimmy Cliff (live)
The Essential Bruce Springsteen

While on tour in 1981, Springsteen bought a Jimmy Cliff cassette at the Amsterdam airport which contained a song called "Trapped!" According to Springsteen biographer Dave Marsh, Springsteen introduced the song at a concert in London's Wembley stadium. But he put his own indelible stamp on it, removing the reggae influences and replacing it with a particularly surging brand of rock 'n' roll.

"This Land Is Your Land" — Woody Guthrie (live)
Springsteen Live

From one kindred spirit to another—that is the appeal that Woody Guthrie, the folkie leftist who took America by storm, had on Springsteen, the working-class kid from New Jersey who lived near the wrong side of the tracks. Springsteen performed an unabridged version of the Guthrie classic at the Nassau Coliseum in late December 1980 (this is the version that appears on the album). On stage, he called it as one of the most beautiful songs ever written. Ironically, he left out the most radical verses, choosing, perhaps unintentionally, to emphasize its poetry rather than its politics although he knew, of course, what Guthrie was singing about. He sang it too in other lands, for other people, people who probably had never even heard of Woody Guthrie. "This is an old song about an old dream," he said while in Paris. "It's hard to think what to say about this song, because it's sung a whole lot in the States and it's been misinterpreted a whole lot. It was written as a fighting song and it was written, I feel, as a question everybody has to ask themselves about the world they live in, every day."

Bruce Springsteen Greatest Hits
(Columbia, 1995)

M ost (but not all) of the hits plus a few extras ("Secret Garden," "Murder Incorporated," "Blood Brothers," and "This Hard Land.")

The E Street Band:

Bruce Springsteen

Roy Bittan

Clarence Clemons

Danny Federici

Nils Lofgren

Patti Scialfa

Garry Tallent

Max Weinberg

...and alumni:

Steve Van Zandt

Ernest "Boom" Carter

David Sancious

Tracks:

"Born To Run" (4:30)

"Thunder Road" (4:48)

"Badlands" (4:03)

"The River" (5:00)

"Hungry Heart" (3:20)

"Atlantic City" (3:56)

"Dancing In The Dark" (4:03)

"Born In The U.S.A." (4:41)

"My Hometown" (4:12)

"Glory Days" (3:49)

"Brilliant Disguise" (4:15)

"Human Touch" (5:10)

"Better Days" (3:44)

"Streets Of Philadelphia" (3:16)

"Secret Garden" (4:27)

"Murder Incorporated" (3:57)

"Blood Brothers" (4:34)

"This Hard Land" (4:50)

Running time: 73:15

"Streets Of Philadelphia"
from *Greatest Hits*
(Columbia, 1995)

In 1994, Academy Award-winning director Jonathan Demme asked Bruce Springsteen to write a song for a movie he was directing, called *Philadelphia*. The movie, about a gay man's struggle with AIDS, starred Tom Hanks, Antonio Banderas, and Denzel Washington. Springsteen had already written a partial lyric about the death from sarcoma cancer of a close friend. But Demme wanted a rock song to open the movie and, more important, a song that would appeal to a broader audience.

Working from his home studio in Rumson, New Jersey, Springsteen began experimenting with various sounds, including a synthesizer played "over a hip-hop influenced beat I programmed on the drum machine." After slowing the rhythm down, the lyrics, he said, fell into place. "I finished the song in a few hours and sent the tape off to Jonathan..."

It begins dirge-like, a haunting, atmospheric lament, as a dying man addresses his companion. Essentially, it is a death bed confessional. The somber music reflects the mood: a mournful voice accompanied by a spare, understated arrangement and a drum loop and synthesizer. The syncopated rhythm sounds like an irregular heartbeat.

Springsteen intentionally made the lyrics vague to emphasize its universal themes. "I wanted it to be read a few different ways."

The protagonist is cut off from himself, lonely, and full of despair. Much in the song is left unsaid, much is implicit, but there is no denying the irrefutable sense of isolation that envelops the character. He hears in his head the voices of friends "vanished and gone." Are they also the victims of AIDS? Springsteen leaves it open to interpretation. No one is going to come to his rescue—"no angel gonna greet me"—it is just himself and his lover/companion at his bedside.

"There was a certain spiritual stillness that I wanted to try to capture," Springsteen told the gay magazine *Advocate*. "Then I just tried to send in a human voice, as human a voice as I possibly could. I wanted you to be in somebody's head, hearing their thought—somebody who was on the cusp of death but still experiencing the feeling of being very alive."

After the words end, the song continues for another minute or so, the drumbeat softly fading as the sound of the organ becomes louder, reflecting the end of a life.

In March 1994, Springsteen performed "Streets Of Philadelphia" at the annual benefit for AIDS Project Los Angeles at the Universal Amphitheatre. It was released as a single and cracked the Top 10, Springsteen's first Top 10 since 1987. It also won several Grammy awards as well as an Academy Award for Best Original Song. During his acceptance speech at the Oscar ceremony, Springsteen commented on the purpose and power of art:

> You do your best work and you hope that it pulls out the best in your audience and some piece of it spills over into the real world and into people's everyday lives and it takes the edge off of your fear and allows us to recognize each other through our veil of differences. I always thought that was one of the things popular art was supposed to be about.

"This Hard Land"
from *Greatest Hits*
(Columbia, 1995)

The Texas-Mexico border runs 1,248 miles along the Rio Grande. It is a remote region of canyons, gorges, and cliffs, the kind of terrain that allows for drifting and sleeping under the stars. The Guthrie-esque "This Hard Land," an idealistic and romantic piece from the Springsteen canon, covers this territory.

A solo harmonica sets the pensive mood before the entire band kicks in, with Max Weinberg's muscular drumming giving the song added strength and a solid boost of high-octane energy. Despite the bleakness of the lyrics ("now even the rain it don't come 'round"), the effect of the E Street Band gives the song a defiant, life-affirming edge. One line, in particular, recalls the stubborn determination of "The Promised Land." When Springsteen sings that the howling of the wind "just stirs you up like it wants to blow you down," one gets the impression that, despite the hardships, these characters haven't given up yet.

The characters include the narrator, his sister, and a friend named Frank, lost souls who move from town to town and sleep on the mountainside or in the fields or by the rivers. In the morning, when they wake up, they make their modest plans to "stay hard, stay hungry," but most of all to "stay alive." These are the same types of characters who populate much of *The Ghost Of Tom Joad* and appear in such songs as "Brothers Under The Bridge."

Although Springsteen and E Street Band re-recorded the song in 1995 for *Greatest Hits,* it is the original version on *Tracks* that remains a favorite among fans—Roy Bittan's evocative piano playing, in particular, garners the most praise. It is also reportedly a particular favorite of Max Weinberg and Springsteen himself.

"When people think back on their closest friends, the friends they had when they grew up, those friendships always go hand in hand with the music and all the strong feelings that the music brought, feelings which were even stronger if you shared them with somebody," Springsteen says. "It was an essential part of what rock 'n' roll was about and I really tried to write songs that captured that. 'This Hard Land' was one of those."

"HOMESTEAD"

"But, oh, there was weeping last night at the Homestead!
The river ran red on its way to the sea,
And curses were muttered and bullets whistling,
And Riot was King of the land of the free."
—Anonymous, "A Man Named Carnegie"

"The essence of good songwriting is actually having something to say."
—Joe Grushecky

Co-written by Joe Grushecky, the Pittsburgh-based lead singer of The Houserockers (formerly the Iron City Houserockers), "Homestead" is a tough little number about the bloody battle between big business and unions in Homestead, Pennsylvania, in 1892, a steel town located seven miles east of Pittsburgh on the Monongahela River. It appears on Gruschecky & The Houserocker's *American Babylon* (Razor & Tie, 1995), which Springsteen produced—the first time Springsteen fully produced the work of another artist. He also co-wrote another cut on the album, "Dark And Bloody Ground" and played on most of the other selections. Although Grushecky wrote most of the lyrics to "Homestead," Springsteen supplied most of the music. What's more, he joined Grushecky & The Houserockers for six dates on their East and Midwestern tour dates during the autumn of 1995.

It is not surprising that Springsteen and Grushecky would have so much in common. They are kindred spirits who share a common background (working-class roots based in the East) and a common interest (inequality, oppression, and injustice). By day, Grushecky teaches socially and emotionally disturbed children.

On May 30, 1892, steelworkers rejected a three-year contract offered by Henry Clay Frick, chairman of Carnegie Steel, and went on strike, effectively shutting down the Homestead Works. In all fairness to the workers, the terms in the contract that Frick offered were so unfavorable that he knew it would be dismissed. He had no desire to negotiate. To Frick, the union had a choice—take it or leave it. Unionism would not be tolerated at Carnegie Steel.

Pinkerton detectives, hired by Frick to protect the plant, traveled up the Monongahela on two barges, the "Monongahela" and "Iron Mountain." Rumors had already spread that a Pinkerton arrival was pending. On July 6,

1892, the workers of the Carnegie Steel and Iron and the Pinkertons clashed, using pistols, muskets, rifles, shotguns, and clubs. When it was all over, six workers were killed (John E. Morris, Silas Waine, Thomas Weldon, Henry Striegel, John Pares, and Joseph Soppo) as were two Pinkerton guards (J. W. Kline and Mike Connors). Seventeen workers and as many as two hundred Pinkertons were wounded. Although the Pinkertons surrendered by the end of the day, the union victory was short-lived at best. Six days later, the state militia took over and protected the strikebreakers until November, when the union finally capitulated.

"Homestead" offers a modern perspective on the town. It takes place in 1973 while the Vietnam War is still raging. The narrator, born in the coal fields of Kentucky, moves north to Pennsylvania and finds a job rolling steel in a foundry in Homestead. He works beside a guy named Grzbowski who offers survival tips ("There's many a man who lost the fingers from their hands," he warns. "You could wind up crippled or dead in Homestead"). Springsteen and Grushecky describe the glow of the steel, the fire and smoke of the furnace, and the dust so thick "you could choke."

The narrator is all too aware of the old stories that circulate around the mill, of the twelve-hour shifts and of the Pinkerton detectives who tried to kill the union workers, about Henry C. Frick, president of Carnegie Steel and Iron, and of Andrew Carnegie himself, the Scottish immigrant who once said that for a rich man to die with money on his hands was a disgrace. He hears stories too of the day the Monongahela River "ran red" and how the union "caved in" in Homestead.

But the mill represented more than just a job to the narrator. It became his life, his family. It provided not only his source of income but his badge of identity. He got married, bought a house, and, on late summer nights when the heat became unbearable, he relished the camaraderie of his fellow workers while having a brew in the local bars.

And then the mills were gone. Instead of working in them, the narrator now demolishes them down "until there's nothing left but the sweat and blood in the ground."

And yet Homestead is in his blood. By the last line, he is still living there.

Homestead remains a crucial part of the cultural heritage of the Pittsburgh area. For weeks and months after the battle ended, it made national and international news. Poets commemorated it, others expressed outrage at the treatment of the workers, and at least one journalist excoriated Andrew Carnegie directly with a parody of "The Blue Bells Of Scotland."

In December 2004, Springsteen, Grushecky, and members of the Houserockers performed at Flood Aid '04, a sold-out concert at Pittsburgh's Heinz Hall to benefit the victims of a major flood that devastated areas of western Pennsylvania, including some 10,000 homes. During the *Devils & Dust* tour, Springsteen performed at the Petersen Events Center in Pittsburgh, and it seemed only appropriate that during the encore Springsteen invited Joe Grushecky to join him onstage.

As far as the Homestead Works themselves, all that remain are twelve 100-foot tall smokestacks. In 1986, U.S. Steel closed its Homestead Works. Demolishment of the site began in 1988 and continued until 1992. Five years later, the Park Corp. and Continental Real Estate transformed the original 270-acre site on the banks of the Monongahela River into The Waterfront, a $300 million, mixed-use complex of dining, shopping, and entertainment. Where once stood steel mills are national chains, bookstores, and a movie theater. The only surviving structure of the Battle of Homestead is the Pump House, built in 1891. It houses events sponsored by the nonprofit Battle of Homestead Foundation.

Andrew Carnegie. (Author collection)

Tracks
(Columbia, 1998)

A massive boxed set of 66 selections spanning 25 years, *Tracks* contains previously unreleased material, early demos, B-sides of hit singles, and alternate takes (including "Stolen Car" and "Born In The U.S.A."). Arranged chronologically from 1972 to 1998, it follows the arc of Springsteen's remarkable career, from his early folkie, Dylanesque days (including his solo auditions for legendary Columbia producer John Hammond) to R&B-influenced material to the post-E Street Band era.

Musicians:

Bruce Springsteen: guitar, vocals, harmonica, bass

Danny Federici: organ, glockenspiel, accordion

Garry Tallent: bass

Vini Lopez: drums

David Sancious: piano, organ

Clarence Clemons: saxophone, percussion

Steve Van Zandt: guitar

Roy Bittan: Piano, keyboards

Max Weinberg: drums

Producers: John Hammond, Mike Appel, Jim Cretecos, Jon Landau, Bruce Springsteen, Steve Van Zandt, Chuck Plotkin, and Roy Bittan

Tracks:

Disc One

"Mary Queen Of Arkansas" (4:27)

"It's Hard To Be A Saint In The City" (2:52)

"Growin' Up" (2:38)

"Does This Bus Stop At 82nd Street?" (1:58)

"Bishop Danced" (4:18)

"Santa Ana" (4:35)

"Seaside Bar Song" (3:33)

"Zero and Blind Terry" (5:56)

"Linda Let Me Be The One" (4:24)

"Thundercrack" (8:25)

"Rendezvous" (2:48)

"Give The Girl A Kiss" (3:51)

"Iceman" (3:17)

"Bring On The Night" (2:36)

"So Young And In Love" (3:47)

"Hearts Of Stone" (4:29)

"Don't Look Back" (3:00)

Running time: 62:94

Disc Two

"Restless Nights" (3:44)
"A Good Man Is Hard to Find (Pittsburgh)" (3:15)
"Roulette" (3:51)
"Dollhouse" (3:31)
"Where The Bands Are" (3:43)
"Loose Ends" (4:00)
"Living On The Edge Of The World" (4:17)
"Wages Of Sin" (4:51)
"Take 'Em As They Come" (4:28)
"Be True" (3:39)
"Ricky Wants A Man Of Her Own" (2:44)
"I Wanna Be With You" (3:21)
"Mary Lou" (3:21)
"Stolen Car" (4:26)
"Born In The U.S.A." (3:10)
"Johnny Bye-Bye" (1:49)
"Shut Out The Light" (3:51)

Running time: 55:20

Disc Three

"Cynthia" (4:13)
"My Love Will Not Let You Down" (4:24)
"This Hard Land" (4:46)
"Frankie" (7:22)
"TV Movie" (2:45)
"Stand On It" (3:05)
"Lion's Den" (2:18)
"Car Wash" (2:06)
"Rockaway The Days" (4:40)
"Brothers Under The Bridge ('83)" (5:06)
"Man At The Top" (3:19)
"Pink Cadillac" (3:33)
"Two For The Road" (1:57)
"Janey Don't You Lose Heart" (3:24)
"When You Need Me" (2:54)
"The Wish" (5:14)

"The Honeymooners" (2:04)
"Lucky Man" (3:31)

Running time: 63:61

Disc Four

"Leavin' Train" (4:05)
"Seven Angels" (3:26)
"Gave It A Name" (2:47)
"Sad Eyes" (3:47)
"My Lover Man" (3:56)
"Over The Rise" (2:38)
"When The Lights Go Out" (3:05)
"Loose Change" (4:19)
"Trouble In Paradise" (4:37)
"Happy" (4:51)
"Part Man, Part Monkey" (4:28)
"Goin' Cali" (2:59)
"Back in Your Arms" (4:34)
"Brothers Under The Bridge" (4:55)

Running time: 51:07

"A Good Man Is Hard To Find (Pittsburgh)"
from *Tracks*
(Columbia, 1998)

A *Born In The U.S.A.* outtake, but thematically similar to the songs on *Nebraska,* "A Good Man Is Hard to Find (Pittsburgh)" is a good example of just how deeply Springsteen delves into the psychological state of his characters and how he, in a few minutes and several precisely etched lines, can evoke the history and emotional state of a person. And it surely is no coincidence that he borrows the title from a Flannery O'Connor short story, a writer he was reading at the time.

According to Springsteen scholar Bob Crane, the songwriter based the story on a 1982 account of a Vietnam War widow, living in Pittsburgh, who, after her husband is killed, raises a young child on her own. She, like her dead husband, is yet another victim of the war.

The opening couplet brings two ostensibly different cities of the world together:

It's cloudy out in Pittsburgh
It's rainin' in Saigon

The setting is Christmas, supposedly the happiest time of the year. The young widow sits by the glow of the Christmas tree lights, listening to a radio playing softly in the background and thinking to herself just how difficult it is to find a "good" man. She reminisces about what she once had (Springsteen employs deliberately old-fashioned language here): A "fella," she was "somebody's girl." Now, in the back room their little girl sleeps. The young mother, herself a lost soul, tries to protect her daughter from "the meanness of this world" (lyrical shades of "Nebraska" here).

By her bedside, she keeps a photograph of her wedding portrait—her husband in his dress greens, she in her white wedding gown, memories of a better time. Although she is still a young woman, she has no time for the usual frivolous activities of youth. No more nights on the town or prowling the bars. Besides, she doesn't want those things anymore, Springsteen sings. Her needs are simpler and more fundamental—just somebody to hold her through the night to make her feel safe, that elusive good man.

In the last stanza, she turns off the television set and then wordlessly climbs into bed, thinking about how wasteful war is, and how expendable the people are who fight in it and who pay the ultimate sacrifice. The sense of isolation that the song conveys is almost unbearable.

"There are things that make sense of life for people: their friends, the work they do, your community, your relationship with your partner," Springsteen says. "What if you lose those things, then what are you left with? The political aspect wasn't something that was really on my mind at the time, it was more just people struggling with those particular kinds of emotional or psychological issues."

"Roulette"
from *Tracks*
(Columbia, 1998)

One of Springsteen's first topical songs, "Roulette" was written just days after the partial core meltdown at the Three Mile Island nuclear power plant on March 28, 1979, in Dauphin County, Pennsylvania, ten miles from the state capitol of Harrisburg. It was recorded a few weeks later on April 3. "Roulette" is a powerful tale of paranoia and misplaced trust. Although originally released in 1988 as the B-side of "One Step Up," it was intended to be on *The River* but Springsteen instead chose not to include it, calling it "too specific." Years later, he admitted he might have made a mistake, "I may have gotten afraid—it went a little over the top, which is what's good about it. In truth it should have probably gotten put on. It would have been one of the best things on the record and it was just a mistake at the time..." Springsteen performed "Roulette" during the *Tunnel Of Love* tour. Finally, it was remixed for *Tracks*.

The incident at Three Mile Island started simply and innocently enough. Around 4 a.m. on March 28, a combination of technical malfunctions, human error, and just plain bad luck led to the worst nuclear accident in American history. A pressure valve suddenly malfunctioned. By failing to close, it caused the cooling water to drain from the open valve. The result was overheating. Confronted by contradictory readings, the operators shut off the emergency water system, exacerbating the situation. Within minutes, hundreds of flashing lights accompanied by horns and sirens went off. By early morning, temperatures in the reactor reached a dangerous 4,300 degrees Fahrenheit—on the verge of a meltdown. Then contaminated water leaked into an adjacent building and started to release radioactive gases inside the plant.

Rumors spread quickly. Within hours of the accident, a local radio station reported trouble at the plant. At one point over the next few days, a civil defense alarm was triggered in Harrisburg. Frightened and confused residents didn't know what to believe or who to trust and braced themselves for the worst.

Two days later, on March 30, Gov. Richard Thornburgh issued an advisory evacuation notice:

> Based on advice of the Chairman of the NRC [Nuclear Regulatory Committee], I am advising pregnant women and pre-school age children, to leave the area within a five-mile radius of the Three Mile Island facility until further notice.

More than 140,000 people fled the area, seeking safety wherever they could and leaving behind veritable ghost towns. Some residents, concerned about their possessions, shouted through open car windows, "Watch the town," to those few souls who chose to stay behind. Tensions were so high at one point that the mayor of one of the nearby towns even threatened to shoot looters on sight.

Springsteen captures this uncertainty beautifully. From the opening chords there is a sense of urgency. The music is ominous, nervy, and jumpy; Springsteen's ferocious vocals seethe with a palpable anger and echo the paranoia of the lyrics. He assumes the voice of a firefighter who has no illusions about his status in the world. He realizes he is just a dispensable pawn in a bigger game. The song itself begins in the middle. Something has already happened. The firefighter, his wife, and children suddenly leave their home, taking whatever they can carry with them, packing their belongings into the car. The children's toys lie scattered in the backyard, innocence interrupted. Meanwhile, the firefighter hears rumors but doesn't know what or whom to believe. All he wants are some answers.

Springsteen paints a picture of a world turned upside down. Chaos reigns, the police patrol the streets. In a panic, the firefighter tries to find a safe haven but the state troopers stop him at a roadblock. They place him in detention— "they said they just want to ask me a few questions"—but he escapes and runs, although where to we don't know. In a voice laced with dread, Springsteen sings as if his life depended on it, as if time is running out, which indeed it is. He spits out the entire middle section. He doesn't let up—indeed, he barely takes a breath, words stumbling over each other—and the band keeps up right along with him: Steve Van Zandt and Garry Tallent accompanying Springsteen on slashing guitars, Max Weinberg relentless on unstoppable drums.

After the situation at Three Mile Island eventually calmed down, President Jimmy Carter ordered a full investigation. Over time, the nuclear power industry introduced new and improved safety and training precautions.

Although even today it is difficult to determine how many people ultimately were affected by the accident, it did negatively impact the entire nuclear power industry—the cleanup process alone was slow and expensive. After Three Mile Island, support for nuclear energy fell considerably. And with the threat of terrorism on everyone's mind, support continues to shrink.

"Wages Of Sin"
from *Tracks*
(Columbia, 1998)

> *"For the Wages Of Sin is death..."*
>
> —Romans 6:23

A tense, moody ballad about a lost relationship, "Wages Of Sin" is full of dark imagery and even darker emotions. It is the kind of song, with its haunting, sinewy melody, that lingers in the memory long after you've first heard it. It is also one of Springsteen's bleakest lyrics, a pessimistic portrait of the worst kind of dysfunction.

The couple in the song has long since stopped talking to each other. He wants to talk, she gives him the silent treatment, and the cycle of non-communication is repeated over and over again. It is a passive-aggressive heart play. He thinks she is punishing him for some wrong that was done in the past, but she won't say exactly what it is. Eventually, this back and forth tug of emotional war becomes a ritualized part of their daily routine.

Thematically, the song returns to the sins of the father topic that is so prevalent in much of Springsteen's work. The lyrics are strikingly similar to "My Father's House" on *Nebraska*—both songs were recorded around the same time. The same dream sequence appears in them. The narrator recalls a nightmarish memory from his boyhood, of trying to make it safely home through the forest "before the darkness falls." As in "My Father's House," he runs, his heart pounding, with "the devil snapping at my heels." He is a ball of nerves, keeping all his fears buried deep inside until, unable to control them, they erupt. He knows it's a losing game but he still plays on, pretending that all is well even though he realizes he is only hurting himself and those he loves. If the biblical Wages Of Sin is death, then this man is experiencing a type of living death.

Musically, the song is darkly menacing, somber, funereal, almost dirge-like. The rumbling drums are as unrelentingly oppressive as the heavy air that pervades the household, snuffing out any possibility of light from seeping through. It is a *Nebraska*-era song with a rock sensibility. It is a song that is hard to shake, its melody as hypnotic as anything Springsteen has recorded. You may not like the message it conveys, but it is difficult to turn away.

Springsteen recorded "Wages Of Sin" for *Born In The U.S.A.* but thought it cut too close to the bone for comfort to include.

Wages of sin. (Theresa Albini)

"Shut Out The Light"
from *Tracks*
(Columbia, 1998)

An outtake from the *Born In The U.S.A.* sessions, "Shut Out The Light" is an acoustic song, chilly and moody, built around simple chord changes about the problems of a man returning home from a war (presumably Vietnam) who is trying, not entirely successfully, to live up to expectations. The music is as simple and spare as the tightly written lyrics: folk guitar, harmonica, and Soozie Tyrell's haunting fiddle.

"Shut Out The Light" originally appeared as the flip side of the "Born In The U.S.A." single in 1984, a masterful choice since the character of Johnson Leneir could very well be the *Born In The U.S.A.* vet, ten years down the road. The original version, according to *Backstreets*, featured two additional verses that fleshed out the story considerably and made "an allusion to the main character's possible drug addiction—lying awake until morning in a back bedroom, 'Just him and a few bad habits he brought back from over there.'" Springsteen, though, deleted the reference from the version that appears on *Tracks*, as well as on the single, making the story ostensibly more universal.

In the first few lines of the song, Springsteen depicts the character's lonely desperation. The exposition is deceptively straightforward. Leneir's plane lands on the tarmac. He takes a taxi from the airport to a have a drink at a local Main Street bar where he sits in a corner in the dark, not quite ready to face his own homecoming. Eventually, he gets up the strength and fortitude to return to his wife but spends a restless night staring up at the ceiling. Overcome by an overwhelming sense of dread, he feels paralyzed and is unable to even move his hands.

A banner on his family's front porch is plastered with a cheery message, "Johnny welcome home." He and his friend Bobby polish the chrome of an old Ford. Johnny's mother says she is so happy to have him back home; his father assures him that he can probably get his job back at the factory. Everyone tries to keep up appearances, pretending everything is okay. But Johnny finds it impossible to connect. Nobody asks questions, nobody dares to discuss what he has gone through. Nobody wants to talk about it, least of all Johnny himself. He is lost in limbo. In the chorus, he cries out at night, but it is a dark prayer that offers no relief. He has the shakes and feels he is going to be sick. Images from his past continue to haunt him—he dreams of where he's been—and we conclude that Johnson Leneir will never be quite the same again. Others may have moved on, but for him, the war will never be over.

"Rockaway The Days"
from *Tracks*
(Columbia, 1998)

A story-song with a particularly memorable melody (and a great title to boot), "Rockaway The Days" boasts one of Springsteen's most unaffected and effortless vocals with a throwaway "alright" at the end of most stanzas that lends the song a folksy inflection.

Billy has just been released from prison, but he remains an incorrigible thug. He returns to his home in Maryland where his mother, who lives in a mobile home, takes him back into the fold. At a picnic he meets a woman with the unlikely name of Mary Dove. It's love at first sight. They get married in a typical Springsteen setting—in a valley "where the river flows."

But the peaceful idyll is short-lived. Billy gets into an argument with a young man at a roadside bar and cuts him with a razor. He returns to Mary who, having had enough of his wild ways, offers little sympathy, and when he tries to see his mother, she turns him away. (The theme of parental rejection resonates with Springsteen. He has written about it often, from "Adam Raised A Cain" on *Darkness On The Edge Of Town* to, most recently, in "The Hitter" on *Devils & Dust*.) Desperate, Billy then pounds on a neighbor's door but again to no avail. Stealing a car and packing a gun, he and his wife (they apparently have made up) try to escape down a highway but are pursued by a series of state troopers. The car crashes into a telephone pole. Billy dies, Mary lives. Only in death is he again accepted by his mother—she buries him down by the riverside.

The rich have the power, Springsteen sings, and the poor want a little bit of the money that comes with that clout (he sings about this dynamic again on "Man At The Top.") Billy feels powerless and weak, tired and confused, but, like so many other characters in the Springsteen canon (Ralph from "Johnny 99" comes to mind), he is also his own worst enemy. The only way he can control his destiny is by resorting to violence, but even the thrill of a fight, of physical aggression, is fleeting at best.

"Rockaway The Days" sounds like the basis of a first-rate screenplay or a Raymond Carver short story or, for that matter, a Sam Shepard play. It is yet another example of Springsteen noir—direct, succinct, an underrated precision-cut gem.

"Pink Cadillac"
from *Tracks*
(Columbia, 1998)

> *My love is bigger than a-Cadillac*
> *I try to show it and you drive a-me back.*
>
> —Buddy Holly, "Fade Away"

A song that even Elvis would love. It's also a song that has absolutely no socially redeeming value about it whatsoever. It's just a pure slice of rockabilly heaven—and one of Springsteen's funniest and most sensuous songs to boot. That, in a nutshell, sums up the rowdy charm of "Pink Cadillac."

Surprisingly, "Pink Cadillac" did not appear on any official album until the release of *Tracks*. It first surfaced as the B-side of "Dancing In The Dark," although ironically given its infectious melody, Springsteen recorded it as an acoustic track for *Nebraska*.

It has everything going for it—an irresistible, instantly hummable melody; loose, tongue-in-cheek vocals from Springsteen; great sax solos from Clarence Clemons; Max Weinberg's patented powerhouse drumming; lyrics that playfully echo both Bo Diddley *and* Buddy Holly; even references to Adam and Eve and all those mysterious goings-on in the Bible. And at its center is the image of a car that features prominently in rock 'n' roll history and lore.

Think the Boss meets Jerry Lee Lewis with a bit of the King's swagger thrown in for good measure.

COVER ME

It takes a particular kind of artist to cover a Springsteen song (there's something about the sheer number of words that can be intimidating). Here's a few of the more notable covers:

- Although "Rendezvous" was one of the first tracks recorded for *Darkness On The Edge Of Town*, Springsteen was never satisfied with the studio version. Instead, it appears as a live performance on *Tracks*. More famously, though, is the version that the Greg Kihn Band recorded on their album *With The Naked Eye*.

- The Knack recorded "Don't Look Back" in 1979 although it did not appear on their album, *Retrospective: The Best Of The Knack*, until 1992.

- "Pink Cadillac," an irresistible rockabilly gem, has been covered by many artists, including Melissa Etheridge, Natalie Cole, Southern Pacific, and the late Carl Perkins.

- Patti Smith rewrote Springsteen's "Because The Night" for her *Easter* album and turned in a smolding performance.

- The late Warren Zevon rewrote "Jeannie Needs A Shooter" for his *Bad Luck Streak In Dancing School* album.

- Robert Gordon covered "Fire" on his *Fresh Fish Special* with Springsteen at the piano. But it was the Pointer Sisters who found just the right groove with their phenomenally successful rendition (they also recorded "The Fever," as did Southside Johnny and the Asbury Jukes on the marvelous *I Don't Want To Go Home* recording).

- Springsteen wrote "Protection" for Donna Summer that appeared on her self-named 1982 album.

- Springsteen has also written songs for Gary "U.S." Bonds, an early influence, including "This Little Girl."

"The Wish"

from *Tracks*

(Columbia, 1998)

"I took after my mom in a certain sense," Springsteen said about his Italian-American mother Adele. "Her life had an incredible consistency, work, work, work every day, and I admired that greatly. I admired her ability to present herself. She would get up in the morning and the bathroom was near my bed, and I could hear the sound of her in the bathroom. The faucet would come on, the make-up kit come out, things clicking on the sink, and I just sat and listened to my mother in the act of getting ready to present herself to the world. And then her high heels, and the sound they made when they left the house. I had a little balcony I used to sleep out on sometimes, and I'd hear her heels going up the street towards the office."

This routine of "presenting herself" forms the core—the heart—of "The Wish," Springsteen's genuinely touching ode to his mother. He captures the pride and dignity of work but it is the mundane, everyday details that make the song come alive.

Adele's office, in Freehold, New Jersey, was two blocks into the center of town. Occasionally Springsteen would visit her there—she was a legal secretary—"...and it was filled with men and women who seemed to have a purpose." To Springsteen, the ordinary tasks that his mother and others like her performed suggested a kind of nobility— a quiet, everyday nobility.

Springsteen first sang "The Wish" publicly at the Christic Institute benefit concert in Los Angeles in November 1990. Initially pegged to appear on *Tunnel Of Love*, it is his most personal song, and clearly one of his most autobiographical, a guitar-based ballad—gentle and sweet and full of fond memories. It opens with a wintry scene, the streets dirty with a messy mixture of rain and snow. A small boy and his mother stand outside a "rundown" music store window. It is Christmas. Under the Christmas tree, the boy soon receives what he wished for—a brand-new Japanese guitar.

Like many children who grew up in the Fifties, Springsteen's introduction to rock 'n' roll was watching Elvis Presley on *The Ed Sullivan Show*. He fell in love with the sound of the music and with the instrument that came to symbolize, for him, freedom. His mother bought him a guitar. At $60, it was a huge sacrifice at the time—money they couldn't afford to part with—but it was also an expression of faith. "It was simply money we just really didn't have," Springsteen says. "My folks were always in debt to the finance company. They'd borrow for this and pay it off just in time for Easter and pay it off in time for the next thing. So buying the guitar was a very meaningful gesture of faith at the time from her."

But his hands were too small to maneuver around the frets. Frustrated, he put it aside for five years. On the eve of The Beatles' arrival in America, he tried again, this time buying his own guitar from a pawnshop for $18. "It was one of the most beautiful sights I've ever seen in my life," he says. "There it is: the Guitar. It was real and it stood for something. I had found a way to do everything I wanted to do." A cousin taught Springsteen a few basic chords, and then he was on his own.

In "The Wish" he sings about wearing his Beatle boots (how many other musicians of his generation had their own Beatle boots?) and of his mother wearing pink curlers and matador pants. She pulls him off the couch, encouraging the young boy (although one senses he doesn't really need too much of a push) to do the twist for his uncles and aunts. His father is here, too, but he remains mostly in the background. If his father looked at the world through "deadly" eyes, his mother gave him hope. While she couldn't stop him from experiencing pain, she did give him the strength to work through it and made it clear that not everything was bleak. She was the anchor, the glue, the one who held the family together. She provided consistency, stability, and a sense of optimism that helped shape and add layers of complexity to his music. Whereas his father represented sorrow, his mother embodied pure joy. She was also the parent who loved popular music, especially Elvis Presley and the love songs that played continuously on the radio.

Later, in the song, Springsteen thinks about everything the guitar has brought him. He doesn't spell out what it is but he doesn't have to. We know.

"Well, I got this guitar, and I learned how to make it talk."

THE KING AND THE BOSS

"To me, he was as big as the whole country itself, as big as the whole dream. He just embodied the essence of it..."

—Bruce Springsteen, *Rolling Stone*, September 22, 1977

As most every Springsteen fan knows, Elvis had a huge artistic influence on the Boss. Mostly in concert but also occasionally on record, Springsteen has paid homage to his musical predecessor:

"Follow That Dream"

According to *Backstreets*, Springsteen first performed a rendition of the Presley classic in Paris during the 1981 *River* tour. Springsteen's version though features an additional verse.

"Johnny Bye-Bye"

Springsteen's song inspired by Elvis' death. Originally called "Bye Bye Johnny" and first performed on his 1981 European tour, it was based on an outtake from the *Darkness* sessions called "Let's Go Tonight." Since the song includes several lines from Chuck Berry's "Bye Bye Johnny," the songwriting credits cite both Berry and Springsteen. It was released in 1985 as the flip side of Springsteen's "I'm On Fire" single and later reissued in slightly different form in 1998 on *Tracks*.

"Pink Cadillac"

Recorded in 1983, it is the flip side of "Dancing In The Dark" and also appears on *Tracks*. Writes Shawn Poole in *Backstreets*: "Elvis first summoned the enduring image/metaphor of the pink Caddy in his Sun Records classic, 'Baby, Let's Play House.' It has since become inextricably linked with Presley, and his '55 model remains on display at Graceland's Automobile Museum."

"Can't Help Falling In Love"

Springsteen sang this Presley weepy as an encore during the *Born In The U.S.A.* tour in early 1985.

"Viva Las Vegas"

Title track of the Presley film of the same name. Springsteen's version was released in 1990 on the benefit tribute album *The Last Temptation Of Elvis* with backup by Ian McLagan on keyboards and Jeff Porcaro on drums (both appeared on *Human Touch* and *Lucky Town*). It also appears on *The Essential Bruce Springsteen*.

"57 Channels (And Nothin' On)"

One of Springsteen's lesser songs, the lyrics recall the apocryphal story of Elvis firing his gun at a television set because he didn't like what he saw ("in the blessed name of Elvis").

"Part Man, Part Monkey"
from *Tracks*
(Columbia, 1998)

"Be it enacted by the General Assembly of the State of Tennessee, That it shall be unlawful for any teacher in any of the Universities, Normals and all other public schools of the State which are supported in whole or in part by the public school funds of the State, to teach any theory that denies the story of the Divine Creation of man as taught in the Bible, and to teach instead that man has descended from a lower order of animals.

Be it further enacted, that any teacher found guilty of the violation of this Act, Shall be guilty of a misdemeanor and upon conviction, shall be fined not less than One Hundred $ (100.00) Dollars nor more than Five Hundred ($500.00) Dollars for each offense."

—Public Acts of the State of Tennessee passed by the Sixty-fourth General Assembly (AKA "The Butler Act"), March 13, 1925

"If evolution wins, Christianity goes."

—William Jennings Bryan

"Scopes isn't on trial, civilization is on trial."

—Clarence Darrow

"There's thems that believe we came from Adam and Eve, and then there's thems that, um, like this."

—Bruce Springsteen, introducing "Part Man, Part Monkey" in concert

What do you get when you mix one part reggae, one part history lesson, and pepper it with a generous sprinkling of double entendres? "Part Man, Part Monkey," an infectious, reggae-based rocker that manages to be hilarious *and* serious. It makes sense that Springsteen, the lapsed Catholic with a love for the rituals of his lost faith, would write a comical, tongue-in-cheek send-up of biblical literalism.

An outtake from *Human Touch*, "Part Man, Part Monkey" was featured prominently during the *Tunnel Of Love* tour and was officially released as the B-side to "57 Channels (And Nothin' On)." More recently, it resurfaced in politicized form during the 2005 *Devils & Dust* tour as a response to the intelligent design controversy that was then sweeping the country.

There are all kinds of monkeys mentioned in the song, from a groom trapped in a monkey suit to the "poor sucker" cited in the first line. "The poor sucker" refers to John T. Scopes, a popular 24-year-old science teacher in Dayton, Tennessee, who, in 1925, assigned readings to his students on evolution for a tenth grade biology class. At the behest of the ACLU, he agreed to be the test-case guinea pig to challenge a law—the recently passed Butler Act—that banned the teaching of evolution in Tennessee's public schools.

Billed as the trial of the century, the Scopes proceedings pitted two larger-than-life public figures against each other: William Jennings Bryan for the prosecution versus Clarence Darrow for the defense (science fiction writer H.G. Wells reportedly was approached, but he rejected the offer). Both volunteered their services. Bryan, a three-time Democratic candidate for president and a devout fundamentalist with a literal belief in the Bible, was considered the greatest living orator of his day; Darrow, an agnostic, was America's most famous defense attorney. Also present during the proceedings was the nation's best-known reporter, the irascible H.L. Mencken of the *Baltimore Evening News,* who sent dispatches across the country to readers eager to hear about the strange goings-on in a tiny Tennessee town located in the heart of the fundamentalist South. Caustic as ever, Mencken called Bryan "a tinpot pope..." and lamented at what he perceived to be as his fall from grace. "It is a tragedy, indeed," he continued, "to begin life as a hero and to end it as a buffoon." Put them all together, and you had the makings of a mighty combustible mix.

The fight against Darwinism did not emerge in a vacuum, though. By 1925, Bryan was strenuously campaigning against the teaching of evolution in public schools. He had already succeeded in getting legislation introduced in 15 states. More than this, he supported the passage of an anti-evolution amendment to the United States Constitution. Bryan, known as "The Great Commoner" because of his populist stance, knew how to connect with the ordinary man and woman on the street, especially in the Bible-haunted South. He knew who his audience was. At one point, he even offered $100 to anyone who could prove that they descended from apes.

Although the trial lasted only 8 days, it captured the imagination of the public, transforming the streets of Dayton, Tennessee (pop. 1,800) into a carnival atmosphere that was the 1920s precursor to the equally bizarre Terry Schiavo case in 2005. Chimpanzees performed in side shows, lemonade stands were set up for passers-by, shouts of street vendors ("ice cream and hot dogs here!") mingled with the hymns coming out of the months of blind singers, and evangelists recited passages from the Bible at the top of their lungs. Outside the courtroom jostled newspaper reporters, photographers, hawkers of both religious tracts and biology texts, holy rollers, and curiosity seekers, ordinary men and women who wanted to be as close to the action as possible.

Ironically, the Great Orator never did get a chance to read his closing statement, a speech he considered, not coincidentally, "the mountain peak of my life's effort" (under a peculiarity of Tennessee law, Bryan could not deliver the speech because Darrow chose not to have one). He died six days after the trial ended. While still in Dayton, and making the finishing touches to his speech, which he hoped to get published, he lay down to take a nap after eating an enormous dinner and died quietly in his sleep.

Toward the close of the trial, Darrow asked the jury to deliver a guilty verdict so that the case could be appealed to the Tennessee Supreme Court and, if necessary, the U.S. Supreme Court. Ultimately, Scopes was indeed found guilty and the court fined him $100. A year later, though, the case was reversed by the Tennessee Supreme Court—not on constitutional grounds, but on a technicality (the fine should have been set by the jury, not the judge). The case was dismissed ("Nothing is to be gained," declared the court, "by prolonging the life of this bizarre case"). Although the Scopes trial represented a major setback for the anti-evolution forces, as the 2005 case in Dover, Pennsylvania, among others indicates, Darwinism continues to be a controversial issue with strong opinions apparent on both sides.

Springsteen's inspiration for the song seems to be the 1960 film *Inherit The Wind,* directed by Stanley Kramer and starring Spencer Tracy as Darrow, Frederic March as Bryan, and Gene Kelly as Mencken, which was based on the play by Jerome Lawrence and Robert E. Lee. (In 1988, it was remade into a television movie starring Jason Robards, Kirk Douglas, and Darren McGavin.) Significantly, Lawrence and Lee wrote *Inherit The Wind* as a pointed response to the anti-communist hysteria of 1950s McCarthyism. And even though the playwrights drew heavily from the trial transcripts, they did not intend the play to be an accurate depiction of the Scopes proceedings. Scopes attended the premiere of the film in Dayton, Tennessee, on the 35th anniversary of the trial. The mayor of Dayton proclaimed Scopes Trial Day and gave the former teacher the key to the city. Two years later, in 1962, Scopes published his memoirs, *Center Of The Storm,* in which he predicted the day would come when "we will not be bothered by Fundamentalists."

But, back to the song itself. The randy narrator in "Part Man, Part Monkey" has no trouble identifying with his simian ancestors. In the last stanza he wonders if God made man "in a breath of holy fire" or, he asks, did he crawl out "out of the muck and mire"? The man on the street, he says, believes what the Bible tells him to believe. But our narrator knows better (or, at least, knows himself better). "Part man, part monkey, baby that's me," he gleefully admits.

The Great Commoner must be turning in his grave.

"Back In Your Arms"
from *Tracks*
(Columbia, 1998)

A Sixties-style soul ballad, and a real beauty, "Back In Your Arms" contains a great Springsteen vocal; passionate, committed, and full of genuine emotion. Accompanied by most of the E Street Band, it even boasts a slow sax solo by Clarence Clemons.

The lyrics are uniformly sad. The love that the narrator sings so passionately about seems all but lost. And yet he still carries a torch for his beloved, hoping that it isn't too late to redeem himself in her eyes. He laments the empty promises they made to each other at night. He recalls his own mistakes, how he was indifferent to her overtures, turning a cold shoulder, but now he realizes that he desperately yearns for the love that he so cavalierly threw away.

The images are stirring too, echoing the sadness and turmoil that the character feels inside: empty roads buffeted by howling winds, dark skies, and deep shadows. It is a wildly romantic song of regret and sorrow, as the singer slowly comes to the realization of just how much he has lost, but it is also tinged with the slightest touch of hope. And in Springsteen song after Springsteen song, hope is sometimes all you need.

"Brothers Under The Bridge"
from *Tracks*
(Columbia, 1998)

The last song on *Tracks* (and an outtake from *The Ghost Of Tom Joad*), "Brothers Under The Bridge" is about a group of homeless Vietnam veterans who leave Los Angeles and set up a camp in the San Gabriel Mountains. "This is the story about one of them who has a grown daughter that he's never seen, and she grows up, and she comes looking for her dad," says Springsteen.

Recorded in May 1995, it is a worthy addition, along with ""Born In The U.S.A." and "Shut Out The Light," to Springsteen's canon of war-related songs. Boasting a fragile but memorable melody and appropriately weary vocals, it tells the story of a lost soul who made a few wrong, and apparently devastating, turns with simplicity and great compassion.

All the Vietnam vet in the song wants is to be left alone ("Ain't lookin'for nothin'") and to live his own life in his own way. He has had enough of the violence of big city street life where, he sings, you can get killed over nothing. He doesn't want any trouble, nor does he have any to give. It's a great line, and it captures perfectly the fatalism and exhaustion of someone who has lowered his expectations and needs very little to get by.

"Brothers Under The Bridge" also acknowledges the very real dangers of living out in the mesquite wilderness, surrounded by brush and canyon. When the hot Santa Ana winds come howling down, the campfire is particularly vulnerable. One winter night, the narrator recalls, a homeless man burned to death in his own campfire, singed by the embers of a deadly blaze. They buried him, he states matter of factly, along the bridge.

We don't know what turn of events led to the narrator's homelessness, but we do feel the sadness and terror and uncertainty that form the crux of his daily life and of the special sense of camaraderie that he feels toward his equally fallen comrades.

18 Tracks
(Columbia, 1999)

 one-CD distillation of the four-CD *Tracks* with several never-before-released bonuses: "Trouble River," "The Fever," and "The Promise."

Musicians:
Bruce Springsteen: vocals, guitar
Danny Federici: organ, glockenspiel, accordion
Garry Tallent: bass
Vini Lopez: drums
David Sancious: piano, organ, keyboards
Clarence Clemons: saxophone, percussion, background vocals
Roy Bittan: piano, keyboards
Max Weinberg: drums
Stevie Van Zandt: guitar
Nils Lofgren: vocals

Additional musicians:
Mario Cruz: tenor sax
Ed Manion: baritone sax
Mark "The Love Man" Pender: trumpet
Richie "La Bamba" Rosenberg: trombone
Mike Spengler: trumpet
Michael Fisher: percussion
Randy Jackson: bass
Jeff Porcaro: drums
Omar Hakim: drums
Gary Mallaber: drums
Marty Rifkin: pedal steel guitar, dobro
Soozie Tyrell: violin

Producers: Bruce Springsteen and Chuck Plotkin

Tracks:
"Growin' Up" (2:38)
"Seaside Bar Song" (3:33)
"Rendezvous" (2:48)
"Hearts Of Stone" (4:29)
"Where The Bands Are" (3:43)
"Loose Ends" (4:00)
"I Wanna Be With You" (3:21)
"Born In The U.S.A." (3:10)
"My Love Will Not Let You Down" (4:24)

"Lion's Den" (2:18)

"Pink Cadillac" (3:33)

"Janey Don't You Lose Heart" (3:24)

"Sad Eyes" (3:47)

"Part Man, Part Monkey" (4:28)

"Trouble River" (4:18)

"Brothers Under The Bridge" (4:55)

"The Fever" (7:35)

"The Promise" (4:48)

Running time: 67:52

"The Fever"
from *18 Tracks*
(Columbia, 1999)

Southside Johnny and the Asbury Jukes may have made it famous but Springsteen's original is still the definitive version.

Recorded in May 1973, "The Fever" has a loose and languid feeling, an R&B style piano-based classic. It takes its time getting its point across. No one's in any particular hurry. It slowly gains momentum, the music moving at a leisurely pace, before Springsteen even starts to sing. The lyrics describe mundane details—a man comes home from work, turns on the television set, but he can't keep his mind on the program because all he's thinking about is his girl. He is a man obsessed—perhaps possessed even. And then it builds— slowly but surely—from there. The chorus repeats in a call-and-response pattern what's on his mind ("He's got the fever, oh he's got the fever") and Springsteen replies, helplessly ("Nothing that a po' boy can do"). The "ooo, ooo" background vocals of Clarence Clemons add to the pleasure of the slow burn. In fact, Springsteen milks it for all that its worth and his band mates gamely accompany him for the ride. Vini Lopez's drums sound appropriately passionate when necessary, pause for a tension-filled moment, and then continue for heightened dramatic effect. It goes on like this for more than seven gorgeous minutes.

"The Promise"
from *18 Tracks*
(Columbia, 1998)

"To me, 'The Promise' is like a story, for a movie, pure Bruce romanticism, absolutely great."

—Graziano Romani, Italian rock star

In June 1977 Springsteen recorded a moody ballad called "The Promise," written during a time when his career was stalled in an ugly lawsuit against ex-manager Mike Appel. He had originally intended to include it on *Darkness On The Edge Of Town* but deleted it because he felt too many reviewers would misinterpret the song, mistakenly believing it was about his legal troubles. Springsteen also thought its message was too bleak to be included on what was turning out to be an already bleak album. So "The Promise," a long-time fan favorite, languished in the vaults until it finally surfaced, more than 20 years after it was written, on *18 Tracks*, Springsteen's one-CD distillation of the four-CD set *Tracks*, albeit in a somber acoustic version that accentuates its stark qualities.

A pensive piano-based ballad, it is reminiscent both musically and thematically of Springsteen's own "Racing In The Street" with traces of Jackson Browne's "For a Dancer." It is also the follow up to "Thunder Road"—as well as its down side.

The story is familiar. It chronicles, methodically and inexorably, the woes of a group of friends. Johnny works in a factory, Billy works downtown, Terry plays in a rock 'n' roll band, and the narrator does unspecified work ("a little job" is how he describes it) but it really doesn't matter since the job itself is immaterial. Some nights instead of going to work, he goes to the drive-in or he just stays home. Springsteen uses a movie metaphor again, comparing the character's modest dreams with the dreams of the characters who appear on the big screen. We know that the narrator takes pride in things that mean something to him, but he's also a bit of a daredevil. He drives a Challenger, a car that he built himself, but he drives it down dead-end streets in the bad parts of town, ostensibly risking life and limb for a cheap thrill.

Broke, he sells his beloved car, and little by little his dreams crumble and then vanish completely. "Every day it just gets harder to live this dream I'm believin' in," he sings. The lyrics mention "Thunder Road" but this Thunder Road is less a form of escape than a situation he can't escape from. Both

"Thunder Road" and "The Promise" may have similar characters and tread similar territory but they arrive at entirely opposite conclusions. It's the difference between breaking free and being irrevocably trapped. And yet even when the promise is broken, even when there is no more fire in the belly, even when there is nothing left to hold onto, Springsteen offers a hard truth—like the characters in *Nebraska's* "Reason To Believe," you simply go on living.

"The Promise" is a humble homage to all the world's lost souls and broken lives as well as those who still cling, however slightly, to the dream of a better day. Cold comfort, perhaps, but it's a start.

The Essential Bruce Springsteen

(Columbia, 2003)

The best of Springsteen in one volume, it features songs from Springsteen's decades-long career, including a selection of rarities and previously unreleased recordings.

Musicians:

Bruce Springsteen: lead vocals, acoustic guitar, electric guitar, harmonica bass, background vocals, recorder, mandolin, handclaps

Mike Appel: background vocals

Roy Bittan: Fender Rhodes, glockenspiel, synthesizer, keyboard, piano, mellotron, kurzweil, pump organ, Korg M1, Crumar, background vocals

Richard Blackwell: congas, percussion

Ernest "Boom" Carter: drums

Clarence Clemons: saxophone, percussion, background vocals, handclaps

Danny Federici: accordion, organ, glockenspiel, piano, Vox continental, Farfisa, background vocals

Jere Flint: cello

Bob Glaub: bass

Jim Hanson: bass

Randy Jackson: bass

Suki Lahav: violin

Larry Lemaster: cello

Nils Lofgren: guitar, dobro, slide guitar, banjo, background vocals

Vincent "Mad Dog" Lopez: drums, background vocals

Gary Mallabar: drums, percussion

Ian McLagan: piano, organ

Jeff Porcaro: drums, percussion

Marty Rifkin: pedal steel

David Sancious: piano, organ, electric piano, clavinet

Jane Scarpantoni: cello

Patti Scialfa: vocals, guitar, harmony

Garry Tallent: bass, tuba, background vocals

Soozie Tyrell: background vocals

Steve Van Zandt: guitar, mandolin, background vocals

Max Weinberg: drums, background vocals

Harold Wheeler: piano

Alliance Singers: Corinda Crawford, Tiffeny Andrews, Michelle Moore, Antoinette Moore, Antonio Lawrence, Jesse Moorer

Horn section: Mark Pender (trumpet), Mike Spengler (trumpet), Rich Rosenberg (trombone), Jerry Vivino (tenor sax), Ed Marion (baritone sax)

Producer: Jon Landau

Tracks:

Disc One
"Blinded By The Light" (5:02)
"For You" (4:39)
"Spirit In The Night" (4:48)
"4th Of July, Asbury Park (Sandy)" (5:36)
"Rosalita (Come Out Tonight)" (7:04)
"Thunder Road" (4:50)
"Born To Run" (4:30)
"Jungleland" (9:33)
"Badlands" (4:01)
"Darkness On The Edge Of Town" (4:28)
"The Promised Land" (4:33)
"The River" (4:59)
"Hungry Heart" (3:19)
"Nebraska" (4:30)
"Atlantic City" (3:57)

Running time: 72:69

Disc Two
"Born In The U.S.A." (4:39)
"Glory Days" (4:15)
"Dancing In The Dark" (4:01)
"Tunnel Of Love" (5:10)
"Brilliant Disguise" (4:15)
"Human Touch" (6:28)
"Living Proof" (4:44)
"Lucky Town" (3:24)
"Streets Of Philadelphia" (3:16)
"The Ghost Of Tom Joad" (4:23)
"The Rising" (4:47)
"Mary's Place" (5:59)
"Lonesome Day" (4:05)
"American Skin (41 Shots)" (Live) (7:50)
"Land of Hope and Dreams" (Live) (9:22)

Running time: 73:98

Disc Three

"*From Small Things (Big Things One Day Come)*" (2:40)
"*The Big Payback*" (1:57)
"Held Up Without A Gun" (Live) (1:18)
"Trapped" (Live) (5:08)
"None But The Brave" (5:34)
"Missing" (5:03)
"Lift Me Up" (5:14)
"Viva Las Vegas" (3:08)
"County Fair" (4:48)
"*Code of Silence*" (Live) (4:30)
"*Dead Man Walkin'*" (2:40)
"Countin' On A Miracle" (Acoustic) (5:00)

Running time: 45:00

"American Skin (41 Shots)"
from *The Essential Bruce Springsteen*
(Columbia, 2003)

and

Bruce Springsteen Live In New York City
(Columbia, 2001)

Just after midnight on February 4, 1999, a West African immigrant by the name of Amadou Diallo breathed his last breath. In the vestibule of the shabby building where he lived at 1157 Wheeler Avenue in the Soundview section of the Bronx, the 22-year-old convenience store worker originally from Guinea (by then, he had only been in New York for two years) was mistaken for an armed serial rapist by four New York City police officers of the plainclothes Street Crime Unit. As he reached for his wallet, the officers shot the unarmed Diallo 41 times; 19 of those struck him.

Springsteen debuted the song during the last leg of the E Street Band's 2000 reunion tour. "This is a new song called 'American Skin, 41 Shots,'" he told the crowd at the Philips Arena in Atlanta on June 4. The following week he and the band performed the song at Madison Square Garden in New York, "where," says Springsteen, "we were the talk of the tabloids." Indeed, the reaction to "American Skin" amounted to the grossest misinterpretation of a Springsteen song since "Born In The U.S.A.," and, in some ways, it was the greatest controversy of his career.

Patrick Lynch, president of New York's Patrolmen's Benevolent Association, representing some 30,000 policemen and women, encouraged officers to boycott Springsteen's Madison Street Garden concerts. In a letter posted on the PBA website he voiced his objections in no uncertain terms:

> Singer Bruce Springsteen has begun performing in concert a song called "American Skin"—the title seems to suggest that the shooting of Amadou Diallo was a case of racial profiling—which keeps repeating the phrase, "Forty-one shots." I consider it an outrage that he would be trying to fatten his wallet by reopening the wounds of this tragic case at a time when police officers and community members are in a healing period, and I have let his representatives and the press know how I feel about this song.

I strongly urge any PBA members who may moonlight as security or in any other kind of work at rock concerts to avoid working Springsteen concerts. He is scheduled to appear at Madison Square Garden for a 10-day stand beginning June 12, and the PBA strongly urges you not only not to work this or any other Springsteen concert but also not to attend.

Let's stick together on this important issue.

Lynch added, "We don't need a millionaire coming down here and making money off our backs…on a terrible, terrible tragedy."

Perhaps the most heinous charge was Lynch's inappropriate claim that accused Springsteen of writing the song to fatten his own wallet—in other words, exploiting the tragedy. Ironically, the largely unheard "American Skin" hadn't even been recorded yet when the tour began. Indeed, it is safe to say that most people in the audience never heard the song before—Lynch certainly did not.

Other officers supported the boycott, including New York City Police Commissioner Howard Safir, who told the *New York Daily News*, "I personally don't particularly care for Bruce Springsteen's music or his song." But the most vehement criticism—a particularly harsh and mean-spirited piece of vitriol—came from Bob Lucente, president of the New York State Fraternal Order of Police, "He's turned into some type of fucking dirtbag. He goes on the boycott list. He has all these good songs and everything, American-flag songs and all that stuff," he said, clearly knowing nothing about Springsteen or his music, "and now he's a floating fag." (Lucente later apologized to gay police officers, but not to Springsteen himself.) Meanwhile, Stanley Crouch, the distinguished African-American critic, offered an African-American perspective, but also misinterpreted it and unintentionally added fuel to the fire by insisting that "American Skin" depicts "Amadou Diallo as a victim of racist cops gone trigger-happy."

Springsteen was taken aback by all the negative response. "I felt the song was simply an extension of the music I had been writing for my whole life," he told Robert Hilburn of the *Los Angeles Times*. "It was a meditation on what it means to be an American at a particular moment in time.

"It felt to me like the most necessary issue to deal with at the turn of the century was the question of race in America and how we deal with one another. To some degree, the answer to that question is going to decide a lot about how the nation as a whole eventually rises or falls. I wanted to point out that people of color are viewed through a veil of criminality and that ultimately means they are thought of as less American than other Americans, therefore people with less rights."

Others came to Springsteen's defense. In a letter to the *New York Times,* New York City police lieutenant Michael J. Gorman argued that "Mr. Springsteen has generally been a supporter of police officers, giving generously to police charities. Attacks on him are not only unfair but also counterproductive."

The incident divided the city into two camps: Those who supported the police and thought the shooting an innocent though tragic mistake and those who cried police brutality, excessive force, and racial profiling; in other words, those who thought Diallo was killed simply for being black. The officers— Kenneth Boss, Sean Carroll, Edward McMellon, and Richard Murphy—were eventually cleared of all charges, which only exacerbated the polarizing feelings that had mounted on both sides. Eventually, Diallo's parents filed a civil suit against the officers and the city, charging the department with racial profiling. In early 2004, the Diallo family agreed to a $3 million settlement.

Springsteen and the E Street Band played the song without incident at the Madison Square Garden concerts, although he did preface it with a warning to the crowd, "We need some quiet."

Significantly, Diallo is never mentioned directly by name in the song, only by inference. Springsteen goes to great lengths to offer a balanced view of the shooting. Repeated throughout though is the mantra, "forty-one shots." The first verse is written from a police officer's perspective. He kneels over Diallo's body. He then asks a series of questions—Is it a gun? Is it a knife? Is it a wallet?—the kinds of questions that would have gone through his head prior to pulling the trigger.

The second verse belongs to a worried mother, Lena, as she issues a cautionary warning to her son, stressing the importance of knowing proper street etiquette; that is, giving him specific instructions about *how* to act. If an officer stops you, she pleads, be polite, never run away, and, above all, always keep your hands in plain sight.

The third verse brings the two voices together and serves as a reminder that a collective responsibility lies with us all ("We're baptized in these waters / and in each other's blood"). The river of blood can also be a river of hope.

In the end, some good did emerge from the tragedy. In 2003, Kadiatou Diallo, Amadou's mother, went on to not only publish a book about the entire experience (*My Heart Will Cross The Ocean: My Story, My Son, Amadou,* with journalist Craig Wolff) but also established the Amadou Diallo Foundation, Inc., which offers scholarships to immigrant students, runs programs in the

New York public schools to advance racial understanding, and works to improve police and community relationships. In 2002, police commissioner Raymond W. Kelly announced an anti-profiling policy, and in Soundview itself, community leaders renamed the block of Wheeler Avenue where the Diallo family lived as Amadou Diallo Place.

"Land Of Hope And Dreams"
from *The Essential Bruce Springsteen*
(Columbia, 2003)

and

Bruce Springsteen Live In New York City
(Columbia, 2001)

> *"Not I, not any one else can travel that road for you / You must travel it for yourself."*
>
> —Walt Whitman, *Leaves Of Grass*

> *"That's where I want to go tonight*
> *And I want you to go with me*
> *Because I need to go with you—that's why I'm here"*
>
> —Bruce Springsteen, in concert

Anyone who has been to a Springsteen concert knows just how genuinely spiritual it can be. His early shows—those legendary performances throughout the country and of course along the Jersey Shore—were justly famous for their intensity but also for their unique blend of spirituality and grit—for their *pure theater*. Some scholars, such as Larry David Smith, have referred to these shows as "a direct extension of the Southern black church and its long, joyous, liberating communal rituals." The Springsteen who stands on stage is the personification of a preacher, and not just any old preacher—but a rock 'n' roll preacher—whose congregation of the faithful is the sea of people dancing in the aisles and pumping their fists in the air in collective unison. Make no mistake. This is a very vociferous congregation whose call and response—its active participation—plays just as crucial a role as the singer. And if the concert happens to take place in New Jersey, all the better, for in the Garden State, Brother Bruce appears at his most glorious. Indeed, to see Springsteen prowling the stage of a Jersey arena is, wrote Greg Tate in the *Village Voice,* like being "under a revival tent. It's in fact where his blue-collar creed connects up with his all-American Confidence Man Carny Barker Televangelist shtick."

Springsteen has said that the spiritual intensity of his shows have their origin in soul music. And so, in his most fervent songs, in his most spiritual songs, he pays witness, cajoles, pleads, and implores for salvation (it can take many forms) or at least some kind of transformation for the "ministry of rock 'n' roll" can make most anything possible. In his own way, then, Springsteen is preaching the social gospel, adopting what music historian Craig Werner calls the gospel notion of conscious living. At times, he offers lamentations (as on *Nebraska* and *The Ghost Of Tom Joad*) rather than anthems. Other times, though, in the best realization of the democratic ideal, he provides a sense of solace.

On stage and on record, Springsteen tries to create a transcendent—fleeting though it may be—community. "In the Pentecostal churches whose gospel music spawned so much of rock 'n' roll," Springsteen biographer Dave Marsh writes, "the purpose of music is to enhance interaction between congregation and performers. What Springsteen idealized in early rock 'n' roll music were attempts to achieve something similar…." That is, suggests Marsh, Springsteen intends to "regain that dialogue with the audience." When The Lights Go Out at a Springsteen concert, you can be sure that you are not alone: thousands of like-minded souls are singing along to the same lyrics and asking the same tough questions. Indeed, Marsh has called Springsteen "a creator of community."

"Pete Townshend said that rock music was one of the big spiritual movements of the second half of the Twentieth century," says Springsteen. "It is medicinal and it does address your spirit, there's no two ways about it. And it came out of the church. Who were the first front men? The preachers!"

If any song best reflects the big-heartedness of Springsteen's music, then it must be the gloriously optimistic "Land Of Hope And Dreams." Introduced during the 1999/2000 reunion tour—the E Street Band's first world tour in 18 years—Springsteen felt he needed a new song "that would reaffirm our sense of purpose and capture our current ambitions, that would let our fans know once again what we were here for."

"Land Of Hope And Dreams" uses the heaven-bound train, the celestial railway, the glory train, the train-as-salvation, as a metaphor. The train features prominently in American song and folklore from heroes and villains ("John Henry," "Railroad Bill," "Casey Jones") to train-wreck songs ("The Wreck Of

The Old 97") to folk songs that romanticize the train journey (Elizabeth Cotten's "Freight Train," Leadbelly's "Rock Island Line" and "Midnight Special," Steve Goodman's "City Of New Orleans," and Johnny Cash's "Hey Porter") to eerie songs with supernatural elements ("Mystery Train") to freedom songs (Bob Marley's "This Train," Curtis Mayfield's "People Get Ready").

The refrain of "Land Of Hope And Dreams" is a twist on the old African-American spiritual "This Train (Is Bound For Glory)." The origins of "This Train" are obscure although it probably dates back to the Nineteenth century when it was sung in rural churches and at camp revival meetings. First recorded in 1925 by Wood's Blind Jubilee Singers and in field recordings for the Library of Congress, it appeared in John and Alan Lomax's 1934 anthology *American Ballads And Folk Songs* and again in Alan Lomax's 1960 anthology *The Folk Songs Of North America* before resurfacing during the folk revivals of the 1950s and early 1960s. Woody Guthrie recorded it several times and others too across musical genres—blues (Big Bill Broonzy), folk (Pete Seeger; Peter, Paul, and Mary; the Kingston Trio), country (Johnny Cash), gospel (The Staple Singers), reggae (Bob Marley), and rock (Indigo Girls).

"This Train" echoes the lyrics of several old gospel songs about the Promised Land, including "Freedom Train-a-Comin'" but especially "The Gospel Train Is Coming." Probably the best known of the Negro spirituals, "The Gospel Train Is Coming" was popularized by the Fisk Jubilee Singers, an African-American choir based at Fisk University in Nashville. During the 1870s they traveled around the world not only raising money for Fisk, but also promoting Negro spirituals to non-black audiences, spreading the word to the uninitiated. Initially, the lyrics of the song appear welcoming, as the train moves full-steam ahead:

> *The gospel train is coming,*
> *I hear it just at hand,*
> *I hear the car wheels moving*
> *And rumbling thro' the land,*
>
> *Get on board, children*
> *Get on board, children*
> *Get on board, children*
> *For there's room for many a more.*

But there is a warning:

O, sinner you're forever lost,
If once you're left behind.

Then again, you can't beat the price:

The fare is cheap and all can go,
The rich and poor are there,
No second-class on board the train,
No difference in the fare.

And the company is certainly above reproach:

There's Moses, Noah and Abraham,
And all the prophets, too,
Our friends in Christ are all on board,
O, what a heavenly crew

Like "The Gospel Train Is Coming," "This Train" also contains its own caveat:

This train is bound for glory, this train (my Lord),
This train is bound for glory, this train;
This train is bound for glory, and if you ride you must be holy,
This train, my Lord, this train.

It then goes on to recite a litany of passengers who are *not* welcome aboard.

This train don't carry no liars, this train (my Lord)...
This train don't carry no gamblers, this train (my Lord)...
This train don't carry no gamblers, this train (my Lord)...
This train don't carry no gamblers, hobo liars, midnight ramblers,
This train, my Lord, this train.
This train don't carry no jokers...no cigarette smokers,
This train, my Lord, this train.

In sharp contrast, Springsteen's heaven-bound train recalls more closely the hopeful optimism of Curtis Mayfield's "People Get Ready"—inspired by the 1963 March on Washington—and, in particular, its luminous refrain that reminds people of an approaching train:

You don't need no baggage, you just get on board
All you need is faith to hear the diesels hummin'
Don't need no ticket, you just thank the Lord

But how does one get to heaven? In the Bible, Elijah was carried to heaven on a chariot ("a chariot of fire and horses of fire"). In the folk tradition, we hear of sacred voyages by ship—the gospel ships. Later on, during the era of the Iron Horse, the train became the preferred mode of transportation and for partly this reason the spiritual railway appears in many Nineteenth-century poems, songs, and stories. But whether it's a song or broadside, poem or short story, the implied message here is that if you wander too far off the path, if you veer from righteousness, you will not go to heaven.

A common theme running through both the old spirituals and the newer songs is the idea of a train that will take the faithful to heaven after their earthly toil is over. But the key word is *faithful*. Like "This Train," its spiritual predecessor, "People Get Ready" does not welcome all, for it includes the telling phrase—this train is "no place for the hopeless sinner."

Not so "Land Of Hope And Dreams." This is a song about redemption and forgiveness and a faith that transcends all earthly and heavenly barriers. It celebrates the humanity of us all, it is about being inclusive. Everyone is welcome. *No one* will be turned away. *No one* will be rejected. Brother Bruce's expansive universe is big enough to hold anyone who wants to join him: white and black, male and female, young and old, rich and poor, friend and foe, fool and king, saint and sinner—*especially* saints and sinners. It is an equal opportunity train.

"Land Of Hope And Dreams" could also be called a rock spiritual, especially as it is performed by Springsteen in concert, with the full force of the band behind him and the presence of the "congregation" at his feet. On stage, the public Springsteen combines the eloquence and passion of a gospel preacher and the slick polish of a carnival barker. He is a man who wants to—needs to—go to, as he calls it, the river of life, the river of love, the river of faith, the river of hope, the river of transformation, the river of sanctification, the river of resurrection. If Springsteen can't promise us life everlasting, he at least does promise us life in the moment.

Like Walt Whitman, Springsteen celebrates community but, unlike the great poet, he also celebrates the notion of a rock 'n' roll brotherhood and sisterhood. "Land Of Hope And Dreams" is, at once, a strikingly democratic vision and a profoundly spiritual one.

During *The Rising* tour, Springsteen dedicated the song to the people of Iraq.

"None But The Brave"
from *The Essential Bruce Springsteen*
(Columbia, 2003)

"None But The Brave" is classic Springsteen, a heartfelt ballad that remained in the vaults for too long. Set in the Asbury Park bar scene of the 1970s and originally recorded for the *Born In The U.S.A.* sessions, it boasts an appealing melody and some great lyrics, along with some nice sax work from Clarence Clemons.

Springsteen breaks no new ground here, but it is a beauty nevertheless. The contemplative lyrics long for the way things used to be, even though the narrator is savvy enough to realize that the old days will never return. Snippets of phrases catch perfectly the fleeting memory of an ex-lover, her words that come back to haunt him from passing cars, the bars where they used to hang out, now empty. He dreams about her at night—about the way she used to look—even though that person no longer exists. Irrationally, he cruises the old hangouts, not expecting, but half wishing that she will walk through the door. Instead, he sees someone else who reminds him of her and asks her to dance. But, of course, it isn't the same.

"Missing"
from *The Essential Bruce Springsteen*
(Columbia, 2003)

A little-known song from a little-known movie. Not to be confused with "You're Missing" from *The Rising* (although it does share some lyrical similarities), "Missing" is an almost-forgotten treasure, a moody, impressionistic ballad about loss and grief.

"Missing" appears in the opening credits of Sean Penn's *The Crossing Guard* (1995), the actor's second attempt at directing (his directing debut, *The Indian Runner*, also had a Springsteen connection—it was inspired by "Highway Patrolman"). A somber Jack Nicholson plays Freddy Gale, a father still grieving after his daughter was killed by a hit-and run driver. He has waited patiently for six years for John Booth (David Morse), the man responsible, to be released from prison. On the day Booth is released, Gale tells Booth he will kill him within the week.

Unfortunately, *The Crossing Guard* is an uneven movie, frustrating and unsatisfying. Despite strong performances by Nicholson and Anjelica Huston as his estranged wife, it is saddled with a weak and oftentimes implausible script, which is a shame since the movie had so much potential.

Springsteen's song is the best thing about the movie.

Experimenting with drum looping, Springsteen creates a chilling mood piece that perfectly matches the film's dark themes. But it also stands on its own. The music sounds distant—it has a drowning effect as if the narrator is being swallowed up by his own pain. The narrator gets up in the morning and although everything seems the same—the same cigarettes lie on the table, the same jacket hangs on the chair—he senses that something is different. In a chilling premonition, he dreams the night before that the sky had turned black. He tried but he could not reach his beloved—she was lost in some kind of limbo and couldn't return home. In the evening, alone, he still hears her footsteps, still hears her voice in the hallway, and still smells her scent drifting through the bedroom.

Then he awakes, and she is gone.

"Lift Me Up"
from *The Essential Bruce Springsteen*
(Columbia, 2003)

Another movie connection, "Lift Me Up" was written for John Sayles' film *Limbo* (1999). Sayles asked Springsteen to write a song for the ending, an ending that many people found frustrating. In the last scene, a small plane approaches the Alaskan island where the main characters are stranded. They look up toward the sky, not sure whether the plane is coming to rescue them or do them harm. We hear the hum of the plane's engine, and then the credits come up and Springsteen's lovely song plays on the soundtrack.

The plot itself sounds like a Springsteen song. Joe Gastineau (David Strathairn) is a gruff former fisherman traumatized by an incident that occurred years ago at sea. He meets lounge singer Donna de Angelo (Mary Elizabeth Mastrantonio) and her troubled teenage daughter Noelle (Vanessa Martinez) and tries, with great difficulty, to start again. But his past comes back to haunt him and things get a bit complicated.

It is not surprising that Sayles, the doyen of independent filmmakers as well as a novelist and short story writer, would turn to Springsteen for musical inspiration. After all, they have a lot in common. Like Springsteen, Sayles shares a working-class background (Sayles grew up in Schenectady, New York) and similar work habits. Sayles does prodigious amounts of research before writing a script. "Two things I try to do," he told a reporter for the English newspaper, the *Guardian,* "one is just meet people and talk to them about their jobs, about their life. The other is very practical—I don't want to invent a location that doesn't exist and have to create it. I don't want to have to put trees up and change the beach, so I say, 'Well, what's there?' and try to write that into the script."

Limbo isn't the first time Springsteen and Sayles worked together. Springsteen also contributed several songs—"Adam Raised A Cain," "She's The One," "It's Hard To Be A Saint In The City"—to an early Sayles effort, the teenage romance, *Baby, It's You* (1983), while Sayles returned the favor by directing a live performance video for the "Born In The U.S.A." single, as well as the "I'm On Fire" and "Glory Days" videos.

Like Springsteen, Sayles isn't afraid to take chances, even if he has the potential to alienate his audience. "Most movies are meant to be about the illusion of risk," says Sayles. "In this movie, I am asking you to get emotionally involved with the characters, but we don't know what's going to happen to them. I don't even give you any warning that it's gonna change from a nice quiet ride to mortal danger."

Using an ethereal falsetto voice—the voice he first used in the Nineties—Springsteen plays up the uncertainty of the ending. Just like we don't know what lies ahead in our own lives, neither can the characters predict their own fate. The haunting quality of "Lift Me Up"—along with its espousal of love no matter what happens—adds layers of depth and poignancy to an already fragile melody.

"County Fair"

from *The Essential Bruce Springsteen*
(Columbia, 2003)

Some may consider this wistful piece of nostalgia too slight to be considered among Springsteen's best, but, to me, "County Fair" is an almost perfect song, an evocative gem with a melody that lingers long after the music stops.

Culled from a collection of acoustic songs that Springsteen cut in California in 1983 after the release of *Nebraska,* Springsteen has described "County Fair" as a portrait of an end-of-summer fair on the outskirts of a town. Although specific sites are mentioned (Telegraph Hill, Soldiers Field), the setting could be anywhere. The location doesn't really matter because it is, after all, a memory song about a particular mind set and about the way something—a sound, a smell—makes you feel during a specific time in your life, about the idyllic charms of a place that is forever etched in memory.

Boasting a warm Springsteen vocal, the song is swathed in the simple pleasures of small-town memories, of the joys—and frights—of riding a rollercoaster as it is ready to drop, the sound of the pipe organ on the merry-go-round, a spinning fortune wheel. It evokes the heady carnival atmosphere of the Asbury Park boardwalk—you half expect the narrator to bump into Madam Marie herself—but transported to a local festival somewhere in the American heartland.

Springsteen proceeds along at a leisurely pace, filling the song with wonderful details. Not satisfied just to tell us that a "little rock 'n' roll band" is playing and that people are dancing out in the open air, he even gives the band a name: James Young and the Immortal Ones (it even sounds like a real Sixties outfit) rocking out on two guitars, bass, and drums. There are moments, too, of gentle self-deprecation (he hopes he remembers where he parked the car) before it turns pensive. The couple sits for a while in the front yard with the radio playing softly in the background, and in a moment of rapturous beauty, the narrator pulls his sweetheart close to his heart, looks up at the stars and wishes that it would never end. Then, of course, it's over.

But rather than repeating the catchy chorus—you're almost ready to start singing along—Springsteen defies expectations and pulls back, ending the song on an uncertain note. A moment has passed, flitting across the universe, and it is now gone forever.

...And Sixty More

Bruce Springsteen.

In alphabetical order:

1. "Ain't Got You"
(Tunnel Of Love)
Autobiographical lyrics ("Been paid a king's ransom for doin' what comes naturally"), acappella vocals, and an irresistible shuffling beat make this one of the more immediately appealing songs on *Tunnel Of Love*.

2. "All That Heaven Will Allow"
(Tunnel Of Love)
Romance and commitment wrapped up in a sweet package.

3. "All The Way Home"
(Devils & Dust)
A catchy song with a great guitar riff about second chances by someone who's seen it all but isn't quite ready to give up. The song itself has been around awhile. According to Christopher Phillips, Springsteen wrote it for Southside Johnny (it appears on Southside's 1991 *Better Days* album); Springsteen also performed it several times while on tour in 1992-1993.

4. "Because The Night"
(Bruce Springsteen & The E Street Band Live/1975–85)

A Top 20 hit for co-writer Patti Smith in 1978, this passionate, slow-burning rocker is all about seizing the moment.

5. "Be True"
(Chimes Of Freedom, Tracks)

"You be true to me / And I'll be true to you"—if any words can sum up Springsteen's philosophy, the lyrics to this solid mid-tempo pop song must be it. Fiercely romantic and rampant with cinematic imagery, "Be True" appeared on the B-side of "Fade Away" in 1981. A live version, recorded in Detroit on March 28, 1988, is on the *Chimes Of Freedom* EP before popping up again on *Tracks*. Sweet and tender, in another era (think the Sixties) it would have soared to the top of the charts.

6. "The Big Payback"
(The Essential Bruce Springsteen)

A short, infectious spurt of robust rockabilly.

7. "Bishop Danced"
(Tracks)

Recorded live at the seminal club Max's Kansas City in 1973, this represents early Springsteen at his surreal best.

8. "Bring On The Night"
(Tracks)

This short (under three minutes) urgent rocker cuts right to the bone as the narrator, confused and sodden with the heartache of an unrequited love, walks the street at night "lookin' for romance," but only ends up "stumblin' in some stupid half-trance." The darkness consumes him in more ways than one.

9. "Cadillac Ranch"
(The River)

Pure rowdy fun. Nothing more, nothing less.

10. "Candy's Room"
(Born To Run)

Danger—or the possibility of it—is everywhere in this song, from Max Weinberg's ominous drumming to Springsteen's barely restrained vocals.

11. "Car Wash"

(Tracks)

Two minutes of working-class angst from the unusual perspective (unusual for a rock song sung by a male, that is) of a young woman who works in a car wash by day with dreams of becoming a nightclub singer.

12. "Code Of Silence"

(The Essential Bruce Springsteen)

A tough, guitar-based rocker, co-written by Joe Gruschecky, about conceit, broken promises, and words left unsaid.

13. "Cover Me"

(Born In The U.S.A.)

A danceable beat with a pleading vocal and a lyric that just begs for protection.

14. "Dead Man Walkin'"

(The Essential Bruce Springsteen)

Title song from the Tim Robbins movie, it offers a terse lyric—powerful in its very conciseness—and keys in decidedly minor chords, altogether appropriate given the subject matter of the movie (the execution of a Louisiana murderer). "I tuned the *E* string of my guitar down to a *D* and cut it as low a key as possible to get as much deepness and darkness I could out of the music," Springsteen explains in the liner notes to *The Essential Bruce Springsteen.*

15. "Dollhouse"

(Tracks)

Nervy and taut rocker from the late Seventies about a relationship on the rocks where pretense can no longer hold a couple together.

16. "Dry Lightning"

(The Ghost Of Tom Joad)

A thoughtful, bare-bones ballad with a slightly Mexican feel, although the imagery itself is strictly Western. In their preciseness alone, the first four lines of the song are reminiscent—in both feel and tone—of Annie Proulx's short story "Brokeback Mountain."

17. "The E Street Shuffle"

(The Wild, The Innocent & The E Street Shuffle)

A young man's paean to summer—buoyant, brassy, and full of life. Springsteen says he based the song on Major Lance's soul classic "Monkey Time."

18. "Frankie"

(Tracks)

From the *Darkness On The Edge Of Town* sessions, this seven-minute plus story-song treads familiar terrain—lovers floundering in a dying town—but the commitment in Springsteen's voice, as well as the harmonica segue and a late appearance of Clarence Clemons' saxophone make it memorable.

19. "From Small Things (Big Things One Day Come)"

(The Essential Bruce Springsteen)

Springsteen gave this energetic, tongue-in-cheek, Chuck Berry soundalike number to Welsh rocker Dave Edmunds with marvelous results but the Boss is no slouch either.

20. "The Fuse"

(The Rising)

Scenes from America immediately after September 11—bringing the flag down at a courthouse, a long black line of cars driving through town in a funereal march, an empty house on a quiet afternoon—set to a sensuous, hypnotic techno rhythm. In the Spike Lee film *25th Hour* composer Terence Blanchard gave the song a new mix, adding an orchestral arrangement to the original.

21. "Glory Days"

(Born In The U.S.A.)

The song is about many things—baseball, rock 'n' roll, the optimism of youth, the agony of aging. The combination of organ, piano, and guitar, coupled with Springsteen's friendly vocals creates a timeless garage band sound, yet its very cheerfulness belies the undercurrent of sadness: Look away and it will all be gone before you know it.

22. "Hearts Of Stone"

(*Tracks*)

A minor hit for Southside Johnny and the Asbury Jukes, "Hearts Of Stone" is a soulful, mournful ballad made even more memorable by Clarence Clemons' sax and a first-class horn section, including trumpets and trombones.

23. "The Hitter"

(*Devils & Dust*)

A quiet, trenchant song, well written with precise details about a down-on-his-luck boxer—weary from having fought too many fights—who returns to his mother's home seeking refuge and, it seems, forgiveness—to no avail. During the *Devils & Dust* tour, Springsteen introduced "The Hitter" by talking about choice: "I always figure we carry with us the seeds of creation—the possibility to build good things and make good things—and, also, the seeds of our destruction. And that is part of the merry human package. I think that was the deal we made with God, supposedly—the whole 'East Of Eden' thing." The title character has made his choices—some good and some bad—he knows who he is and what he has done and, for better or worse, he has made peace with his decisions and the course of his life's path.

24. "Hungry Heart"

(*The River*)

Springsteen's huge hit—a fun song with an infectious melody, although the too-short lyric hints of darker undercurrents.

25. "Iceman"

(*Tracks*)

A haunting piano-based song that starts slowly but gains power along the way. It also features the quintessential Springsteen lyric, "I wanna go out tonight, I wanna find out what I got" and several striking examples of Old Testament imagery, particularly "white angels of Eden with their flamin' swords" and "glory roads of heaven."

26. "Incident On 57th Street"

(*The Wild, The Innocent & The E Street Shuffle*)

An operatic tale, part *West Side Story*, part Wild West yarn set in the East with a cast of colorful characters (pimps and street thugs carrying switchblade knives with names like Spanish Johnny and Puerto Rican Jane) with a fairy-tale-like piano coda.

27. "Janey Don't You Lose Heart"

(Tracks)

A gentle, soothing mid-tempo rocker about trying to keep dreams alive.

28. "Johnny Bye-Bye"

(Tracks)

Recorded in 1983 at Thrill Hill in Los Angeles in a converted garage, Springsteen recorded every part himself using a drum machine and keyboards. A homage to Elvis Presley, this exceptionally short song (just over two minutes) with the rockabilly beat evolved from a *Darkness On The Edge Of Town* outtake called "Let's Go Tonight" and was first performed on the European leg of *The River* tour with the title of "Bye Bye Johnny." Springsteen rightly credits Chuck Berry as the co-author since Berry's "Bye Bye Johnny" provided the basic structure and several of the lines. Slightly adjusting the title, Springsteen released "Johnny Bye Bye" as the B-side of "I'm On Fire" in 1985, although the version heard on *Tracks* is considerably different. Specifically, writes Erik Flannigan and Christopher Phillips in *Backstreets Liner Notes,* "It begins with a count-in not found on the 1985 issue, and lead guitar and keyboard overdubs heard on the end of the B-side have disappeared. Most significantly, the *Tracks* version uses a drum machine, which was replaced on the B-side by a simple snare, bass, and hi-hat part...."

29. "Jungleland"

(Born To Run)

Although it sounds overwrought to these ears, there is no denying its power and the almost mythic place it holds for many fans in the Springsteen canon. And, indeed, the characters are either larger than life (Magic Rat, Flamingo) or archetypal ("barefoot girl sitting on a hood of a Dodge"). It is full of lonely and desperate lovers lurking in dark corners while gunshots echo in the night as the misfits and outcasts take their "honest stand" on the city streets. The introduction has an elegant feel to it, almost classical, before a mournful sax and atmospheric piano give it a tougher, more urban sound. Most Springsteen fans love "Jungleland" but even for those who, like me, don't accept it wholeheartedly, to ignore it would be foolhardy.

> ### LITERARY SPRINGSTEEN
> Writers as varied as Bobbie Ann Mason, Richard Ford, and Stephen King refer back to Springsteen. King opens *The Stand* with a quotation from "Jungleland" while T.C. Boyle's title story from his short story collection *Greasy Lake* directly invokes Springsteen.
>
> In 2005, two literary works used Springsteen's work as inspiration. Tennessee Jones's *Deliver Me From Nowhere* contains 10 linked stories suggested by Springsteen's stark masterpiece *Nebraska* while the short story anthology *Meeting Across The River* edited by Jessica Kaye and Richard J. Brewer consists of 20 stories inspired by Springsteen's cryptic song of the same name about two small-time hoods reaching one last time for the brass ring

30. "Kitty's Back"

(The Wild, The Innocent & The E Street Shuffle)

Sophisticated, urbane, and jazzy, if at times strident, Springsteen describes it as "a swing tune, a shuffle, a distorted piece of big band music." The minute-long guitar introduction is reminiscent of James Brown's "It's A Man's World," before it shifts gear into a looser, frenetic, jazzy homage to the night.

31. "Leap Of Faith"

(Lucky Town)

A joyous rocker that straddles the sacred with the profane.

32. "Living On The Edge Of The World"

(Tracks)

The alternate version of "State Trooper"—sounds like the Clash meets Sam the Sham and the Pharoahs with a cheesy Tex-Mex organ thrown in the loop. With its jerky punk rhythms, harmonica, and hand claps, it's a pure adrenaline rush.

33. "Loose Change"

(Tracks)

Dark tale about a drifter with no connections. Another chilling example of Springsteen noir.

34. "Loose Ends"
(Tracks)

An end of a relationship song, this one boasts pungent lyrics and a soulful solo sax.

35. "Lost In The Flood"
(Greetings From Asbury Park, N.J.)

An anti-war precursor to "Born In The U.S.A.," this rambling, complex tale about a soldier returning home from the war features profane imagery (bald nuns running through the Vatican, wretched souls on Main Street drinking unholy blood) and colorful characters with equally colorful nicknames (Sticker, Gunner, Jimmy the Saint) before culminating in a violent but wildly stylized shoot-out in the Bronx. Frustrating, maddening, and brimming with ideas, it captures Springsteen at a moment early in his career where the words just spewed forth like an unstoppable geyser.

36. "Man At The Top"
(Tracks)

An excellent little parable with an especially fetching melody about never being satisfied with what you have and always looking for more. E Street Band member Nils Lofgren performed a fine rendition on the Springsteen tribute album *Light Of Day.*

37. "Meeting Across The River"
(Born To Run)

Moody slice of music noir about small-time hoods and a last chance illegal scam. Enigmatic and jazz-infused, Randy Brecker's lonely horn gives it an almost unbearably poignant air.

38. "Murder Incorporated"
(Greatest Hits)

A fierce little rocker about living life dangerously—whether by choice or circumstance.

39. "My Love Will Not Let You Down"
(Tracks)

Lyrically similar to "Bring On The Night," this is another philosophical statement courtesy of the Boss—about another desperate character who is not afraid to make a commitment. Depending on your point of view, it could be honorable or just plain scary.

40. "New York City Serenade"
(The Wild, The Innocent & The E Street Shuffle)

Piano, keyboards, and jazz set the urban nightclub mood for this nearly 10-minute epic of midnight in Manhattan. Here, Springsteen sounds strikingly like Van Morrison circa *Astral Weeks.*

41. "Over The Rise"
(Tracks)

A stark, Sixties-style ballad about lost love and soured dreams. Forever the movie buff, Springsteen even quotes a line from Pauline Kael's *I Lost It At The Movies:* "Is a promise that love couldn't keep same as a promise broken?" A latter-day variation of "The River's" "Is a dream a lie if it don't come true or is it something worse?"

42. "Ramrod"
(The River)

Sure this retro rockabilly piece of fluff is sexist at heart but who cares when you're having so much fun?

43. "Real World"
(Human Touch)

About a man who has had it with pretense, phoniness, and the charade of modern life (Springsteen himself?). He is still a seeker but, this time around, he is not afraid to ask for a little help.

44. "Reno"
(Devils & Dust)

Some love it but probably a lot more hate it. Despite the sexually explicit lyrics, "Reno," about a man who is having a fling with a prostitute, is actually quite sweet-tempered (with a lovely, unobtrusive melody) albeit in a rough-edged way. It is historically important for earning Springsteen his first advisory warning label on the album cover.

TEN FUNNIEST SPRINGSTEEN SONGS

There's *Serious Bruce,* and there's *Funny Bruce.* The following are the ten funniest, friendliest songs in the Springsteen canon:

"Cadillac Ranch"
"Crush On You"
"I'm A Rocker"
"Part Man, Part Monkey"
"Pink Cadillac"
"Ramrod"
"Rosalita (Come Out Tonight)"
"Sherry Darling"
"Stand On It"
"TV Movie"

45. "Ricky Wants A Man Of Her Own"

(*Tracks*)

Growing up is hard to do. The mother says her "little girl" won't talk to her anymore and the father is just plain exasperated—he doesn't know what to do and how to behave around his teenage daughter. It isn't often puberty is taken seriously in a pop song. Springsteen adds an extra bit of spice with a tasty Tex-Mex organ sound.

46. "Sad Eyes"

(*Tracks*)

A fan favorite, "Sad Eyes" is a gorgeously poignant ballad about elusive love. Although recorded in 1990, during the *Human Touch/Lucky Town* era and using some of the same musicians, it sounds almost anachronistic, like a long lost 1960's song, complete with chiming falsetto and ringing guitar. The intoxicating melody makes the slightly arrogant (and ominously paranoid) lyrics easier to swallow. Is this guy really in love with her or does he simply want to control her? Springsteen playfully experiments with phrasing too, embellishing the word "sad" in almost melismatic fashion until it becomes barely recognizable.

47. "Santa Ana"
(*Tracks*)

An early, impressionistic bar song that features Daniel "whupping" the devil, the Giants of Science (presumably J. Robert Oppenheimer and company) in the New Mexican desert, Sam Houston in Texas fighting for his life at the Alamo, and a mythic gunslinger named Kid Cole. Weird, strange, and set in a universe strictly all its own.

48. "Seaside Bar Song"
(*Tracks*)

Springsteen's early obsessions are all represented here: cars, sand, rock 'n' roll, and, of course, "the night." A lyrical precursor to "Rosalita," Springsteen would lift many lyrics and themes from "Seaside Bar Song" for other, better-known songs. "The highway is alive tonight" appears here, as does his fixation with cars (chrome wheels, stick shift), along with some evocative Jersey Shore imagery (running barefoot in the sand listening to Bo Diddley's guitar).

49. "Sherry Darling"
(*The River*)

Hilarious lyrics, a catchy chorus, *and* plenty of Clarence's sax makes for sheer joy.

50. "She's The One"
(*Born to Run*)

Springsteen gives this *Born to Run* rocker an infectious Bo Diddley beat with lyrics filled with angst, yearning, and the pleasures of long summer nights.

51. "Soul Driver"
(*Human Touch*)

An underrated soul ballad, it features some gorgeous organ work from ex-E Street member David Sancious and lovely harmony vocals courtesy of Sam Moore (of Sam and Dave fame), as well as striking lyrics laced with Old Testament imagery ("Rode through 40 nights of the gospel's rain").

52. "Stand On It"

(*Tracks*)

Anyone who insists Springsteen doesn't have a healthy sense of humor should listen to this hilarious rockabilly raver, ostensibly about a car race but somehow Columbus and Queen Isabella manage to get into the picture too. "A lot of my favorite rock performers were clowns," says Springsteen—and it shows. Who says rock can't be clever? To these ears, Springsteen's hyperkinetic "Stand On It" echoes both in spirit and language a rock and roll version of punster poet Ogden Nash's humorous "Columbus." Compare Springsteen's version:

> *Well now, Columbus, he discovered America even though he hadn't planned on it.*
> *He got lost and woke up one morning when he's about to land on it.*

...with Nash's couplet:

> *So Columbus said, Somebody show me the sunset and somebody did and he set sail for it*
> *And he discovered America and they put him in jail for it*

53. "Thundercrack"

(*Tracks*)

Before there was "Rosalita," there was "Thundercrack," a sloppy, chaotic mess of a song where a very young and undisciplined Springsteen throws everything he has into the mix. Does it work? Not completely, but it is undeniably fun just the same.

54. "TV Movie"

(*Tracks*)

A cousin of "Stand On It" (see above) and for that matter "Pink Cadillac," this piano-based rockabilly gem is worthy of Jerry Lee Lewis and is funny and self-deprecating as hell. Underneath all the fun though lies a (gently) biting social commentary about pop culture, identity, and commercialization.

55. "Used Cars"

(*Nebraska*)

A poignant tale about a young boy, trapped in a cycle of poverty and humiliation, who vows when he grows up to never ride "in no used car again."

56. "Waitin' On A Sunny Day"

(*The Rising*)

Funny and bouncy; a pure pop guilty pleasure.

57. "When You Need Me"

(*Tracks*)

One of Springsteen's sweetest songs and most heartfelt vocals.

58. "When You're Alone"

(*Tunnel Of Love*)

A moving song about the pain—and cost—of isolation.

59. "Where The Bands Are"

(*Tracks*)

Another long-time fan favorite, this infectious rocker, with its guitar solo, sax break, vigorous drumming, and handclaps is just about sheer fun and the joy that rock music can bring.

60. "Zero And Blind Terry"

(*Tracks*)

The first of Springsteen's romantic epics, it's full of teenage angst and urban myths: street gangs with names like the Skulls and the Pythons and the ill-fated love between a gang leader named Zero and his girlfriend Terry (whose father thinks Zero is a "no good"..."thief" and "liar"). Springsteen would revisit this milieu to better effect in songs like "Backstreets" and "Jungleland," but it pretty much started here.

TEN WORST SPRINGSTEEN SONGS

The best of the worst:

"Mary Queen Of Arkansas"

"The Angel"

"Mary's Place"

"My Best Was Never Good Enough"

"Roll Of The Dice"

"The Long Goodbye"

"Gloria's Eyes"

"With Every Wish"

"Cross My Heart"

"All The Way Home"

Further Reading

Arax, Mark, and Tom Gorman. "California's Illicit Farm Belt Export." *Los Angeles Times,* March 13, 1995.

Binelli, Mark. "Bruce Springsteen's American Gospel." *Rolling Stone,* August 22, 2002.

Bonca, Cornel. "Save Me Somebody: Bruce Springsteen's Rock 'n' Roll Covenant." Killingthebuddha.com. Accessed November 3, 2002.

Boxer, Sarah. "New Jersey Selects Its Sept. 11 Memorial." *New York Times,* July 1, 2004.

Carlozo, Louis R. "Beyond Oscars, Nominees Speak of Subtler Rewards." *Chicago Tribune,* February 21, 2006.

Carr, Patrick, ed. *The Illustrated History of Country Music.* Foreword by Johnny Cash. New York: Random House/Times Books, 1995.

Cohen, Norm. *Long Steel Rail: The Railroad in American Folksong.* Urbana, Ill.: University of Illinois Press, 1981.

Corn, David. "Born in th USA: Bruce Springsteen Rocks the American Folk Tradition or *We Shall Overcome: The Seeger Session. Guitar World Acoustic,* August 2006.

Corn, David. "Bruce: Springsteen tells the story of the secret America." Mother Jones. www.motherjones.com. Accessed November 3, 2002.

Cowie, Jefferson. "Fandom, Faith, and Bruce Springsteen." *Dissent*, Winter 2001.

Coyne, Kevin. "The Faulkner of Freehold." *Asbury Park Press*, March 14, 1999.

Coyne, Kevin. "His Hometown." *New Jersey Monthly*, January 2003.

Croft, Karen. "A Saint in the City." Salon.com, July 17, 1999.

Cullen, Jim. *Born In The U.S.A.: Bruce Springsteen and the American Tradition.* New York: HarperCollins Publishers, 1997; Wesleyan University, 2005.

Dalton, Joseph. "My Home Town." *Rolling Stone*, October 10, 1985.

Dann, Trevor. "Reborn in the USA" BBC1 transcript. February 25, 1996. *www.greasylake.com.*

Dawidoff, Nicholas. *In the Country of Country: A Journey to the Roots of American Music.* New York: Vintage, 1997.

Dees, Morris. *A Season for Justice.* New York: Charles Scribner's Sons, 1991.

Demarest, David P., Jr. *"The River Ran Red": Homestead 1892.* Pittsburgh Series in Local and Labor History. Pittsburgh: University of Pittsburgh Press, 1992.

Diallo, Kadiatou, and Craig Wolff. *My Heart Will Cross This Ocean: My Story, My Son, Amadou.* New York: One World/Ballantine, 2003.

Duckworth, Cheryl. "A Runaway American Dream: Springsteen Sings Whitman's America." *Washington Times*, 1999. Online: www.greasylake.org. Accessed February 22, 2003.

Dunn, Geoffrey. "Can Bruce Springsteen catch up to his own past as a populist?" www.metroactive.com. Accessed June 28, 2002.

Dunning, Jennifer. "Swaying, Rocking, Running and Spinning to Springsteen." *New York Times*, January 26, 2006.

Escott, Colin. *Lost Highway: The True Story of Country Music.* Washington, D.C.: Smithsonian Books, 2003.

Feuer, Alan. "$3 Million Paid in Police Killing of Immigrant." *New York Times*, January 7, 2004.

Filene, Benjamin. *Romancing the Folk: Public Memory & American Roots Music.* Chapel Hill, NC: University of North Carolina Press, 2000.

Flannigan, Erik, and Christopher Phillips. The *Backstreets* Liner Notes.

Frank, Robert. *The Americans.* New York: Grove Press, 1959.

Gardner, Elysa. "Springsteen 'Rising.'" *USA Today*, July 14, 2002.

Gifford, Matt. "Jordan Revisited: Rethinking 'Empty Sky.'" *Backstreets*, Spring 2004.

Gleason, Ralph J. "Hank Williams, Roy Acuff, and Then God!" *Rolling Stone*, June 28, 1969.

Goldstein, Stan, and Jean Mikle. *Rock 'n' roll Tour of the Jersey Shore.* Rev. ed. Self-published, 2005.

Gray, Michael. *Song and Dance Man III: The Art of Bob Dylan.* London: Continuum, 2000.

Gullason, Thomas A., ed. *The Complete Short Stories and Sketches of Stephen Crane.* New York: Doubleday, 1963.

Guterman, Jimmy. *Runaway American Dream: Listening to Bruce Springsteen.* New York: Da Capo Press, 2005.

Hagen, Mark. "Springsteen Interview." *Mojo Magazine,* January 1999.

Hampton, Henry. "Nebraska." *In The Rose & the Briar: Death, Love, and Liberty in the American Ballad.* Edited by Sean Wilentz and Greil Marcus. New York: W. W. Norton, 2005.

Hedin, Benjamin, ed. *Studio A: The Bob Dylan Reader.* New York: W. W. Norton, 2004.

Henderson, Lyndee Jobe, and Ro Dean Jobe. *Johnstown.* Images of America series. Charleston, S. C.: Arcadia Publishing, 2003.

Hepworth, David. "The Q Interview." *Q Magazine,* August 1992.

Hermes, Will. "Born to Strum." *New York Times,* April 16, 2006.

Hilburn, Robert. "Under the Boss' Skin." *Los Angeles Times,* April 1, 2001.

Horan, Stephen. "Springsteen's Religious Narrative and the Politics of Culture." Unpublished manuscript presented at "Glory Days: A Bruce Springsteen Symposium" organized by Penn State University. Held at Monmouth University and Sheraton Eatontown Center, New Jersey, September 8-11, 2005.

Jones, Tennessee. *Deliver Me from Nowhere.* Brooklyn, N.Y.: Soft Skull Press, 2005.

Judge, Mark Gauvreau. "The Cult of Bruce." *Wall Street Journal,* August 23, 2002.

Kaye, Jessica, and Richard J. Brewer, eds. Meeting Across The River: Stories *Inspired by the Haunting Bruce Springsteen Song.* New York: Bloomsbury, 2005.

Kot, Greg. "After 30 Years, Springsteen's 'Run' Is Music to Live For." *Chicago Tribune,* November 13, 2005.

Kot, Greg. "Night of Renewal: Springsteen Adopts Preacher's Role, Delivers the Goods." *Chicago Tribune,* September 29, 1999.

Landau, Jon. "Growing Young with Rock 'n' roll." *The Real Paper,* May 22, 1974.

Lee, Felicia R. "Still a Song to Sing All Over This Land." *New York Times*, June 14, 2006.

Lindberg, Peter Jon. "Forever Asbury." *Travel + Leisure*, August 2004.

Loeffler, William. "'Springsteen & Seeger' Blends Rock Music with Ballet." *Pittsburgh Tribune-Review*, April 29-May 5, 2004.

Loder, Kurt. "Gimme Shelter: Springsteen Searches for Love and Faith in the Ruins. Bruce Springsteen: *The Rising*." *Rolling Stone*, August 22, 2002.

Maharidge, Dale, and Michael Williamson. *Journey to Nowhere: The Saga of the New Underclass*. Introduction by Bruce Springsteen. New York: Hyperion, 1996.

Malone, Bill C. *Country Music, U.S.A.: A Fifty-Year History*. Austin, Tex.: University of Texas Press, 1968.

Marcus, Greil. *Invisible Republic: Bob Dylan's Basement Tapes*. New York: Henry Holt, 1997.

Marsh, Dave. *Glory Days: Bruce Springsteen in the 1980s*. New York: Pantheon Books, 1987.

Marsh, Dave. *Bruce Springsteen: Two Hearts: The Definitive Biography, 1972–2003*. New York: Routledge, 2004.

Martin, Gavin. "Hey Joad, Don't Make It Sad…(Oh, Go On Then): NME Interview with Bruce Springsteen." *New Musical Express*, March 9, 1996.

Masur, Louis P. "The Long Run with Springsteen: Bruce Is the Boss of the Road and Our Dreams." *Chicago Tribune*, August 21, 2005.

Mayshark, Jesse Fox. "A Guitar Festival Begins with a Trip to 'Nebraska.'" *New York Times*, January 13, 2006.

McCullough, David. *The Johnstown Flood*. New York: Simon & Schuster, 1968.

McMurtry, Larry. *Roads: Driving America's Great Highways*. New York: Simon & Schuster, 2000.

Metcalf, Stephen. "Faux Americana: Why I Still Love Bruce Springsteen." *Slate*, May 5, 2005.

Millman, Joyce. "To Sleep, Perchance to Dream about the Boss." Salon.com, August 8, 1997.

Morthland, John. *The Best of Country Music*. Garden City, NY: Doubleday & Company, 1984.

New Jersey's Monmouth County Music Heritage: Map & Guide Volume 1: Musical Snapshot 1970–2003. Monmouth County, NJ: Monmouth County Music Heritage Map Committee, 2204.

Newman, Cathy. "Greetings from the Jersey Shore." *National Geographic*, August 2004.

O'Connor, Flannery. *The Complete Stories.* New York: Noonday Press, 1996.

O'Connor, Flannery. *Everything That Rises Must Converge.* New York: Farrar, Straus and Giroux, 1993.

O'Connor, Flannery. *A Good Man Is Hard to Find and Other Stories.* San Diego: Harvest/Harcourt Brace & Company, 1983.

Pareles, Jon. "'Born To Run' Reborn 30 Years Later: The Young Boss, Seen in a Documentary and a London Concert." *New York Times,* November 15, 2005.

Pareles, Jon. "His Kind of Heroes, His Kind of Songs." New York Times, July 14, 2002.

Pareles, Jon. "Bruce Almighty: Having lost his bet on John Kerry, the Boss turns to a higher authority." *New York Times,* April 24, 2005.

Percy, Will. "Rock and Read: Will Percy Interviews Bruce Springsteen." *Doubletake Magazine,* Spring 1998.

Phillips, Christopher. "Citizen Bruce: Interview." *Backstreets,* Summer/Fall 2004.

Phillips, Christopher. "The Devil's in the Details." *Backstreets,* Winter 2005/Spring 2006.

Phillips, Christopher. "With These Hands." *Backstreets,* Winter 2005/Spring 2006.

Piazza, Tom. "Just Plain Folk: Pete Seeger Shares His Views on Bruce Springsteen's New Album..." *Guitar World Acoustic,* August 2006.

Pike, Helen-Chantal. *Asbury Park. Images of America.* Charleston, S.C.: Arcadia Publishing, 1997.

Poole, Shawn. "Is Elvis Home? Springsteen Jumps the Wall." *Backstreets,* Summer/Fall 2004.

Poole, Shawn. "Bruce's Golden Records: Springsteen Recordings that Reference Elvis." *Backstreets,* Summer/Fall 2004.

Prial, Dunstan. *The Producer: John Hammond and the Soul of American Music.* New York: *Farrar, Straus and Giroux,* 2006.

Rockwell, John. "Baby, We Were Born to Dance: The Boss Goes to the Ballet." *New York Times,* January 22, 2006.

"Rock and Remembrance." *The Economist,* August 1, 2002.

Rolling Stone, eds. *Bruce Springsteen: The Rolling Stone Files.* Introduction by Parke Puterbaugh. New York: Hyperion, 1996.

Rotella, Sebastian. "Children of the Border: Caught in a Makeshift Life, Immigrants, Youth Eke Out a Living in San Diego's Balboa Park." *Los Angeles Times,* April 3, 1993.

Santelli, Robert. Liner notes. *Badlands: A Tribute to Bruce Springsteen's Nebraska,* 2000.

Santelli, Robert, and Emily Davidson, eds. *Hard Travelin': The Life and Legacy of Woody Guthrie.* Hanover, N.H.: Wesleyan University Press, 1999.

Sawyers, June Skinner, ed. *Racing In The Street: The Bruce Springsteen Reader.* New York: Penguin Books, 2004.

Sawyers, June Sawyers. "Deliver Me from Nowhere: Spiritual Longing in the Music of Bruce Springsteen." Unpublished manuscript presented at "Glory Days: A Bruce Springsteen Symposium" organized by Penn State University. Held at Monmouth University and Sheraton Eatontown Center, New Jersey, September 8-11, 2005.

Scott, A. O.. "The Boss Bibliography." *New York Times,* July 3, 2005.

Sinclair, Tom. "'Born' Supremacy: Thirty Years after It Made Bruce the Boss, Born To Run Is Back." *Entertainment Weekly,* November 18, 2005.

Smith, Larry David. *Bob Dylan, Bruce Springsteen, and American Song.* Westport, Conn,: Praeger, 2002.

Smith, Martha Nell. "Sexual Mobilities in Bruce Springsteen: Performance as Commentary." *South Atlantic Quarterly,* Fall 1991.

Springsteen, Bruce. "Chords for Change." *New York Times,* August 5, 2004.

Springsteen, Bruce. *Songs.* Rev. ed. New York: Harper Entertainment/ Harper Collins Publishers, 2003.

Springsteen, Bruce. Letter to the Editor. "Greetings from Rumson, N.J." *New York Times,* July 31, 2005.

Springsteen, Bruce. As told to Cal Fussman. "It Happened in New Jersey." *Esquire,* August 2005.

Steinbeck, John. *The Grapes Of Wrath.* New York: Viking Press, 1939.

Steinbeck, John. *The Harvest Gypsies: On the Road to "The Grapes Of Wrath."* Introduction by Charles Wollenberg. Berkeley, Calif.: Heyday Books, 1996.

Sweeting, Adam. "Into The Fire." *Uncut,* September 2002.

Tate, Greg. "Tear the Roof Off Jungleland." *Village Voice,* August 11-17, 1999.

Tichi, Cecelia. *High Lonesome: The American Culture of Country Music.* Chapel Hill, N.C: University of North Carolina Press, 1994.

Tutelian, Louise. "Betting On (and In) Atlantic City." *New York Times,* March 3, 2006.

Tyrangiel, Josh. "Bruce Rising." *Time,* August 5, 2002.

Vranish, Jane. "Songs of Springsteen, Seeger Inspire Working-class Ballets at PBT." *Pittsburgh Post-Gazette,* April 25, 2004.

Weiner, Jonah. "'Cold Case,' Hot Tunes: Springsteen's Soundtrack." *New York Times,* January 7, 2006.

Wilentz, Sean, and Greil Marcus, eds. *The Rose & the Briar: Death, Love, and Liberty in the American Ballad.* New York: W. W. Norton, 2005.

Wilkinson, Alec. "The Protest Singer: Pete Seeger and American Folk Music." *New Yorker,* April 17, 2006.

Wolff, Daniel. "Directions to the Promised Land." *Doubletake Magazine,* Spring 2000.

Wolff, Daniel. Fourth of July, *Asbury Park: A History of the Promised Land.* New York: Bloomsbury, 2005.

About the Author

Born in Glasgow, Scotland, June Skinner Sawyers has written extensively about music, travel, history, spirituality, and popular culture. She contributes regularly for the *Chicago Tribune*, where she used to write a nightlife column, and the *San Francisco Chronicle*. She has taught numerous classes in the humanities at the Newberry Library in Chicago, including a course that studied the music of Bruce Springsteen. She is the author or editor of more than a dozen books, including *Celtic Music* (Da Capo Press), *Racing in the Street: The Bruce Springsteen Reader* (Penguin), and the forthcoming *About a Lucky Band that Made the Grade: The Beatles Together...and Apart* (Penguin). She lives in Chicago.

Index

A

"Across The Border," 110, 153–54, 178; mystical qualities of, 154. *See also* "Matamoros Banks"

"Across The Borderline," 4, 154

Acuff, Roy, 64, 70, 74

"Adam Raised A Cain," 40–42, 46, 213, 245

Agee, James, 140

"Ain't Got You," 247

Alamo Bay (film), 157

"All Or Nothin' At All," 124

"All That Heaven Will Allow," 247

"All The Way Home," 260

Amadou Diallo Foundation, 237

Amazing Grace: The Lives Of Children And The Conscience of a Nation (Kozol), 40

America: A Tribute To Heroes (television concert), 162, 169

American Babylon, 200

American Ballads And Folk Songs, 240

American Industrial Ballads, 182

"American Land," 180, 181

"American Skin (41 Shots)," 91, 147, 235–38; misinterpretation of, 235

The Americans (Frank), 75

And Their Children After Them: The Legacy Of Let Us Know Praise Famous Men (Maharidge and Williamson), 140

"The Angel," 7, 260

"Angel From Montgomery," 99

Animals, 37, 39

Another Side Of Bob Dylan, 138

"Another Thin Line," 117

Anthology of American Folk Music, 78, 79, 80, 183

Aplin, Billy Joe, 155

Appel, Mike, 7, 229

Arax, Mark, 143

Arlen, Alice, 157

Arquette, Patricia, 82

"Around And Around," 44

Asbury, Francis, 16

Asbury Park (New Jersey), 12, 13, 19, 27, 42; history of, 15–16; and "My City Of Ruins," 169; renewal, talk of, 171; riots in, 17, 18; as rock 'n' roll landmark, 172; and Stone Pony, 172; Tillie, as personification of, 114; and *Tunnel Of Love*, 113, 114

Astral Weeks, 255

Atlantic City (New Jersey), 19, 76

"Atlantic City," 63, 76–77, 79, 95; video of, 76

B

Baby, It's You (film), 245

"Baby, Let's Play House," 218

"Back In Your Arms," 222

"Backstreets," 29–30, 146, 259

"Back In The U.S.A.," 44

"Badlands," 37–38, 40, 45

Badlands (film), 69, 70, 71, 73

Badlands: A Tribute To Bruce Springsteen's Nebraska, 77, 84, 97

Bad Luck Streak In Dancing School, 215

"Balboa Park," 149, 150–51, 178

The Band, 1

Banderas, Antonio, 197

Bangs, Lester, 5, 33

Battle of Homestead Foundation, 202

Beach Boys, 25, 44

Beam, Louis, 155

Beatles, 3, 39, 217

Beaver, Ninette, 73

"Because The Night," 215, 248

Belmar (New Jersey), 27

Bernsen, Corbin, 156

Berry, Chuck, 4, 20, 39, 84, 218, 250, 251; Mann Act, violation of, 44

"Better Days," 127

Better Days, 247

"Be True," 248

"The Big Muddy," 128–29, 146

"The Big Payback," 248

Binelli, Mark, 162

"Bishop Danced," 248

Bittan, Roy, 29, 43, 58, 99, 199

"Black Cowboys," 40, 147, 150

Blanchard, Terence, 250

"Blinded By The Light," 3, 5, 151, 146, 148

"Blood Brothers," 195

"The Blue Bells Of Scotland," 202

"Bobby Jean," 63, 147

Bob Dylan, Bruce Springsteen, And American Song (Smith), 53

"Bob Dylan's Dream," 181

Bond, Julian, 156

Bonds, Gary "U.S.," 215

"Book Of Dreams," 130–31

The Border (film), 154

Born On The Fourth Of July (Kovic), 92

Born To Run, 23, 25, 49, 63, 64; as transitional, 32; as turning point, 31, 34

"Born To Run," 31–34, 117, 137, 146; as rock anthem, 31

Born To Run: 30ᵗʰ Anniversary Edition, 23

Born In The U.S.A., 89, 98, 133, 159, 207, 211, 212, 243; tour of, 80, 94, 192, 218

"Born In The U.S.A.," 48, 91–95, 162, 203, 212, 223, 254; misinterpretation of, 91, 93, 235; origin of, 92, 93; video of, 245

Boross, Bob, 167

Boss, Kenneth, 237

Boyle, T.C., 10, 253

Bradley, Ed, 14

Bradley, James A., 16, 17

Bragg, Billy, 39, 182

Brecker, Randy, 254

Brewer, Richard J., 253

"Brilliant Disguise," 63, 115–16; video of, 116

"Bring 'Em Home (If You Love Your Uncle Sam)," 180, 182

"Bring On The Night," 248, 254

"Brokeback Mountain" (short story), 112, 249

Broonzy, Big Bill, 240

"Brothers Under The Bridge," 94, 199, 223

Brown, James, 253

Browne, Jackson, 229

Bryan, William Jennings, 219, 220, 221

Bruce Springsteen & The E Street Band Live/1975–85, 75, 98, 187, 193, 194

Bruce Springsteen Greatest Hits, 137, 195, 199

Bruce Springsteen Live In New York City, 235, 238

Bull, Debby, 97

Burns, Robert, 181

Bush, George H.W.: and new world order, 137

Bush, George W., 183

"Bye Bye Johnny," 218

C

"Cadillac Ranch," 149, 248, 256

Cain, James M., 39

"Candy's Room," 146, 248

"Can't Help Falling In Love," 218

Carnegie, Andrew, 81, 142, 200, 201, 202

Carter Family, 38, 80, 183

Caril (Beaver), 73

Carroll, Sean, 237

Carter, Jimmy, 209

Carver, Raymond, 213

"Car Wash," 48, 248

"Casey Jones," 239

Cash, Johnny, 57, 97, 240

Castello, Marie (Madam Marie), 14, 172

Castiles, 6

"Cautious Man," 46, 110–11, 149

Center Of The Storm (Scopes), 221

Chabon, Michael, 31, 33

Chandler, Raymond, 59, 63

Child ballads, 57, 85, 109

"Child Bride." *See* "Working On The Highway"

"Chimes Of Freedom," 193

Chimes Of Freedom, 193, 248

"City of New Orleans," 240

The Clash, 84, 253

Claudius II, 119

Clemons, Clarence, 29, 53, 55, 149,

214, 222, 228, 243, 250, 251, 257

Cliff, Jimmy, 92, 193

Cocks, Jay, 105

"Code Of Silence," 249

Cold Case (television series), 62, 63

Cole, Natalie, 215

Collins, Tom, 136, 137

"Columbus," 258

Connors, Mike, 201

Cooder, Ry, 154, 182

Cooke, Sam, 3, 39

Corn, David, 139, 144

Cotten, Elizabeth, 240

"County Fair," 246

"Cover Me," 249

"Cowboys of the Sea," 7

Cox, Courteney, 100

Coyne, Kevin, 103, 163

Crane, Bob, 10, 102, 207

Crane, Stephen, 13, 16, 17

Creedence Clearwater Revival, 4

The Crossing Guard (film), 243

"Cross My Heart," 260

Crouch, Stanley, 236

"The Cruel Mother," 109

Cruise, Tom, 92

"Crush On You," 256

Cullen, Jim, 41, 79, 131, 157

Curtis Mayfield and the Impressions, 28

D

Dalton, Joseph, 102

"Dancing In The Dark," 5, 99–101, 214, 218; video of, 76, 99, 100

"Dancing In The Street," 44

Daniels, Julius, 78, 80

"Dark And Bloody Ground," 200

Darkness On The Edge of Town, 35, 37, 38, 44, 49, 63, 111, 213, 215, 218, 229, 250, 251; drive-in quality of, 47; writing of, 48

"Darkness On The Edge of Town," 49–50; mood of, 49

"Darlington County," 147

Darrow, Clarence, 219, 220, 221

Davis, Clive, 3

Days Of Heaven (film), 72

"Dead Man Walkin'," 249

Dean, James, 40, 41, 70, 149

DeCurtis, Anthony, 93, 113, 121

Dees, Morris, 156

Deliver Me From Nowhere (Jones), 253

Demme, Jonathan, 197

Denison, Iowa: Searching For The Soul Of America Through The Secrets Of A Midwest Town (Maharidge and Williamson), 140

DePalma, Brian, 100

"Deportee (Plane Wreck At Los Gatos)," 4, 39

Devils & Dust, xiv, 38, 173, 213; tour of, 7, 45, 55, 83, 118, 124, 153, 154, 176, 178, 202, 219, 251

"Devils & Dust," 94, 147, 175

Dexter, Pete, 40, 128, 129

Diallo, Amadou, 235, 236, 237

Diallo, Kadiatou, 237

Diddley, Bo, 214, 257

DiFranco, Ani, 39, 182

Dion, 131

"Dirty Water," 4

"Does This Bus Stop At 82nd Street?" 7, 146, 147

"Dollhouse," 249

Domino, Fats, 3

"Don't Look Back," 215

"Don't Worry Baby," 44

Dorsey, Tommy, 17

Douglas, Kirk, 221

"Downbound Train," 96–97, 147

"Do You Love Me?" 4

"Dream Baby Dream," 4

Drifters, 54

"Drive All Night," 62–63

"Dry Lightning," 249

Dust Bowl Ballads, 135, 138

Dylan, Bob, 1, 3, 7, 23, 34, 39, 57, 76, 138, 181, 193

E

Earle, Steve, 64, 96, 182

East of Eden (film), 40

East of Eden (Steinbeck), 39, 41

Easter, 215

Edmunds, Dave, 250

The Ed Sullivan Show (television series), 216

18 Tracks, 225, 229

Elliott, Ramblin' Jack, 39

Ely, Joe, 96

"Empty Sky," 163–64

"Empty Sky" (memorial), 163

"empty sky...*The Rising*" (dance piece), 167

Escott, Colin, 73, 74

Espinoza, Maria, 149

The Essential Bruce Springsteen, 193, 218, 231, 249

E Street Band, 38, 105, 127, 159, 193, 199, 222; reunion tour of, 235

"The E Street Shuffle," 148, 151, 250

Etheridge, Melissa, 215

Evans, Walker, 140

"Every Picture Tells A Story," 5, 100

F

"Factory," 47, 48, 53

"Fade Away," 59, 248

"Fade Away" (Holly), 214

Farina, Sandy, 94

Federici, Danny, 15, 53, 55, 59, 60, 154, 171

"The Fever," 225, 228

"57 Channels (And Nothing On)," 149, 218, 219

"Fire," 215

Fisk Jubilee Singers, 240

Flannigan, Erik, 252

Floyd, Harmonica Frank, 84

The Folk Songs Of North America (A. Lomax), 240

Folkways: A Vision Shared: A Tribute to Woody Guthrie and Leadbelly, 39

"Follow That Dream," 41, 218

Fonda, Henry, 135, 137

"For A Dancer," 229

Ford, John, 39, 48, 73, 135, 136, 137

Ford, Richard, 253

"Forever Young," 7

"For You," 8–9

Fourth of July, Asbury Park: A History Of The Promised Land (Wolff), 15

"4th of July, Asbury Park (Sandy)," 11, 13–19, 48, 146

Fox, Michael J., 93

Frank, Robert, 75

"Frankie," 94, 250

Frankie Lymon and the Teenagers, 17

"Freedom Train-A-Comin'," 240

Freehold (New Jersey), 102, 103, 163; racial tensions in, 101

The Freewheelin' Bob Dylan, 138
"Freight Train," 240
Fresh Fish Special, 215
Frick, Henry Clay, 81, 142, 200, 201
"Froggie Went A' Courtin'," 181
"From Small Things (Big Things One Day Come)," 250
Fugate, Caril, 70, 72
"The Fuse," 250

G
Gabriel, Peter, 165
"Galveston Bay," 155–57, 150; inspiration behind, 156
Garman, Bryan K., 78
Gathering Storm: America's Militia Threat (Dees), 156
Gelasius, 119
"The Ghost of Tom Joad," 27, 135–39, 149
The Ghost of Tom Joad, 38, 105, 150, 154, 193, 199, 223, 239; authenticity, lack of in, 139; Border Suite of, 178; and Woody Guthrie, 133; influences on, 138; tour of, 93, 154, 173; as social commentary, 133
Gilmore, Mikal, 40, 133
Gilmore, Patrick, 182
"Give The Girl a Kiss," 39
"Give Him A Great Big Kiss," 39
Glenn, Thomas Jefferson "Alabama," 152
"Gloria's Eyes," 147, 260
"Glory Days," 63, 147, 250; video of, 245
"Goin' Cali," 27
Goodman, Benny, 3, 17

Goodman, Steve, 240
"A Good Man Is Hard To Find" (short story), 74, 207–8
"A Good Man Is Hard To Find (Pittsburgh)," 94
Gordon, Robert, 215
Gorman, Michael J., 237
Gorman, Tom, 143
"The Gospel Train Is Coming," 240, 241
The Grapes Of Wrath (film), 39, 73, 135, 136, 138
The Grapes Of Wrath (Steinbeck), 39, 136, 137, 144, 151, 192
"Greasy Lake" (short story), 10
Greasy Lake (Boyle), 253
Great Revival, 26
Greeley, Andrew, 109, 118, 119
Green, Al, 28
Greetings From Asbury Park, N.J., xiv, 1, 5, 9, 18, 23, 114
Greg Kihn Band, 8, 215
Griffin, Patty, 61
"Growin' Up," 5–7
Grubb, Davis, 111
Grushecky, Joe, 117, 200, 201, 202, 249
Gulf War, 137
Gun Crazy (film), 48
Guterman, Jimmy, 15, 67, 95, 121
Guthrie, Arlo, 39
Guthrie, Woody, 37, 38, 78, 80, 93, 96, 136, 138, 181, 183, 194, 240; and *The Ghost of Tom Joad*, 133, 135

H
Haggard, Merle, 69, 96

Hagen, Mark, 32, 49

Hammond, John, 7, 203

Hank III, 77

Hanks, Tom, 197

Hanson, Jim, 141

"A Hard Rain's A-Gonna Fall," 181

Harrelson, Woody, 70

Harris, Ed, 157

Harris, Emmylou, 64

The Harvest Gypsies: On The Road To The Grapes Of Wrath (Steinbeck), 137. *See also* Their Blood Is Strong

Hate On Trial: The Case Against America's Militia Threat (Dees), 156

Hatfield, Bobby, 124

"Hearts Of Stone," 251

Heaton, James and Daniel, 141, 149

"He Lies In The American Land," 181, 182

Hepworth, David, 123

Heyday Books, 137

"Hey Porter," 240

Hiatt, Brian, 175

Hiatt, John, 78

"Highlands," 181

"Highway Patrolman," 81–82, 111, 146, 149, 243

"Highway 61 Revisited," 4

Hilburn, Robert, 74, 236

A History Of Violence (film), 111

"The Hitter," 149, 150, 213, 251

Holly, Buddy, 214

Homeland (Maharidge and Williamson), 140

"Homestead," 200–2

Homestead (Pennsylvania), 200, 201, 202

Hooker, John Lee, 74

Hopper, Edward, 67

Hornby, Nick, 27, 43

The Houserockers, 200

"How Can A Poor Man Stand Such Times and Live?" 180, 182, 183

Human Touch, 121, 125, 130, 218, 219, 256; making of, 123

"Human Touch," 123; religious imagery in, 123

"Hungry Heart," 51, 59, 251

"Hurricane," 76

Hurricane Katrina, 183; and New Orleans, 182

Huston, Anjelica, 243

Huston, John, 40, 73

I

"I Ain't Got No Home," 39, 183

"Iceman," 251

I Don't Want To Go Home, 215

"I Dreamed I Saw Joe Hill," 181

"I Dreamed I Saw St. Augustine," 181

"If I Should Fall Behind," 127

"If I Was the Priest," 7

I Lost It At The Movies (Kael), 255

"I'm A Coward," 117

"I'm Goin' Down," 99

"I'm A Long Gone Daddy," 91

"I'm On Fire," 63, 97, 218, 252; video of, 245

"I'm A Rocker," 256

"Incident On 57th Street," 46, 148, 151, 251

In Country (Mason), 94, 99

In Country (film), 94

"Independence Day," 53–54

The Indian Runner (film), 82, 243

Indigo Girls, 39, 240

"In Freehold," 102, 149

Inherit The Wind (film), 221

"Into The Fire," 46, 48, 162–63, 166

Iraq War, 182

"It's All Right," 28

"It's Hard To Be A Saint In The City," 7, 46, 149, 245

"It's The Little Things That Count," 117

"It's A Man's World," 253

"I Wanna Be With You," 39, 48

"I Wanna Marry You," 55–56

"I Want You," 4

"I Wish I Were Blind," 124

J

"Jacob's Ladder," 46

Jagger, Mick, 34, 124

James, Jesse, 73

"Janey Don't You Lose Heart," 252

Jeanette Blast Furnace Preservation Association, 141

"Jeannie Needs A Shooter," 215

"Jersey Girl," 193

Jersey Shore, 19; towns of, 27

"Jesus Was An Only Son," 46, 149, 176–77

Jett, Joan, 93

"Johnny Bye-Bye," 27, 39, 218, 251–52

Johnny Cash and the Tennessee Three, 97

"Johnny 99," 48, 76, 78–80, 95, 146, 149, 213, 252

"John Hardy Was A Desperate Little Man," 80

"John Henry," 136, 239

Johnson, Robert, 38, 73–74, 78, 81, 85

Johnstown Flood, 81, 82

"Jole Blon," 4

Jones, Tennessee, 253

Journey To Nowhere: The Saga Of The New Underclass (Maharidge and Williamson), 140, 141, 151, 152

"Jungleland," 30, 149, 252, 253, 259

"Just Around The Corner To The Light Of Day," 93

K

Kael, Pauline, 255

Kalifornia (film), 70

Kaye, Jessica, 253

Kelly, Gene, 221

Kelly, Raymond W., 238

Kerry, John, 45, 98

Khan, Asif Ali, 165

King, Stephen, 253

Kingston Trio, 240

Kinsey, Leroy, Jr., 101

"Kitty's Back, 146, 148, 253

Klein, Joe, 80, 138, 183

Kline, J.W., 201

The Knack, 215

Kot, Greg, 32, 127

Kovaly, Andrew, 181, 182

Kovic, Ron, 92

Kozol, Jonathan, 40

Kramer, Stanley, 221

Ku Klux Klan, 155, 156

L

Lahav, Suki, 15

Lance, Major, 39, 250

Landau, Jon, 32

"Land Of Hope And Dreams," 193, 238–43; as rock spiritual, 242; train metaphor in, 239; vision in, as democratic, 242

Lange, Dorothea, 137

The Last Temptation Of Elvis, 218

Laughton, Charles, 111

Lawrence, Jerome, 221

"Layla," 34

Leadbelly, 240

"Leah," 39, 46, 147

"Leap Of Faith," 46, 149, 253

Leaves Of Grass (Whitman), 238

Lee, Spike, 250

Lee, Robert E., 221

Lennon, John, 34

"Let's Go Tonight." *See* "Johnny Bye-Bye"

Levin, Joseph J., 156

Lewis, Dean, 101

Lewis, Jerry Lee, 28, 214, 258

Lewis, Juliette, 70

"Lift Me Up," 244–45

Light Of Day: A Tribute To Bruce Springsteen, 61, 96, 254

Light Of Day (film), 93

Limbo (film), 244, 245

"The Line," 145, 147, 149, 178

Line of Fire: The Morris Dees Story (television movie), 156

"Lion's Den," 46

"Little Queenie," 44

"Living On The Edge Of The World," 83, 84, 253

"Living Proof," 129–30

Lloyd, Emily, 94

Lofgren, Nils, 254

Lomax, Alan, 240

Lomax, John, 240

"Long Black Veil," 4

"Long Gone Lonesome Blues," 56, 57

"The Long Goodbye," 260

"Long Time Comin'," 147

"Loose Change," 253

"Loose Ends," 254

Lopez, Vini, 10, 228

"Lord Franklin's Dream," 181

"Lord Randal," 181

"Losin' Kind," 117

"Lost In The Flood," 147, 254

"Love Is Strange," 73

Lowell, Lisa, 154

Lucente, Bob, 236

"Lucky Man," 48, 118

Lucky Town, 121, 125, 127, 130, 131, 218, 256

Lynch, David, 70

Lynch, Patrick, 235, 236

M

Madam Marie. *See* Marie Castello

Madigan, Amy, 157

Maharidge, Dale, 140, 141, 151

Malick, Terrence, 69, 70, 72, 73

Mallaber, Gary, 141

Malle, Louis, 157

Malone, Bill C., 58

"Man At The Top," 213, 254

Mann, Manfred, 3

"A Mansion On The Hill," 77

"Mansion On The Hill, 77–78, 131

"Man's Job," 123

March, Frederic, 221

Marcus, Greil, 34, 79–80, 91

"Maria's Bed," 147

Marley, Bob, 240

Marsh, Dave, 28, 56, 57, 59, 70, 73, 84, 93, 94, 97, 100, 139, 154, 193, 239

Martha and the Vandellas, 44

Martin, Gavin, 93

Martinez, Vanessa, 244

"Mary Hamilton," 109, 110

"Mary Queen of Arkansas," 7, 146, 260

"Mary's Place," 25, 39, 146, 260

Massey, Raymond, 41

Mason, Bobbie Ann, 53, 94, 99, 253

Mastrantonio, Mary Elizabeth, 244

"Matamoros Banks," 154, 178. *See also* "Across the Border"

Mayfield, Curtis, 170, 240, 241

McCartney, Paul, 39

McDonald, Gabrielle Kirk, 156

McGavin, Darren, 221

McLagan, Ian, 131, 218

McMellon, Edward, 237

McMurtry, Larry, 72

"Meeting Across the River," 63, 76, 146, 253, 254

Meeting Across The River (Kaye and Brewer), 253

"Meet Me At Mary's Place," 39

Mellon, Andrew, 81

Mencken, H.L., 220

Metzger, Tom, 156

"Midnight Special," 240

"The Mighty Quinn," 3

Millman, Joyce, 50

"Missing," 243–44

Mitchum, Robert, 25, 111

Mizell, Hank, 84

Moffat, Donald, 157

"Monkey Time," 250

Monroe, Bill, 57

"Mony Mony," 4

Moore, Bill, 140

Moore, Sam, 123, 257

Morris, John E., 201

Morrison, Van, 1, 18, 31, 39, 255

Morse, David, 82, 243

Mortensen, Viggo, 82

"Mountain Of Love," 4

"Mrs. McGrath," 182

Muller, Bobby, 92, 93

"Murder Incorporated," 195, 254

Murphy, Elliott, 61

Murphy, Richard, 237

"My Beautiful Reward," 127, 131

"My Best Was Never Good Enough," 260

"My Bucket's Got A Hole In It," 57

"My City of Ruins," 14, 46, 162, 169–72; and Asbury Park, 169

"My Father's House," 85–86, 96, 210

My Heart Will Cross The Ocean: My Story, My Son, Amadou (Diallo and Wolff), 237

"My Heart's In The Highlands," 181

"My Hometown," 101–3, 147

"My Love Will Not Let You Down," 255

The Mysteries of Pittsburgh (Chabon), 31, 33

"Mystery Train," 112, 240

N

Nam, Nguyen Van, 156

Nash, Ogden, 258

Natural Born Killers (film), 70

Nebraska, 38, 45, 51, 67, 79, 80, 81, 86, 87, 93, 95, 97, 105, 207, 210,

214, 239, 253; as immoral, accusations of, 75; and Flannery O'Connor, 74; and Robert Frank, 75; reaction to, 67; and Hank Williams, 57; writing of, 73
"Nebraska," 69–75, 151, 207
Nelson, Paul, 44
New Jersey: boardwalk culture of, 19; and Jersey Turnpike, 84
Newman, Cathy, 19
"The New Timer," 46, 140, 147, 149, 151–53
"New York City Serenade," 146, 148, 151, 255
New York Guitar Festival: and "The Nebraska Project," 67
New York Times: September 11 obituaries in, 162
Nicholson, Jack, 154, 243
The Night of the Hunter (film), 39, 111
"99 Year Blues," 78, 80
"No Money Down," 44
"None But The Brave," 243
"No Nukes" concert, 57
"No Surrender," 63; as anthemic, 98
"Nothing Man," 147

O

O'Brien, Brendan, 159, 175
Ocean Grove (New Jersey), 16, 27
O'Connor, Flannery, 39, 73, 128, 207; and *Nebraska*, 74
"Oklahoma Hills," 4
Olson, Josh, 111
"On The Prowl," 117
"One Step Up," 117–18, 208
One Step Up/Two Steps Back: The Songs of Bruce Springsteen, 61, 78

"On Top of Old Smokey," 4
"Open All Night," 39, 83, 84–85, 146
Orbison, Roy, 23, 25, 31, 39
Out Of The Past (film), 48
"Out In The Street," 48
"Over The Rise," 255

P

"The Pace Of Youth" (short story), 17
"Paradise": and September 11 attacks, 168
Pareles, Jon, 32
Pares, John, 201
Paris Trout (Dexter), 40, 128
Paris Trout (television movie), 129
"Part Man, Part Monkey," 219–22, 256; and intelligent design controversy, 219
Payne, Rufe, 74
Pearl Jam, 159
Peckinpah, Sam, 87
Penn, Sean, 82, 243
"People Get Ready," 170, 240, 241, 242
Percy, Will, 138
Perkins, Carl, 215
Peter, Paul, and Mary, 240
Peters, Gretchen, 58
Philadelphia (film), 197
Phillips, Christopher, 92, 247, 252
Pickett, Wilson, 3, 39
"Pilgrim In The Temple Of Love," 117
"Pink Cadillac," 214, 215, 218, 258
Pirner, Dave, 39
Pitt, Brad, 70
"Pittsburgh Town," 181
Plotkin, Chuck, 141
"Point Blank," 58–59

Pointer Sisters, 215

Pond, Steve, 105

Poole, Shawn, 218

Porcaro, Jeff, 218

Powers, Harry, 111

"Precious Memories," 4

Presley, Elvis, 3, 34, 39, 112, 149, 214, 216, 251; Springsteen, influence on, 217–18

"Pretty Flamingo," 3

"The Price You Pay," 27, 46, 61–62; biblical imagery in, 62

Prine, John, 99–100

"The Promise," 225, 229–30

Promised Land, 61, 62; notion of, 44, 45, 240

"Promised Land," 44

"The Promised Land," 27, 44–46, 48, 199

"Protection," 215

"Proud Mary," 4

Proulx, Annie, 112, 249

"Prove It All Night," 47

Prozac Nation (Wurtzel), 8

Q

"Quarter to Three," 4

R

"Racing In The Street," 27, 42–44, 146, 229

Rage Against the Machine, 159

"Railroad Bill," 239

"Rain," 39

"Ramblin' Man," 64, 77

"Ramrod," 255, 256

Raspberries, 39

Reagan, Ronald, 40, 79, 91, 95

"Real World," 255

"Reason To Believe," 86–87, 146, 147, 154, 230

Redding, Otis, 3

Reed, Blind Alfred, 182, 183

"Rendezvous," 215

"Reno," 255

Retrospective: The Best Of The Knack, 215

Reynolds, Burt, 149

"Ricky Wants A Man Of Her Own," 256

Rifkin, Marty, 141, 154

Ripley, Arthur, 48

The Rising, 25, 39, 167, 243; and September 11 attacks, 159; tour of, 164, 242

"The Rising," 46, 48, 146, 162, 166–68; and Asbury Park, 167; reaction to, 167

"The Rising" (sculpture), 164

The River, 51, 59, 208; tour of, 80, 127, 218, 251; and Hank Williams, 57

"The River," 48, 56–58, 146, 255

Roads: Driving America's Great Highways (McMurtry), 72

road songs, 96

Robards, Jason, 221

Robbins, Tim, 39, 249

Robinson, Smokey, 39, 54

"Rockaway The Days,: 213

"Rockin' All Over the World," 4

"Rock Island Line," 240

Rodgers, Jimmie, 49, 57, 79, 96

Rogers, Kenny, 94

"Roll Of The Dice," 260

Romani, Graziano, 229

The Ronettes, 25, 131

"Rosalita (Come Out Tonight)," 11, 20–21, 49, 146, 148, 256, 257, 258

Ross, Alex, 181

Rotella, Sebastian, 150

"Roulette," 48, 208–10

"Run Through The Jungle," 4

Runaway American Dream (Guterman), 15

S

Sacramento Bee, 140

"Sad Eyes," 256

Safir, Howard, 236

Sam & Dave, 123, 257

Sam the Sham and the Pharoahs, 253

Sancious, David, 15, 27, 257

"Santa Ana," 257

"Satan's Jewel Crown," 4

Sayles, John, 97, 244, 245

Schiavo, Terry, 220

Schrader, Paul, 92, 93

Schwartz, Frederic, 163, 164

Scialfa, Patti, 27, 154

Scopes, John T.: trial of, 220, 221

The Searchers (film), 39

"Seaside Bar Song," 20, 257

A Season For Justice (Dees), 156

"Secret Garden," 63, 195

"Seeds," 192–93

Seeds: The Songs Of Pete Seeger, Vol. III, 182

Seeger, Pete, 129, 135, 136, 179, 181, 182, 240

"Sell It And They Will Come," 117

Sena, Dominic, 70

September 11 attacks, 159, 162, 163, 165, 167, 168, 250; Monmouth

County, casualties in, 166, 169

Shangri-Las, 39

Sheen, Martin, 69, 70, 72

Shepard, Sam, 97, 213

Shepherd, Jan, 84

"Sherry Darling," 146, 257, 256

"She's The One," 245, 257

"Shut Out The Light," 48, 94, 212, 223

Simon J. Lubin Society, 137

"Sinaloa Cowboys," 143–44, 149, 151, 178

Smith, Harry, 78, 79, 80, 183

Smith, Larry David, 45, 53, 238

Smith, Patti, 215, 248

"Song Of Myself," 47

"Song Of The Open Road," 26

Songs (Springsteen), 32, 37, 60, 93, 116, 123, 151, 164

songwriting: American noir tradition of, 111

Son Volt, 84

Soppo, Joseph, 201

"Soul Driver," 46, 123, 257

"Souls Of The Departed, 94, 149

Southern Pacific, 215

Southern Poverty Law Center, 156

"Southern Son," 7

Southside Johnny and the Asbury Jukes, 215, 228, 247, 251

Spacek, Sissy, 70, 72

"Spare Parts," 46, 107–10, 147

Spector, Phil, 23, 49

Spring Lake (New Jersey), 18, 27

"Spirit In The Night," 5, 9–10, 148, 151

Springsteen, Adele, 216

Springsteen, Bruce: and Asbury Park,

significance of, 13; biblical
imagery, use of, 46; and blues, 73;
on Catholic upbringing, 34, 176;
childhood of, 6; in concert,
intensity of, 238, 239; country
music, effect on, 37, 57, 64, 69; as
country singer, 64; covers by,
193–94; as disconnected, 69, 73;
dream imagery of, 96; fans,
connection to, xiv, 29; father,
relationship with, 53, 54, 139; folk
music, effect on, 37; as folk singer,
179; Freehold, as patron saint of,
102; on good songs, xiv; influences
on, 38–39, 78, 79; and hope, 50,
222; as lapsed Catholic, 109, 170,
176; as loner, 6; masculinity,
definition of, 107; mother,
relationship with, 139, 216, 217;
persona of, 5; as phenomenon, 34;
and promised land, 26, 27, 44, 46,
50; rock and roll, importance of on,
xiv; as romantic, 74; sincerity of,
58; themes of, 29; as synthesist, 38,
44; vulnerability of, 8; on war, 94
Springsteen, Douglas, 54, 102, 112
Springsteen, Virginia, 57
The Stand (King), 253
"Stand On It," 258, 256
Stanton, Harry Dean, 97
Staple Singers, 240
Starkweather, Charles, 69, 70, 71, 78;
execution of, 72; victims of, 75
Starr, Edwin, 94, 192
"State Trooper," 83, 84, 253
St. Dominic's Preview, 39
Steel Mill, 18
Steinbeck, John, 39, 40, 41, 42, 136,

137, 144, 151, 192
Stewart, Rod, 5, 100
Stiehm, Meredith, 63
"Stolen Car," 60–61, 63, 203
Stone, Oliver, 70
"Straight Time," 147
Strathairn, David, 244
Strauss, Neil, 27
"Street Queen," 7
"Streets Of Philadelphia," 197–98
Streigel, Henry, 201
Strummer, Joe, 84
Stuart, Marty, 57, 58
St. Valentine, 119
Styron, William, 129
"Subterranean Homesick Blues," 1
"Sugarland," 117
Summer, Donna, 215
Swaggart, Jimmy, 28
"Sweet Little Sixteen," 44
Sweeting, Adam, 164

T
"Take 'Em As They Come," 39
"Take Me To the River," 28
Tallent, Garry, 39, 138, 209
Tate, Greg, 101, 239
"Tenth Avenue Freeze-Out," 27–29,
148, 149
Testa, Philip, 76
Texas: Vietnamese refugees in, 155
Their Blood Is Strong (Steinbeck), 137.
See also The Harvest Gypsies
"This Hard Land," 147, 195, 199
"This Land Is Your Land," 39, 80, 93,
194
"This Little Girl," 215
"This Train," 240

"This Train (Is Bound For Glory)," 241, 242; origins of, 240

"This World Is Not My Home," 183

Thompson, Jack, 149

Thompson, Jim, 39

Thornburgh, Richard, 209

Three Mile Island, 208, 210

"Thundercrack," 20, 258

"Thunder Road," 25–27, 39, 55, 117, 123, 146, 162, 229, 230; cinematic quality of, 25

Thunder Road (film), 25

'Til We Outnumber 'Em: Live from Cleveland, 38

The Times They Are A-Changin', 138

"Tom Joad," 135, 138

"Tougher Than The Rest," 107

Tourneur, Jacques, 48

Townshend, Pete, 239

Tracks, 60, 61, 83, 84, 203, 208, 214, 215, 218, 223, 229, 248, 252

train songs, 96

"Trapped!" 193

"Trouble River," 225

Tunnel Of Love, 60, 105, 111, 113, 115, 118–19, 216; motivations behind, 116; religion in, 109; tour of, 114, 208, 219

"Tunnel Of Love," 112–14; funhouse metaphor in, 113

"TV Movie," 256, 258

25ᵗʰ Hour (film), 250

"Twist And Shout," 4

"Two Faces," 115

"Two Steps Back," 63

Tyrell, Soozie, 141, 154, 212

U

United States: Vietnamese refugees in, 155

"Used Cars," 259

V

"Valentine's Day," 118–19; religious imagery in, 118

Van Zandt, Steve, 98, 209

"Vietnam," 92, 93

Vietnamese Fishermen's Association, 156

Vietnam Veterans Of America, 93

Vietnam War: Khe Sahn, battle of, 92; refugees of, 155; Saigon, fall of, 155

"Vigilante Man," 39

"Viva Las Vegas," 218

W

"Wages Of Sin," 210–11

Waine, Silas, 201

"Waist Deep In The Big Muddy," 129

"Waitin' On A Sunny Day," 259

Waits, Tom, 193

"Walk Like A Man," 63, 111–12

"Waltz Across Texas," 4

"War," 94, 192

Ward, Ed, 11

Washington, Denzel, 197

Weinberg, Max, 75, 91, 99, 101, 107, 199, 209, 214, 248

Weldon, Thomas, 201

Werner, Craig, 38, 239

West, George, 136

"We Shall Overcome," 38

We Shall Overcome: The Seeger Sessions, xiv, 10, 38, 136, 179–80; and *American Land Edition*, 180;

eclecticism of, 179, 183; tour of, 84, 181, 182

"When Johnny Comes Marching Home," 182

"When The Lights Go Out," 117

"When The Saints Go Marching In," 4

"When You Need Me," 250

"When You're Alone," 147, 259

"Where The Bands Are," 259

Whiteman, Paul, 17

Whitman, Walt, 26, 38, 47, 238, 242

"Who'll Stop the Rain?" 4

Wild At Heart (film), 70

"Wild Billy's Circus Story," 148, 149, 179, 183

The Wild, The Innocent & The E Street Shuffle, 11, 20, 97, 114, 179

Will, George F., 91, 94

Williams, Hank, 37, 38, 49, 56, 58, 64, 69, 70, 79, 85, 91, 92, 96, 138; influences on, 74; and *Nebraska*, 57, 73, 77; and *The River*, 57

Williamson, Michael, 140, 151

Willis, Bruce, 94

Wings For Wheels: The Making of Born To Run, 23

Wise Blood (film), 40, 73

Wise Blood (O'Connor), 40, 73

"The Wish," 48, 216–17; as autobiographical, 216

"With Every Wish," 147, 260

With The Naked Eye, 215

Wolff, Craig, 237

Wolff, Daniel, 15, 17, 18, 53

Wollenberg, Charles, 137

Wood's Blind Jubilee Singers, 240

Woody Guthrie: A Life (Klein), 80, 138

"Wooly Bully," 4

"Working On The Highway," 95–96

"Worlds Apart," 164–65

"Wreck On The Highway," 64–65

"The Wreck On The Highway," 64

"The Wreck Of The Old 97," 240

Wurtzel, Elizabeth, 8, 9

Y

Yarrow, Peter, 179

"You Can Look (But You Better Not Touch)," 149

"You Can't Catch Me," 84

"You Never Can Tell," 44

"Youngstown," 94, 140–42, 149

"You're Missing," 165–66, 243

Z

"Zero And Blind Terry," 259

Zevon, Warren, 194, 215